HAWAII

TOP SIGHTS, AUTHENTIC EXPERIENCES

Amy Balfour, Jade Bremner, Kevin Raub,
Ryan Ver Berkmoes, Greg Ward

Contents

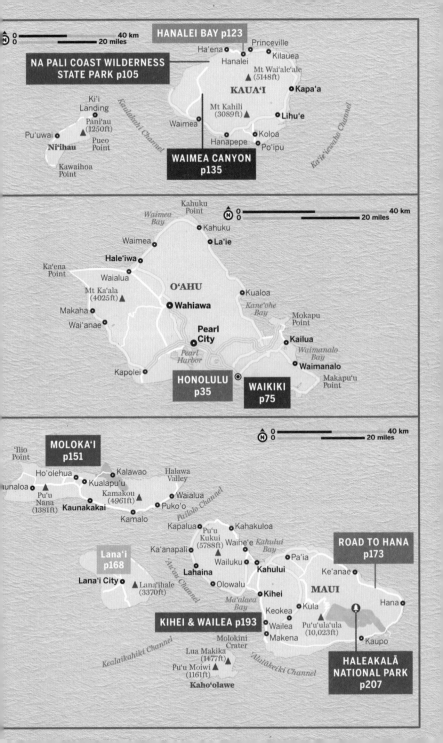

Welcome to Hawaii

There's no place quite like Hawaii. Floating in the vast Pacific, shaped by volcanic blasts and mighty seas, Hawaii boasts spectacular scenery, superb beaches and, above all, its own unique cultural identity.

Six Hawaiian islands now welcome visitors. The most popular and populated, O'ahu, is home to the only city, Honolulu, and the most famous resort, Waikiki. The next most visited is Maui, circled by perfect beaches and lined by plush resorts. Further south, the island of Hawai'i itself, once powerful enough to conquer its neighbors and give the archipelago its name, is still growing thanks to its active volcanoes, and is known as the Big Island. Wind and water have sculpted Kaua'i, the oldest major island, into a wonderland of cliffs and chasms, while smaller Lana'i and Moloka'i offer a sense of Hawaiian life in centuries gone by.

Life in Hawaii is very much lived outdoors. Whether you're here to surf, swim, kayak or hike, you'll soon realize that for the locals, every encounter with nature is infused with *aloha 'aina* – love and respect for the land. The islands are proud of their multicultural heritage; the descendants of ancient Polynesians and immigrants from all over the world – drawn equally from America and Asia – coexist with ease. At its best, everything in Hawaii feels easygoing and casual, bursting with genuine aloha and fun. Even the smells are sublime thanks to flower leis and tropical blooms, not to mention all that fish and fruit.

Every encounter with nature is infused with aloha 'aina – love and respect for the land.

Na Pali Coast Wilderness State Park (p105)

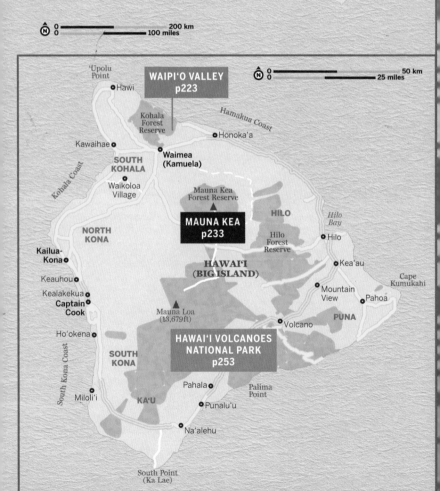

PACIFIC
OCEAN

Ni'ihau   Kaua'i

O'ahu

Moloka'i

Lana'i   Maui

Kaho'olawe

Hawai'i
(Big Island)

0 — 200 km
0 — 100 miles

0 — 50 km
0 — 25 miles

'Upolu
Point

Hawi

WAIPI'O VALLEY
p223

Kohala
Forest
Reserve

Hamakua Coast

Honoka'a

Kawaihae

**SOUTH
KOHALA**

Waimea
(Kamuela)

Kohala Coast

Waikoloa
Village

Mauna Kea
Forest Reserve

HILO

Hilo
Bay

**NORTH
KONA**

MAUNA KEA
p233

Hilo

Hilo
Forest
Reserve

**Kailua-
Kona**

**HAWAI'I
(BIG ISLAND)**

Kea'au

Cape
Kumukahi

Keauhou

Kealakekua

**Captain
Cook**

Mauna Loa
(13,679ft)

Mountain
View

Pahoa

PUNA

Ho'okena

Volcano

South Kona Coast

**SOUTH
KONA**

**HAWAI'I VOLCANOES
NATIONAL PARK**
p253

Pahala

Palima
Point

Miloli'i

KA'U

Punalu'u

Na'alehu

South Point
(Ka Lae)

Plumeria Blossoms
FOCALPOINT/SHUTTERSTOCK ©

COVID-19

We have re-checked every business in this book before publication to ensure that it is still open after 2020's COVID-19 outbreak. However, the economic and social impacts of COVID-19 will continue to be felt long after the outbreak has been contained, and many businesses, services and events referenced in this guide may experience ongoing restrictions. Some businesses may be temporarily closed, have changed their opening hours and services, or require bookings; some unfortunately could have closed permanently. We suggest you check with venues before visiting for the latest information.

Hawaii's Top 12

Na Pali Coast, Kaua'i

Rugged adventures on land and sea

The Na Pali Coast (pictured above: p105) deserves to top every Kaua'i visitor's to-do list. Admire it from a cruising catamaran, or pit your paddle and kayak against the elements. Hikers can see it close up on the demanding 11-mile Kalalau Trail (p112). Whether you're on a day hike or a backpacking expedition, you'll encounter a place like no other, where verdant cliffs soar above the waterfalls of wilderness valleys.

1

YIN YANG/GETTY IMAGES ©

WRITEFULLY SAID/SHUTTERSTOCK ©

Haleakalā National Park, Maui

Otherworldly beauty from shore to summit

As you hike into Haleakalā (p210), you notice the crumbly lunar landscape and the volcanic cinders beneath your feet. The trail continues through a tableau of stark lava, cinder cones and ever-changing clouds. In the coastal section, waterfalls tumble into pools flanked by trails, viewpoints and a bamboo forest.

2

DAVID MADISON/GETTY IMAGES ©

Hawai'i Volcanoes National Park, Big Island

Hotspots abound in this awe-inspiring park

Set on the flanks of the world's most active volcano – whose latest eruption ended in 2018 – this extraordinary park (p253) is a dramatic reminder that nature remains very much alive and in perpetual motion. Incredible hiking trails take in lava flows and tubes, steam vents and wild beaches. Above: Kilauea Iki (p256)

3

4

Road to Hana, Maui

Hold on tight for a dramatic drive

A white-knuckle roller-coaster of a ride, the Hana Highway (p173) twists through dense, jungle-fringed valleys and skirts beneath mighty cliffs, curling around 600 twists and turns along the way. Fifty-four one-lane bridges cross nearly as many waterfalls – some eye-popping torrents, others soothing and gentle. Driving is only half the thrill. Get out and swim in a Zen-like pool, hike a ginger-scented trail and savor fresh guava and coconuts.

5

Waikiki, O'ahu

Waikiki is back, baby! Dig in

Hawaii's most famous resort, Waikiki (p75) had become a haven for tacky plastic lei, coconut-shell bikini tops and motorized, hip-shaking hula dolls – but real aloha and chic-modern style have returned. Beach boys and girls surf legendary waves by day, and after sunset tiki torches light up the sand. Every night hula dancers – backed by slack key guitars and ukuleles – sway to ancient and modern rhythms at oceanfront hotels, open-air bars and even shopping malls.

FIRE TATOR/SHUTTERSTOCK ©

Moloka'i

History, indigenous culture and stunning views

More than half of Moloka'i's people have indigenous heritage,
and locals favor preservation of land and culture over tourism
schemes. Yet visitors to Moloka'i (p151) find the welcoming
aloha spirit is everywhere. As well as the spectacular Kalaupapa
Peninsula, island sights include the Halawa Valley, home to
hundreds of sacred taro patches, ancient temples, and waterfalls
pounding into swimmable pools.

MNSTUDIO/SHUTTERSTOCK ©

Waimea Canyon, Kaua'i

Lush, dramatic and divine for exploring

Carved by aeons of erosion and the collapse of the volcano that formed Kaua'i, Waimea Canyon (p135) stretches 10 miles long, 1 mile wide and more than 3600ft deep. Roadside lookouts along the sinuous, scenic drive survey russet cliffs, towering waterfalls and endless abysses. Steep trails lead hikers down to the canyon floor, out to coastal headlands, and deep into the mountaintop swamps.

7

Honolulu, O'ahu

A multicultural extravaganza

In Honolulu (p35), Hawaii's vibrant, cosmopolitan capital on O'ahu's southern shoreline, you can eat your way through the pan-Asian alleys of Chinatown, gaze out to sea from the landmark Aloha Tower and explore the USA's only royal palace, where Hawaii's last monarch languished under house arrest. Browse at the world's largest open-air shopping center, then pay your respects at Pearl Harbor.

CHRISTIAN MUELLER/SHUTTERSTOCK ©

Kihei & Wailea, Maui

Golden-sand beaches and pristine resorts

Famed for phenomenal swimming, snorkeling, sunbathing and sunny skies, the beaches of Kihei & Wailea (p193) are world class. In winter whales congregate immediately off shore, while snorkel cruises head out year-round. The further south you go, the more magnificent the beaches become, culminating in the superb, mile-long Big Beach. If you're not staying in exclusive Wailea, thank Hawaii's beach-access laws, which allow you to visit these beautiful strands, with dedicated public parking lots.

CLOCKWISE FROM TOP: ALEXEY KAMENSKIY/SHUTTERSTOCK ©; ALEXANDER CASPARI/SHUTTERSTOCK ©; MICHELE FALZONE/GETTY IMAGES ©

Mauna Kea, Big Island

A white peak beneath a blanket of stars

In Hawaiian tradition, the summit of the islands' tallest mountain, Mauna Kea (p233), is the point where the earth and the heavens meet. Astronomers have in the past 50 years taken advantage of the clearest air on the planet to erect powerful observatories. While science and spirituality remain at loggerheads, visitors can still join mountaintop stargazing sessions.

10

Hanalei Bay, Kaua'i

Where beach life is the best life

Repeatedly voted among the USA's very best beaches, this crescent-shaped bay (p123) on Kaua'i's North Shore delights lazy sunbathers and active beachgoers alike. Surfers can charge massive (and some beginner) waves, while onlookers amble along the golden sands. Surf lessons take place near the pier, and every afternoon locals and visitors fire up barbecue grills, crack open cold brews and watch the daylight fade.

11

Waipi'o Valley, Big Island

A fascinating and alluring Polynesian valley

The Waipi'o Valley (p223) is a mysterious green bowl filled with ghosts and legends. It's a sacred site, a retreat from the outside world. The special distillation of all these makes it irresistible. Some simply snap their photos from the panoramic overlook, one of the Big Island's most iconic views. Others trek down to the valley floor to stroll a black sand beach and peer at distant waterfalls. Access is limited beyond that, which only enhances the mystery.

12

Plan Your Trip
Need to Know

When to Go

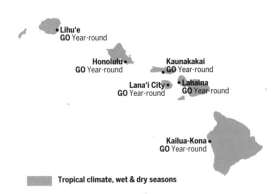

• Lihu'e
GO Year-round

Honolulu•
GO Year-round

Kaunakakai
•GO Year-round

Lana'i City• •Lahaina
GO Year-round GO Year-round

Kailua-Kona •
GO Year-round

Tropical climate, wet & dry seasons

High Season (Dec–Apr & Jun–Aug)

○ Accommodations prices up 50–100%.

○ Christmas to New Year and around Easter are the most expensive and busy periods.

○ Winter is rainier (but best for whale-watching and surfing), summer is slightly hotter.

Shoulder (May & Sep)

○ Crowds and prices drop slightly between schools' spring break and summer vacation.

○ Temperatures are mild, with mostly sunny, cloudless days.

Low Season (Oct & Nov)

○ Fewest visitors, airfares to Hawaii are at their lowest.

○ Accommodations rates drop by up to 50%.

○ Weather is typically dry and hot (not ideal for hiking).

Currency
US dollar ($)

Language
English, Hawaiian

Visas
Visitors from Canada, the UK, Australia, New Zealand, Japan and many EU countries don't need visas for stays of less than 90 days. Other nations see http://travel.state.gov.

Money
ATMs are widespread in cities and larger towns. Credit cards are almost universally accepted and are usually required for reservations. Tipping is customary.

Cell Phones
Foreign phones that use tri- or quad-ban frequencies work in Hawaii. It's also possible to buy inexpensive cell phones with pay-as-you-go plans.

Time
Hawaiian–Aleutian Standard Time (GMT/UMC minus 10 hours)

Daily Costs

Budget: Less than $150

- Dorm bed: $25–60
- Local plate lunch: $8–10
- Bus fare (one way): $2–4

Midrange: $150–300

- Double room with private bath at midrange hotel or B&B: $125–200
- Rental car (excluding insurance and gas) per day/week: from $35/200
- Dinner at casual sit-down restaurant: $20–50

Top End: More than $300

- Beach-resort hotel room or luxury condo rental: more than $300
- Three-course meal with a cocktail in a top restaurant: $75–150
- Guided outdoor adventure tour: $80–250

Useful Websites

Hawaii Visitors and Convention Bureau (www.gohawaii.com) Official tourism site, events calendar, multilingual planning guides and inspiring Instagram photos.

Hawai'i Magazine (www.hawaiimagazine.com) All-island news, features, food and drink and travel tips.

Lonely Planet (www.lonelyplanet.com/usa/hawaii) Destination information, hotel bookings and more.

Hana Hou! (www.hanahou.com) Hawaiian Airlines' engaging in-flight magazine; feature stories available free online.

Opening Hours

Banks 8:30am – 4pm Monday to Friday; some to 6pm Friday and 9am – noon or 1pm Saturday.

Bars Honolulu and major resorts: noon–midnight, some to 2am Thursday to Saturday. Bars typically close at 10pm in smaller towns.

Government offices 8:30am – 4:30pm Monday to Friday; some post offices open 9am–noon Saturday.

Restaurants Breakfast 6:30am – 10am, lunch 11:30am – 2pm, dinner 5pm – 9:30pm.

Shops 9am–5pm Monday to Saturday, some noon to 5pm Sunday. Malls in resort areas have extended hours.

Arriving in Hawaii

Honolulu International Airport (HNL; ☎808-836-6411; www.airports.hawaii.gov/hnl; 300 Rodgers Blvd; 🛜)

Car Most car-rental agencies are on-site. Drive takes 25 to 45 minutes to Waikiki via Hwy 92 (Nimitz Hwy/Ala Moana Blvd) or H-1 (Lunalilo) Fwy.

Taxi Reach Honolulu or Waikiki by taxi, Uber, or Lyft; average cab fare $35 to $50.

Door-to-door shuttle One-way trip to Waikiki costs $17; operates 24 hours (every 20 to 60 minutes).

Bus TheBus 19 or 20 to Waikiki ($2.60) every 20 minutes from 6am to 11pm daily (large baggage prohibited).

Getting Around

Almost all interisland travel is by plane, while traveling around each individual island usually requires renting a car.

Air Interisland flights are short, frequent and surprisingly expensive.

Boat Limited ferry services connect Maui only with Moloka'i and Lana'i.

Bus Public buses run on the larger islands, but you'll probably find it time-consuming and difficult to get around by bus, except on O'ahu.

Car Rent a car if you want to explore, especially on the Neighbor Islands. A 4WD vehicle may come in handy on Lana'i and Hawai'i, the Big Island.

For more on **getting around**, see p314

Plan Your Trip
Hot Spots For...

WOLFSO/SHUTTERSTOCK ©

Beaches

Thinking of Hawaii instantly conjures images of golden sands backed by tropical palm trees. With hundreds of miles of coastline, you'll be spoiled for choice.

O'ahu
There's just so much happening on O'ahu, especially if you like sun, sand, and adventure.

Waikiki (p75)
Learn to surf, then join a sunset cruise.

Maui
On the Valley Isle, the strands are golden and perfect for sunbathing.

Big Beach (p202)
A mile-long sweep of glorious sand and turquoise waters.

Kaua'i
Enticing beaches attract outdoor adventurers of every skill level.

Hanalei Bay (p123)
For surfers, paddlers, and beach bums alike.

LAURASLENS/SHUTTERSTOCK ©

Adventures on Land

The Hawaiian islands have as much to offer landlubbers as water babies. Strap yourself into a zipline harness, lace up those hiking boots or climb into the saddle.

Maui
An ancient footpath encircles the island, passing centuries-old temples and dwellings.

Pi'ilani Trail (p180)
This coastal footpath crosses 14th-century stepping stones.

The Big Island
Lofty volcanoes offer extraordinary wilderness sights on hikes for every ability level.

Hawai'i Volcanoes National Park (p253) High, low, there's fire wherever you go.

Moloka'i
History and scenery collide on the striking trails of the most Hawaiian island of all.

Kalaupapa Trail (p158)
Descend to a remote peninsula by foot or by mule.

Scenic Drives

Ready to hit the road? These islands may be small, but you can still take unbelievably beautiful road trips, climbing volcano summits and squeezing below soaring pali (cliffs).

RACHEL MARIE PHOTOS/SHUTTERSTOCK ©

Maui
Ancient sights, towering waterfalls and intriguing communities are linked by gorgeous roads.

Road to Hana (p173)
Coastal drive passes waterfalls and 54 stone bridges.

O'ahu
Cosmopolitan, yes. But even the most ardent city denizen needs to let their hair down.

Pu'uohi'a–Round Top (p63)
Take in the views around this lush, ocean-view route.

The Big Island
Pockets of organized activity dot the volcanic regions, with roads leading to wild adventure.

Chain of Craters Road (p267)
Descend through a volcanic zone to old lava flows.

Waterfalls & Swimming Holes

Wade through the mud and step over slippery tree roots on jungle trails, all so you can swim in a crystal-clear pool under a rainforest cascade.

PIERRE LECLERC/SHUTTERSTOCK ©

Kaua'i
The folds of crinkled Na Pali coastline hide a bounty of waterfalls – although they're not always easy to reach.

Hanakapi'ai Falls (p113)
High in a remote valley lies a gem ready for swimmers.

Maui
Head to the Road to Hana and the rain-loving East Side for a gorgeous waterfall lineup.

'Ohe'o Gulch (p212)
Waterfalls tumble into the sea in Haleakalā National Park.

Moloka'i
The mysterious Halawa Valley is replete with ancient history and lush beauty.

Mo'oula & Hipuapua Falls (p157) Hire a local guide to hike to these twin beauties.

Essential Hawaii

FERNANDO MARGOLLES/SHUTTERSTOCK ©

Drinking & Nightlife

For the most part, Hawaii is not a late-night-party kind of place. The sun sets early and things typically quiet down long before the wee hours (thus on Maui, 10pm is often called 'Maui midnight'). Oceanfront bars serve up mai tais and tropical drinks, but it's the cocktail bars and upscale restaurants that are really having fun, creating delicious concoctions using locally sourced spirits and ingredients. Craft breweries are firmly established on the larger islands.

Entertainment

Restaurants, bars and hotels in resort areas often feature live musicians from late afternoon onward, generally solo guitarists performing easy-going island favorites. Big-name Hawaiian musicians appear at Waikiki's major hotels, and larger cities like Honolulu and Kahului hold performance halls where you may be lucky enough

to coincide with slack key and ukulele concerts. Annual festivals on each island showcase the finest Hawaiian artists too, while at its best a Hawaiian luau is a true feast of traditional food, music and hula.

Eating

Hawaii's cuisine is a multicultural explosion of flavor, influenced by the Pacific Rim and rooted in the natural bounty of the islands. The first Polynesian settlers brought nourishing staples such as *kalo* (taro), *niu* (coconut), chickens and pigs. Later plantation-era immigrants imported rice, *shōyu* (soy sauce), chilies and other Asian and Spanish influences. Over time, all these wildly different flavors became 'local.'

Sample local specialties such as *loco moco* (a dish of rice, fried egg and hamburger patty topped with gravy), Spam *musubi* (rice balls with, you guessed it, Spam), *poke* (spiced-up cubes of raw

FROM MY POINT OF VIEW/SHUTTERSTOCK ©

marinated fish) and shave ice. Many top menus offer Hawaii regional cuisine, with chefs adding a gourmet spin to island-produced fish, beef and produce.

Activities

Mark Twain explored Hawaii for the *Sacramento Union* in the 1860s, and enthused in vivid detail about his many adventures. After climbing Haleakalā in 1866, he described the sunrise as 'the sublimest spectacle I ever witnessed.' Modern-day adventurers might pay the same compliment to the whole state. On the water, kiteboarders skip across swells, surfers ride monster waves, snorkelers float beside sea turtles and rafters bounce over choppy winter seas to see humpback whales. On land, hikers climb misty slopes while mountain bikers hurtle through leafy forests. Everyone stops to watch the latest fiery outburst on the Big Island. A truly sublime spectacle indeed.

★ Best Plate Lunches

Super J's (p249), Big Island

Ishihara Market (p148), Kaua'i

Da Kitchen Express (p203), Maui

Mana'e Goods & Grindz (p166), Moloka'i

Kahai Street Kitchen (p96), O'ahu

Shopping

Arts and crafts purchased in Hawaii can become treasures for a lifetime. Start your search at the many shops and galleries run by local art co-ops that sell members' work. Crafts with deep roots in the Polynesian past include *lauhala* weaving, the making of *kapa* (pounded-bark cloth) for clothing and woodworking. You can also find interesting art and jewelry at the islands' annual festivals, which typically stage art fairs along with food and live music.

From left: Haleakalā National Park (p207); *Loco moco* (p304)

Plan Your Trip
Month by Month

January

In Hawaii's wettest and coolest month, the tourist high season gets into full swing as snowbirds travel to escape winter.

♣ Chinese New Year

Between late January and mid-February, Honolulu's Chinatown (p38) erupts with lion dances, firecrackers and parades.

February

Peak tourist season continues, though winter storms bring rainfall and cool temperatures.

♣ Waimea Town Celebration

Festivities on Kaua'i's Westside spread across two weekends, with rodeo, hula, and canoe and stand-up paddleboarding (SUP) races.

March

A busy month, despite lingering rainfall. College students and families take a one- or two-week 'spring break' around Easter.

♣ Whale & Ocean Arts Festival

(http://visitlahaina.com) Maui honors its most famous wintertime visitors – migratory humpback whales – with an art show, live entertainment and kids' activities.

♣ Honolulu Festival

(www.honolulufestival.com) Mixing Hawaiian, Asian, and Polynesian traditions, this three-day festival culminates with a parade and fireworks.

April

Peak tourist season winds down as rains lessen. Resorts grow quieter after Easter.

♣ Merrie Monarch Festival

(www.merriemonarch.com) On Hawai'i (Big Island), Easter Sunday kicks off Hilo's week-long celebration of Hawaiian culture, featuring troupes from all over the world.

✗ Waikiki Spam Jam

(www.spamjamhawaii.com) Waikiki's wacky one-day street festival in late April/early May celebrates Hawaii's love affair with Spam with plenty of *ono kine grinds* (good eats).

YI-CHEN CHIANG/SHUTTERSTOCK ©

May

Crowds thin and prices drop slightly, while temperatures remain mild. Hotels sell out for late May's Memorial Day weekend.

☆ Lei Day

(www.kauaimuseum.org) The traditional Hawaiian art of lei making gets its own holiday on May 1. Waikiki crowns a lei queen, Lihu'e holds workshops and a lei contest, and Hilo on the Big Island hosts lei-making demonstrations and hula.

June

Early-June visitors take advantage of warm, dry weather plus hotel and flight discounts.

✿ Moloka'i Ka Hula Piko

(www.kahulapiko.com) Hawaiian oral history hails Moloka'i as the birthplace of hula. In May or early June, this free three-day hula festival draws huge crowds to sacred hula performances.

★ Best Festivals

Aloha Festivals, September

Triple Crown of Surfing, November & December

Merrie Monarch Festival, March/April

Moloka'i Ka Hula Piko, May & June

Kona Coffee Cultural Festival, November

✿ King Kamehameha Day

(www.kamehamehadaycelebration.org) All islands celebrate a state holiday on June 11. North Kohala (Big Island), the king's birthplace, holds all-day festivities.

July

Temperatures rise and rain is scarce. School vacations make this a busy travel month. Book early and expect high prices.

From left: Surfer in the Triple Crown of Surfing (p24); Lei Day, Honoloulu

✥ Pineapple Festival

(www.lanaipineapplefestival.com) Even though Lana'i no longer grows any pineapples, this early-July festival in Lana'i City celebrates the island's special relationship with the prickly fruit, featuring kid-friendly activities, live music and food.

✥ Independence Day

The biggest Fourth of July fun comes at rodeos held in the *paniolo* (Hawaiian cowboy) towns of Waimea (Kamuela) on Big Island and Makawao on Maui.

✥ Koloa Plantation Days

(www.koloaplantationdays.com) This nine-day festival celebrates Kaua'i's sugar plantation heritage, with a parade, rodeo and live entertainment.

August

Families taking summer vacations keep things busy all around the islands. Hot, sunny weather prevails, especially on the islands' leeward sides.

☆ Hawaiian Slack Key Guitar Festival

Open-air concerts by ukulele and slack key legends in mid-August on O'ahu.

September

After Labor Day weekend in early September, crowds start to fade away at beach resorts. Hot, dry weather continues.

✥ Aloha Festivals

(www.alohafestivals.com) An almost nonstop series of events on all the main islands during September. On O'ahu, look for a Hawaiian royal procession and Waikiki's block party.

October

The slowest month for tourism, October brings travel bargains. Weather is sunny, but humid when the trade winds don't blow.

✕ Hawaii Food & Wine Festival

(www.hawaiifoodandwinefestival.com) Hawaii's hottest chefs and artisan farmers gather for this homegrown celebration, in mid-October to early November on O'ahu, Maui and the Big Island.

⚡ Ironman Triathlon World Championship

This fabled mid-October triathlon on the Big Island's Kona coast is the ultimate endurance contest.

✥ Eo e Emalani I Alaka'i

(www.kokee.org) In early October, Kaua'i's Koke'e State Park re-enacts) Queen Emma's historic 1871 journey to Alaka'i Swamp with a royal procession, and music and hula performances.

November

Vacationing crowds (and scattered rainfall) start returning toward the end of the month. Thanksgiving is a popular and pricey time to arrive.

☕ Kona Coffee Cultural Festival

(www.konacoffeefest.com) For 10 days in early November, the Big Island honors Kona brews with a cupping competition, a coffee-picking contest, a cook-off, farm tours, live music and hula.

⚡ Triple Crown of Surfing

(www.vanstriplecrownofsurfing.com) O'ahu's North Shore – specifically Hale'iwa, Sunset Beach and Pipeline – hosts pro surfing's ultimate contest. Thrill-a-minute competitions for women and men run from early November through mid-December, depending on when surf's up.

December

As winter rainstorms return and temperatures cool slightly, peak tourist season begins in mid-December, making the Christmas to New Year's holiday period extremely busy – and expensive.

⚡ Honolulu Marathon

(www.honolulumarathon.org) On the second Sunday in December, Hawaii's biggest and most popular foot race brings more than 30,000 runners (over half of them from Japan) to Honolulu.

Plan Your Trip
Get Inspired

Read

Shark Dialogues (Kiana Davenport; 1994) Multigenerational saga, from ancient times to the plantation era.

Wild Meat and the Bully Burgers (Lois-Ann Yamanaka; 1996) Contemporary novel about growing up in Hilo, written in both English and pidgin.

Volcano: A Memoir of Hawai'i (Garrett Hongo; 1996) A poet expores his roots in the rainforests and lava flows.

Hotel Honolulu (Paul Theroux; 2001) Satirical tale of a washed-up writer managing a Waikiki hotel.

Honor Killing (David E. Stannard; 2006). Eye-opening story of a real-life 1930s murder on O'ahu.

Above: Maui's Big Beach (p202)

Watch

The Descendants (2011) Contemporary island life, with all its heartaches and blessings.

From Here to Eternity (1953) Classic drama about the build-up to the Pearl Harbor attack.

Forgetting Sarah Marshall (2008) Entertaining rom-com filmed in Hawaii's fanciest resorts.

Blue Hawaii (1961) Romp poolside on Kaua'i with a ukulele-playing Elvis.

Blue Crush (2002) Cheesy, but a local favorite for its surf cinematography.

Moana (2016) Controversial Disney animation, weaving a tale of ancient Polynesia.

Listen

The Folk Music of Hawaii (The Sons of Hawaii; 1971). Slack key guitarist Gabby Pahinui, plus superb ukulele and steel guitar.

Facing Future (Israel Kamakawiwo'ole; 1993) Still the all-time bestselling album by a Hawaiian artist: the late, beloved Iz.

The Remarkable Voice of Hawaii's Mahi Beamer (Mahi Beamer; 1959). Quite astonishing male falsetto singing in a deeply traditional style.

Hawaiian Song Bird (Lena Machado; 1962). Modern re-release of classic, jazz-tinged falsetto recordings.

Hawaiian Slack Key Guitar Masters (Dancing Cat Records; 1995) All the modern greats.

Plan Your Trip
Five-Day Itineraries

Big Island: Hilo to Mauna Kea

Only on the Big Island can you fully appreciate the power of Pele, goddess of fire and volcanoes. Here, pass lava deserts, hike across huge craters and see red-hot steam vents. Stay in Hilo, Puna or Volcano and reserve one day for Mauna Kea.

③

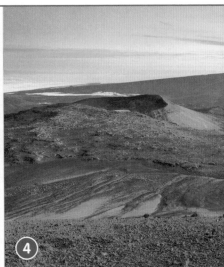

④

Mauna Kea (p233) Explore the summit area then enjoy the stunning sunset and magnificent stargazing.

④

Hilo (p270) Learn about volcanoes at the 'Imiloa Astronomy Center then picnic at Lili'uokalani Park, with views of Mauna Kea as your backdrop. 🚗 40 mins to Hawai'i Volcanoes National Park

①

③ **Puna** Seek out lava attractions, from tide pools to the newest black sand. 🚗 80 mins to Mauna Kea

②

Hawai'i Volcanoes National Park (p253) Check out Kilauea's ever-changing caldera before descending the scenic Crater Rim Drive. Spend another day hiking. 🚗 20 mins to Puna

Maui to Lana'i

You've got time, you've got money and you want outdoor adventures and tranquil relaxation in equal measure. But you're also willing to rough it when the rewards – hidden waterfalls and geological wonders – make it worthwhile.

Lana'i (p168) Hop off the ferry and explore Lana'i City followed by swimming or snorkeling at Hulopo'e Beach. ⚓ 1 hr to Lahaina, then 🚗 45 mins to Wailea

Kihei (p193) Spend two days snorkeling the coast, relaxing on the beach, eating local food and learning about humpback whales. 🚗 75 mins to Haleakalā National Park

Haleakalā National Park (p207) Rise early to watch the sunrise – make a reservation! – then hike into the crater moonscape. Camp in the park or overnight in Kula. 🚗 50 mins from Kula to Lahaina, then ⚓ 1 hr to Lana'i

Wailea (p193) Spend your last day on another glorious beach then savor a top-notch dinner at a restaurant with an ocean view.

Plan Your Trip
10-Day Itinerary

O'ahu to Kaua'i

Think of this as your 'town and country' trip to Hawaii. Start off in the breezy streets of Honolulu, sleeping in mod style at the classic beach resort of Waikiki. Then trade the big-city buzz for the small-town scene on verdant Kaua'i.

Waimea Canyon (p135)
Lace up your hiking boots and spend a couple of days hiking the canyon and Koke'e State Park.
🚗 2 hrs to Hanalei Bay

Na Pali Coast Wilderness State Park (p105) In summer, kayak 17 miles beside Kaua'i's epic sea cliffs. Otherwise, backpack 11 miles to Kalalau Valley. Either way, you've saved the best for last.

Hanalei Bay (p123) Win down again with a stay o Kaua'i's North Shore, swimming and stand-up paddle boarding in Hanalei. Take the gorgeously scenic road trip to Ha'ena State Par
🚗 25 mins to Na Pali Coas Wilderness State Park

SURAT KULAPATANA/SHUTTERSTOCK ©

North Shore Wend your way along O'ahu's lush Windward Coast, with jungle hiking trails, ancient lava-rock fishponds and captivating offshore islands. Save at least an afternoon for the world-famous beaches of the North Shore. Return to Honolulu.
✈ 40 mins to Lihue, then 🚗 1 hr to Waimea

Waikiki (p75) Laze on the sand, learn to surf and pose for a pic with Duke Kahanamoku. Catch the evening hula and light show at Kuhio Beach Park.
🚗 20 mins to Hanauma Bay

Hanauma Bay Spend a morning snorkeling in the bay, then swim off the beaches of Waimanalo, and surf, kayak, windsurf or kiteboard at Kailua Bay.
🚗 20 mins to Turtle Bay, then 🚗 5 mins to Waimea Bay

Honolulu (p35) Shake off the jet lag and explore the museums and historic sites of Hawaii's capital city then dive into the fun of Chinatown. 🚗 20 mins to Waikiki Beach

Plan Your Trip
One-Week Itinerary

Maui & Hawai'i

Looking for tropical adventures? Hit up Maui for its postcard-perfect honeymoon beaches, serpentine coastal drives and hang-loose surf scene. When you're ready for bigger thrills, jet over to the Big Island, where active volcanoes, mysterious valleys and deserted beaches await.

Road to Hana (p173) Drive this cliff-hugging road at a leisurely pace, stopping to kick back on the black-sand beach at Wai'anapanapa State Park. 🚗 3 hrs to Hana

Haleakalā National Park (p207) Spend a day hiking an ancient volcanic caldera and watching the clouds roll over the summit. Camp or overnight in Kula. 🚗 35 mins to Road to Hana

Hana (p186) Go horseback riding, grab lunch at a food truck and sunbathe on gorgeous Hamoa Beach. 🚗 2 hrs to Kahului airport, then ✈ 45 mins to Kona airport

Wailea (p193) Get into resort mode by strolling the sumptuous beaches, getting a seaside massage and dining on Maui-grown beef and produce. 🚗 90 mins to Haleakalā National Park

Hilo (p270) Wander through this harborfront city, exploring its historic architecture, eclectic shops and astronomy center. 🚗 40 mins to Hawai'i Volcanoes National P

Kailua-Kona (p246) Base yourself here to take advantage of the great local beaches and farm tours. 🚗 90 mins to Hilo

Hawai'i Volcanoes National Park (p253) Spend a full day here hiking the otherworldly Kilauea Iki Trail; driving Chain of Craters Rd; and taking in views of the newly widened caldera.

Plan Your Trip
Family Travel

With its phenomenal natural beauty, Hawaii appeals to families. Rather than hanging out in shopping malls, kids can play on sandy beaches, snorkel amid colorful tropical fish and romp through some of the world's most spectacular scenery. Then get them out of the sun for a spell by visiting museums, aquariums and historical attractions.

Hawaii for Kids

There's not too much to worry about when visiting Hawaii with children, as long as you keep them covered in sunblock and heed lifeguards' advice on ocean safety. Coastal temperatures rarely drop below 65°F and driving distances are short.

Just don't try to do or see too much, especially on a first trip. Slow down and hang loose!

Eating Out

Hawaii is a family-oriented and unfussy place, so most restaurants – with the exception of a small number of high-end dining rooms – welcome children. Kid's menus, booster seats and high chairs are usually available everywhere – but if you're going to need it at every meal, bring a collapsible seat.

If restaurant dining is inconvenient, no problem. Eating outdoors at a beach park is among the best island pleasures. Pack finger foods for a picnic, pick up fruit from farmers markets, stop for smoothies at roadside stands and order plate lunches at drive-in counters.

Grocery and convenience stores stock national brands, but the local diet, with its varied cuisines, brightly colored fruit and plethora of sweet treats, may tempt kids away from mainland habits.

BENNY MARTY/SHUTTERSTOCK ©

Entertainment

Even if commercial luau can seem like cheesy dinner shows to adults, many kids love the flashy dances. Children typically get a discount (and sometimes free admission).

If parents need a night out, the most reliable way to find a babysitter is to ask a hotel concierge. On O'ahu, you can also contact **Nannies Hawaii** (📞808-754-4931; http://nannieshawaii.com).

Cultural Activities

Hawaiian Islands Humpback Whale National Marine Sanctuary (p196) Visit Maui in winter and you'll have plenty of company – 10,000 humpback whales! Learn about their role in Hawaiian culture and see them on an unforgettable cruise.

Pearl Harbor (p50) Squeeze inside a WWII-era submarine; pace the decks of a battleship; or learn to fly in virtual reality, on O'ahu.

★ Best Beaches for Kids

Kuhio Beach Park (p78), Waikiki

'Anaeho'omalu Beach (p300), Waikoloa, Big Island

Wailea Beach (p202), South Maui

Halawa Valley (p154) Few places are so steeped in Hawaiian legend as this unspoiled valley on Moloka'i. Giant lizards are said to lurk in its remote waterfalls.

Hawai'i Volcanoes National Park (p253) Hike to petroglyph fields on the Big Island, or watch traditional *hula kahiko* dancing and chanting.

Hanalei National Wildlife Refuge (p129) Polynesian farmers grew taro in Hanalei Valley for a thousand years before Captain James Cook reached Hawai'i. Learn how to make poi on a farm tour.

From left: Hawaiian Islands Humpback Whale National Marine Sanctuary (p196); Kuhio Beach Park (p78)

Ala Moana
Regional Park (p59)

Royal Hawaiian
Hotel (p82)

HONOLULU, O'AHU

In this chapter

Honolulu at a Glance...

In Honolulu, you get to enjoy a boisterous, vibrant Polynesian capital, which delivers an island-style mixed plate of experiences. The city is steeped in history. Tour Victorian-era royal buildings and plunge into the warren that is Chinatown, Honolulu's oldest neighborhood, where 19th-century whalers once brawled and immigrant traders thrived.

Across the city you'll find appealing shops, restaurants and pubs. On the shore, ocean breezes rustle palm trees along beaches, while in the cool, mist-shrouded Ko'olau Range, lush tropical forest hiking trails offer postcard city views.

Honolulu in Two Days

Visit **'Iolani Palace** (p44), then look around the **State Capitol** (p54). Nearby have lunch at **Artizen by MW** (p68) in the **Hawai'i State Art Museum** (p54). Walk down to **Aloha Tower** (p58) to see the views, then have dinner at **Senia** (p70) in Chinatown.

On day two, breakfast at the legendary **Cafe Kaila** (p67). Head to the **Pearl Harbor National Memorial** (p52) to visit the **USS Arizona Memorial** (p53) and other WWII exhibits. Finish with beach time at **Ala Moana Regional Park** (p59) and dinner at **Alan Wong's** (p70).

Honolulu in Four Days

On the third day, spend the morning amidst the beauty of the **Honolulu Museum of Art** (p59), then lunch at its courtyard **cafe** (p69). Afterwards, drive up the Manoa Valley and walk up to beautiful **Manoa Falls**. Have dinner at **Sushi Izakaya Gaku** (p70).

Head out on day four to wander around **Chinatown** (p38)and its **markets**. Have Vietnamese fusion for lunch at **Pig & the Lady** (p69), before visiting the extraordinary **Bishop Museum** (p46). Unwind in Kaka'ako at **Honolulu Beerworks** (p72), then have dinner at **Fête** (p69).

BISHOP MUSEUM

Upper Manoa
Honolulu's green belt, with exclusive residences and the quiet retreats of forest reserve land.

MANOA FALLS TRAIL

CHINATOWN

'IOLANI PALACE

TheBus Central Terminal

University Area
A youthful area in the foothills of the Manoa Valley, filled with eclectic cafes and shops.

Downtown Honolulu & Chinatown Map (p56)
Ala Moana & University Area Map (p60)

Pu'uohi'a–Round Top
Scenic Drive (p63)

University Area
(p61)

Manoa Falls Trail
(p48)

PEARL HARBOR

✈
Daniel K Inouye
International
Airport

Downtown
The bustling heart
of Honolulu, and
the center stage of
Hawaii's political
upheavals.

Mamala
Bay

Ala Moana & Around
The 'Path to the Sea'
connecting Waikīkī
to Honolulu, home
to O'ahu's biggest
beach park.

PACIFIC
OCEAN

Hawaii State Capitol (p54)

Arriving in Honolulu

When you're on O'ahu, getting to Honolulu is easy using either your own rental wheels or TheBus public transportation system. Major car-rental companies are found at Daniel K Inouye International Airport and in Waikiki.

Where to Stay

Honolulu doesn't have much in the way of accommodations. The vast majority of rooms are in Waikiki (p75), which is really just a Honolulu neighborhood, so staying there means you're still close to much of what the city offers.

There are a few places to stay out near the airport, plus a couple of upscale hotels around Ala Moana Shopping Center that might as well be in Waikiki. You will find vacation rentals and bed and breakfasts in various neighborhoods across the city. Those on the hillsides can have sweeping views, but the vacation rental law means that this type of accommodation is in flux.

Buddhist ceremony

CHRISTIAN MUELLER/SHUTTERSTOCK ©

Chinatown

The scent of burning incense still wafts through Chinatown's buzzing markets, fire-breathing dragons spiral up the columns of buildings and steaming dim sum awakens even the sleepiest of appetites.

Great For...

☑ **Don't Miss**

Blooming orchids at Foster Botanical Garden, which is entered on the National Register of Historic Places.

The location of this mercantile district is no accident. Between Honolulu's busy trading port and what was once the countryside, enterprises selling goods to city folks and visiting ships' crews sprang up in the 19th century. Many of these shops were established by Chinese laborers who had completed their sugarcane-plantation contracts. Today, the neighborhood is a mix of immigrant-run businesses with links to the past and some of Honolulu's hippest and best restaurants and bars.

Chinatown Markets

The commercial heart of Chinatown revolves around its markets and food shops. Noodle factories, pastry shops and produce stalls line the narrow

Foster Botanical Garden

PHILLIP B. ESPINASSE/SHUTTERSTOCK ©

Foster Botanical Garden

Chinatown River St

Chinatown Markets

Ala Moana Blvd

N King St

Chinatown

Nu'uanu Ave

S Beretania St

S Vineyard Blvd

Honolulu Harbor

❶ Need to Know

There are pay parking garages scattered across the neighborhood.

✖ Take a Break

Enjoy incredibly fresh seafood in a market setting at Maguro Brothers (p67).

★ Top Tip

Visit in the morning as many of the food vendors and stalls begin running out of prepared foods and treats around lunch.

sidewalks, always crowded with cart-pulling grandmothers and errand-running families. In these busy warrens you'll see the whole range of O'ahu's bounty from both the sea and the land.

An institution since 1904, the **O'ahu Market** (Map p56; ☑808-538-6179; 145 N King St; ⊗6am-5pm) sells everything a Chinese cook needs: ginger root, fresh octopus, quail eggs, jasmine rice, slabs of tuna, long beans and salted jellyfish. At the start of the nearby pedestrian mall is the newer, but equally vibrant, **Kekaulike Market** (Map p56; 1039 Kekaulike St; ⊗7am-5pm). At the top end of the pedestrian mall is **Maunakea Marketplace** (Map p56; ☑808-524-3409; 1120 Maunakea St, Chinatown; mains from $5; ⊗5:30am-4pm), with its popular food court.

Dr Sun Yat-sen Statue

This **statue** (Map p56; 100 N Beretania St) honors the man known as the 'Father of the Nation' in the Republic of China and the 'forerunner of democratic revolution' in the People's Republic of China. Sun Yat-sen traveled to Hawaii in 1879 and was educated at 'Iolani School and O'ahu College (which later became Punahou School and had Barack Obama as a student). He learned the ideals of the French and American Revolutions and became president of the Republic of China (effectively now Taiwan) in 1912.

Foster Botanical Garden

You can spot tropical plants you've only ever read about in all their glory at this spectacular **botanic garden** (Map p56;

[P]808-522-7135; www.honolulu.gov/parks/
hbg; 180 N Vineyard Blvd; adult/child $5/1;
⊘9am-4pm, guided tours 10:30am Mon-Sat;
[P]), which took root in 1850. Among its
rarest specimens are the Hawaiian *loulu*
palm and the East African *Gigasiphon
macrosiphon*, both thought to be extinct
in the wild. Several of the towering trees
are the largest of their kind in the USA.
The self-guided tour is excellent and gives
an introduction to plants and trees found
across Hawaii.

Oddities include the cannonball tree, the
sausage tree, and the double coconut palm
capable of producing a 50lb nut – watch
your head! Follow your nose past fragrant
vanilla vines and cinnamon trees in the
spice and herb gardens, then pick your way
among the poisonous and dye plants. Don't
miss the blooming orchids or the elegant –
and appropriately named – royal palms.

Kuan Yin Temple

With its green ceramic-tile roof and bright
red columns, this ornate Chinese Buddhist
temple (Map p56; [P]808-533-6361; 170
N Vineyard Blvd; ⊘8:30am-2pm) **FREE** is
Honolulu's oldest. The richly carved interior
is filled with the sweet, pervasive smell of
burning incense. The temple is dedicated
to Kuan Yin, bodhisattva of mercy, whose
statue is the largest in the interior prayer
hall. Devotees burn paper 'money' for
prosperity and good luck, while offerings
of fresh flowers and fruit are placed at the
altar.

Sunday-morning market

Hawaii Theater

This neoclassical landmark (p72) first opened in 1922, when silent films were accompanied by a pipe organ. Dubbed the 'Pride of the Pacific,' the theater ran regular shows during WWII, but the development of Waikiki cinemas in the 1960s finally brought down the curtain.

After a multimillion-dollar restoration, this nationally registered historic site reopened in 1996 and now is a major venue for live performances.

By night, the elaborate neon signage has a seductive glow.

Izumo Taishakyo Mission

This Shintō **shrine** (Map p56; ☎808-538-7778; www.izumotaishahawaii.com; 215 N Kukui St; ⊗8:30am-4:45pm) **FREE** was built by Japanese immigrants in 1906. It was confiscated during WWII by the city and wasn't returned to the community until the early 1960s. Ringing the bell at the shrine entrance is considered an act of purification for those who come to pray. Thousands of good-luck amulets are sold here, especially on January 1, when the temple heaves with people who come seeking New Year's blessings. The original Izumo Taisha is in Shimane Prefecture, Japan.

THEODORE TRIMMER/SHUTTERSTOCK ©

Chinatown Walking Tour

Honolulu's neighborhood with the most foot traffic, Chinatown is also the city's most historic district. Soak up the atmosphere with this walk through the colorful streets.

Start Dr Sun Yat-sen Memorial Park

End Dr Sun Yat-sen statue

Duration 0.8 mile

0 — 100 m
0 — 0.05 miles

'A'ala Park

Take a Break Grab a bite to eat at the Maguro Brothers (p67).

Nu'uanu Stream

River St

4 On King St, continue past the red pillars coiled with dragons, then visit the buzzing 1904 **O'ahu Market** (p39).

Kekeaulike St Pedestrian Mall

Maunakea St

Classic Photo Wo Fat Building

Maunakea St

N King St

Martin St

3 At the corner of Maunakea St, the ornate facade of the **Wo Fat Building** resembles a Chinese temple.

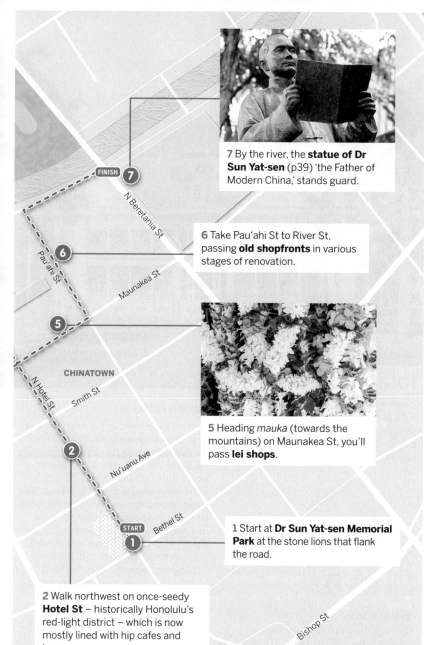

7 By the river, the **statue of Dr Sun Yat-sen** (p39) 'the Father of Modern China,' stands guard.

6 Take Pau'ahi St to River St, passing **old shopfronts** in various stages of renovation.

5 Heading *mauka* (towards the mountains) on Maunakea St, you'll pass **lei shops**.

1 Start at **Dr Sun Yat-sen Memorial Park** at the stone lions that flank the road.

2 Walk northwest on once-seedy **Hotel St** – historically Honolulu's red-light district – which is now mostly lined with hip cafes and bars..

FINISH

N Beretania St

Pau'ahi St

Maunakea St

CHINATOWN

Smith St

N Hotel St

Nu'uanu Ave

START

Bethel St

Bishop St

NAGEL PHOTOGRAPHY/SHUTTERSTOCK ©

'Iolani Palace

No other place evokes a more poignant sense of Hawaii's history. Built in 1882, the palace was modern and opulent for its time, but did little to secure Hawaii's sovereignty.

Great For...

☑ **Don't Miss**

The huge banyan tree on the palace grounds, allegedly planted by Queen Kap'iolani.

Palace History

The palace was built on the instructions of King David Kalakaua in 1882. At that time, the Hawaiian monarchy observed many of the diplomatic protocols of the Victorian world. The king traveled abroad, meeting with leaders around the globe, and received foreign emissaries here. Although impressive for its era, the palace did little to help the monarchy assert Hawaii's sovereignty over powerful US-influenced business interests, who overthrew the kingdom in 1893.

Two years after the coup, the former queen, Lili'uokalani, who had succeeded her brother David to the throne, was convicted of treason and spent nine months imprisoned in her former home. Later the palace served as the capitol of the republic, then the territory and later the state of Hawaii. In 1969 the government

ⓘ Need to Know

Map p56; ☎808-522-0822; www.iolani
palace.org; 364 S King St; grounds free,
basement galleries adult/child $5/3, self-
guided audio tour $20/6, guided tour $27/6;
⏰palace 9am-4pm Mon, from 10:30am Tue-
Thu & Sat, from noon Fri, basement galleries
9:30am-4pm Mon-Sat, tours 9-10am Tue-Thu
& Sat, to 11:15am Fri

✕ Take a Break

Sip Kona-estate coffee and savor city
views at Brue Bar (p72).

★ Top Tip

Call ahead to confirm tour schedules
and reserve tickets during peak
periods.

finally moved into the current state capitol,
leaving 'Iolani Palace a shambles. After
a decade of painstaking renovations, the
restored palace reopened as a museum,
although many original royal artifacts had
been lost or stolen before work even began.

Interior Tours

Visitors must take a docent-led or self-
guided tour (no children under five) to see
'Iolani's grand interior, including recreations
of the throne room and residential quarters
upstairs. The palace was quite modern by
Victorian-era standards. Every bedroom
had its own bathroom with flush toilets
and hot running water, and electric lights
replaced the gas lamps years before the
White House in Washington, DC, installed
electricity. If you're short on time, you can
independently browse the historical exhibits
in the basement, including royal regalia,
historical photographs and reconstructions
of the kitchen and chamberlain's office.

Palace Grounds

The palace grounds are open during daylight
hours and are free of charge. The ticket
booth is in the former barracks of the Royal
Household Guards, a building that looks like
the uppermost layer of a medieval fort.

Keliiponi Hale

A domed pavilion, originally built for the
coronation of King Kalakaua in 1883, is
still used for state governor inaugurations.
Underneath the huge banyan tree,
supposedly planted by Queen Kapi'olani,
the Royal Hawaiian Band (p73) gives
free concerts on most Fridays from noon
to 1pm, weather permitting.

Bishop Museum

Honolulu's local treasure, this museum celebrates the extraordinary natural history and cultures of Hawaii and Polynesia.

Great For...

☑ Don't Miss

The two-story exhibits inside Pacific Hall covering Polynesian, Micronesian and Melanesian culture.

Hawaii's version of the Smithsonian Institute in Washington, DC, the Bishop Museum showcases a remarkable array of cultural and natural history exhibits. It is often ranked as the finest Polynesian anthropological museum in the world. Founded in 1889 in honor of Princess Bernice Pauahi Bishop, a descendant of the Kamehameha dynasty, it originally housed only Hawaiian and royal artifacts. These days it honors all of Polynesia and is an unmissable part of Honolulu's cultural fabric.

Hawaiian Hall

The main gallery, the Hawaiian Hall, resides inside a dignified three-story Victorian building. The three floors are designed to take visitors on a journey through the different realms of pre-contact Hawai'i. On the first floor is *Kai Akea*, which represents

PHILLIP B. ESPINASSE/SHUTTERSTOCK ©

Kamehameha Park
Lunalilo Fwy
Kalihi St
Bishop Museum
Bernice St
Kapalama Ave

❶ Need to Know

☎808-847-3511; www.bishopmuseum.org; 1525 Bernice St; adult/child $25/17; ⊙9am-5pm; P🚹

✗ Take a Break

Feast on local faves *kalua* pork and *lomilomi* salmon (minced, salted salmon, diced tomato, and green onion) at Helena's Hawaiian Food (p68).

★ Top Tip

The gift shop sells high-quality Hawaiian art, crafts and souvenirs.

the Hawaiian gods, legends, beliefs, and the world of precontact Hawai'i. One floor up, *Wao Kanaka* focuses on the importance of the land and nature in daily life. The top floor, *Wao Lani,* is inhabited by the gods.

Pacific Hall

The fascinating two-story exhibits inside the adjacent Pacific Hall cover the myriad cultures of Polynesia, Micronesia and Melanesia. It shows how the peoples of Oceania are diverse, yet deeply connected, and is filled with cultural treasures such as canoes, woven mats and contemporary artwork.

Planetarium

The museum is also home to O'ahu's only planetarium, which has an ever-changing range of shows, including traditional

Polynesian methods of wayfaring (navigation). Check the museum website for upcoming shows.

Other Exhibit Areas

The state-of-the-art, multisensory **Science Adventure Center** is geared towards better understanding of Hawaii's environment. You can explore areas of science in which Hawaii has gained international recognition, including volcanology, oceanography and biodiversity.

The **Na Ulu Kaiwi'ula Native Hawaiian Garden** features species important to Hawaiian culture, ranging from endemic plants to those such as breadfruit that were brought to Hawaii by Polynesians centuries ago.

Manoa Falls Trail

The city's most rewarding short hike leads to a lacy cascade inside Honolulu's green belt.

Great For...

☑ **Don't Miss**

The unique and colourful plants growing near the falls.

The Hike

Honolulu's most rewarding short hike, this 1.6-mile, two-hour round-trip trail runs above a rocky streambed before ending at a pretty little cascade. Tall tree trunks line the often muddy and slippery path. Wild orchids and red ginger grow near the falls, which drop about 100ft into a small, shallow pool. It's illegal to venture beyond the established viewing area.

The photo opportunities are the stuff of tropical fantasy, but note that the trail can get crowded, especially in the afternoon. Come during the cooler, quieter morning hours.

Watch Your Step

Falling rocks and the risk of leptospirosis (a waterborne bacterial infection) make entering the water dangerous.

ℹ Need to Know

For more info on the island's trail system, see http://hawaiitrails.ehawaii.gov.

✕ Take a Break

Enjoy excellent breakfast and lunch fare just south down the valley at Waioli Kitchen & Bake Shop (p68).

★ Top Tip

Need more mileage? There are several trails near Manoa Falls in the Honolulu Watershed Forest Reserve.

Getting There

On public transport, take bus 5 Manoa Valley to the end of the line; from there, it's a half-mile walk uphill to the trailhead. By car, drive almost to the end of Manoa Rd, where a privately operated parking lot charges $5 per vehicle. Don't expect to find free parking.

'Aihualama Trail

Just before Manoa Falls, the marked 'Aihualama Trail branches off the falls trail to the left and scrambles over boulders. The trail quickly enters a bamboo forest with some massive old banyan trees, then contours around the ridge, offering broad and beautiful views of Manoa Valley.

After 1.3 miles of gradual switchbacks and a climb of 1200 feet, hikers reach an intersection with the Pauoa Flats Trail, which ascends to the right for more than

half a mile over muddy tree roots to the spectacular Nu'uanu Valley Lookout. High atop the Ko'olau Range, with O'ahu's steep *pali* (cliffs) visible all around, it's possible to peer through a gap over to the Windward Coast. The total round-trip distance to the lookout from the Manoa Falls trailhead is approximately 5.5 miles. You can also get to the lookout on tracks from the Makiki Valley and Tantalus Dr.

Makiki Valley Trails

A favorite workout for city dwellers, the 2.5-mile Makiki Valley Loop links three Pu'uohi'a-area trails. These paths are usually muddy, so wear shoes with traction and pick up a walking stick. The loop cuts through a lush tropical forest, mainly composed of non-native species introduced to reforest an area denuded by Hawaii's 19th-century *'iliahi* (sandalwood) trade.

USS *Missouri* (p53)

Pearl Harbor

Pearl Harbor has a resonance for all Americans. The site of the December 7, 1941 attack that brought the US into WWII is accessible, evocative and moving.

Great For...

🛈 Need to Know

☑808-422-3399; www.nps.gov/valr;
1 Arizona Memorial Pl; ⏱visitor center
7am-5pm **FREE**

☑ **Don't Miss**

A shoreside walk passes signs illustrating how the attack unfolded in the now-peaceful harbor.

A Surprise Attack

The bombing raid on December 7, 1941 – 'a date which will live in infamy,' President Franklin D Roosevelt later said – began at 7:55am with a wave of more than 350 Japanese planes swooping over the Ko'olau Range, headed toward the unsuspecting US Pacific Fleet in Pearl Harbor. The battleship USS *Arizona* took a direct hit and sank in less than nine minutes, with most of its men killed in the explosion that destroyed the ship. The average age of the 1177 enlisted men who died in the attack on the ship was just 19. It wasn't until 15 minutes after the bombing started that American antiaircraft guns began to shoot back at the Japanese warplanes. Twenty other US military ships were sunk or seriously damaged and 347 airplanes were destroyed during the two-hour attack.

Ultimately, the greatest cost of the Pearl Harbor attack was human. Except for three ships sunk that day – the *Arizona*, the USS *Oklahoma* and the USS *Utah* – almost all of the rest of the navy ships damaged were repaired and fought in WWII. And while the destruction and damage of the US battleships was massive, events soon proved that such vessels were already obsolete. The war in the Pacific was primarily fought by aircraft carriers, none of which were in Pearl Harbor during the attack.

Pearl Harbor National Memorial

One of the USA's most significant WWII sites, this National Park Service monument narrates the history of the Pearl Harbor attack and commemorates fallen service members. The monument is entirely wheelchair accessible. The main entrance also leads to Pearl Harbor's other parks and museums.

The memorial grounds are much more than just a boat dock for the USS *Arizona* Memorial. Be sure to stop at the two superb museums, where multimedia and interactive displays bring to life the Road to War and the Attack & Aftermath through historic photos, films, illustrated graphics and taped oral histories. A shoreside walk passes signs illustrating how the attack unfolded in the now-peaceful harbor.

USS *Bowfin* Submarine Museum & Park

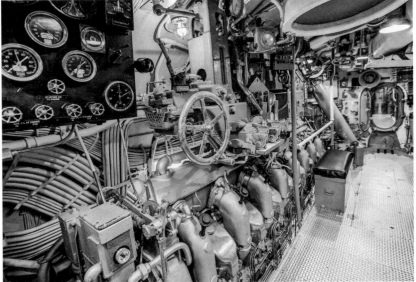

BENNY MARTY/SHUTTERSTOCK ©

The bookstore sells many books and movies about the Pearl Harbor attack and WWII's Pacific theater, as well as informative illustrated maps of the battle. If you're lucky, one of the few remaining, nonagenarian Pearl Harbor veterans who volunteer might be out front signing autographs and answering questions.

Various ticket packages are available for the three attractions that have admission fees. The best deal is a seven-day pass that includes admission to all. Tickets are sold online at www.pearlharborhistoricsites.org, at the visitor center ticket counter, and at each attraction.

USS Arizona Memorial

This somber **memorial** (boat-tour reservation fee $1; ⊗7am-5pm, boat tours 7:30am-3pm) **FREE** commemorates the Pearl Harbor attack and the military personnel who died in it with an iconic offshore monument reachable by boat. The memorial was built over the midsection of the sunken USS Arizona, with deliberate geometry to represent initial defeat, ultimate victory and eternal serenity. In the furthest of three chambers inside the shrine, the names of crewmen killed in the attack are engraved onto a marble wall. In the central section are cutaways that allow visitors to see the skeletal remains of the ship, which even now oozes about a quart of oil each day into the ocean. In its rush to recover from the attack and prepare for war, the US Navy decided to leave the bodies of more than 900 servicemen inside the sunken ship; they remain entombed in its hull.

Boat Tours to USS Arizona Memorial

Boat tours to the shrine depart every 15 minutes from 7:30am until 3pm (weather permitting). For the 75-minute tour program, which includes a 23-minute documentary film on the attack, make reservations online (fee per ticket $1) at www.recreation.gov up to 60 days before your visit. You can also try to secure tickets on the website the day before your visit, beginning at 7am Hawaii time – but these are very limited. It's best to reserve in advance.

Battleship Missouri Memorial

The last battleship built by the US (it was launched in 1944), the **USS Missouri** (☑877-644-4896; www.ussmissouri.com; 63 Cowpens St, Ford Island; admission incl tour adult/child from $29/13; ⊗8am-4pm) provides a unique historical 'bookend' to the US campaign in the Pacific during WWII. Nicknamed the 'Mighty Mo,' this decommissioned battleship is where General MacArthur accepted the Japanese surrender on September 2, 1945.

USS Bowfin Submarine Museum & Park

Adjacent to the visitor center for the Pearl Harbor historic sites, this **exhibit** (☑808-423-1341; www.bowfin.org; 11 Arizona Memorial Dr; self-guided tour $15/7; ⊗7am-5pm, last entry 4:30pm) harbors the moored WWII-era submarine USS Bowfin and a renovated museum that traces the development of submarines from their origins to the nuclear age, including wartime patrol footage. Undoubtedly, the highlight is going aboard the historic submarine.

Pearl Harbor Aviation Museum

This **military aircraft museum** (☑808-441-1000; www.pearlharboraviationmuseum.org; 319 Lexington Blvd, Ford Island; adult/child $25/12, incl guided tour $35/12; ⊗9am-5pm, last entry 4pm) covers WWII and the US conflicts in Korea and Vietnam. The first aircraft hangar has been outfitted with exhibits on the Pearl Harbor attack, the Doolittle Raid on mainland Japan in 1942 and the pivotal Battle of Midway, when the tides of WWII in the Pacific turned in favor of the Allies.

✖ Take a Break

Settle in at **Restaurant 604** (☑808-888-7616; www.restaurant604.com; 57 Arizona Memorial Dr; mains $12-25; ⊗10:30am-10pm Mon-Fri, from 9:30am Sat & Sun) on the waterfront for burgers and salads.

⊙ SIGHTS

Honolulu's compact downtown is just a lei's throw from the harborfront. Nearby, the buzzing streets of Chinatown are packed with food markets, antiques shops, art galleries and hip restaurants. Between downtown and Waikiki, Ala Moana has Hawaii's biggest mall and the city's best beach.

The University of Hawai'i campus is a gateway to the lush and historic Manoa Valley. Various outlying sights, including the fabulous Bishop Museum, are worth putting into your schedule.

◉ Downtown

This area was center stage for the political intrigue and social upheavals that changed the fabric of Hawaii during the 19th century. Major players ruled here, revolted here, worshipped here and still rest, however restlessly, in the graveyards. You can take in a lot of Hawaii history on a short stroll.

Note that the Fort St pedestrian mall suffers from all the social problems in evidence in Honolulu, including many homeless people.

Hawai'i State Art Museum   Museum
(Map p56; ☑808-586-0900; http://hisam. hawaii.gov; 2nd fl, No 1 Capitol District Bldg, 250 S Hotel St; ⊙10am-4pm Mon-Sat & 6-9pm 1st Fri of month) ✔ **FREE** With its vibrant, thought-provoking collections, this public art museum brings together traditional and contemporary art from Hawaii's multiethnic communities. The museum inhabits a grand 1928 Spanish Mission Revival–style building, formerly a YMCA and today a nationally registered historic site. The museum is also home to a fine gift shop and an excellent cafe, Artizen by MW (p68).

Hawaii State Capitol   Notable Building
(Map p56; ☑808-586-0178, tours 808-586-0034; 415 S Beretania St; ⊙7:45am-4:30pm Mon-Fri) **FREE** Built in the architecturally interesting 1960s, Hawaii's state capitol is a poster child of conceptual postmodernism: two cone-shaped legislative chambers have sloping walls to represent volcanoes; the supporting columns shaped like coconut palms symbolize the archipelago's eight main islands; and a large encircling pool represents the Pacific Ocean surrounding Hawaii. Visitors can walk through the

From left: Cathedral of St Andrew (p59); Queen Lili'uokalani Statue; Ali'iolani Hale and Kamehameha the Great Statue

open-air rotunda and peer through viewing windows into the legislative chambers. Pick up a self-guiding tour brochure from the governor's office, Room 415.

Queen Lili'uokalani Statue   Statue

(Map p56; State Capitol) Pointedly positioned between the state capitol building and 'Iolani Palace is a life-size bronze statue of Queen Lili'uokalani, Hawaii's last reigning monarch. She holds a copy of the Hawaiian constitution she wrote in 1893 in an attempt to strengthen Hawaiian rule; 'Aloha 'Oe,' a popular song she composed; and *kumulipo,* the traditional Hawaiian chant of creation.

Father Damien Statue   Statue

(Map p56; State Capitol) In front of the capitol is a highly stylized statue of Father Damien, the Belgian priest who lived and worked with victims of Hansen's disease (leprosy) who were exiled to the island of Moloka'i during the late 19th century. He later died of the disease himself. In 2009 the Catholic Church canonized Father Damien as Hawaii's first saint, after the allegedly miraculous recovery from cancer in 1988 of a Honolulu schoolteacher who

had prayed over the priest's original grave site on Moloka'i.

Ali'iolani Hale   Historic Building

(Map p56; ☎808-539-4999; www.jhchawaii.net; 417 S King St; ☺8am-4pm Mon-Fri) FREE The first major government building ordered by the Hawaiian monarchy in 1874, the 'House of Heavenly Kings' was designed by Australian architect Thomas Rowe to be a royal palace, although it was never used as such. Today, it houses the Supreme Court of Hawaii. Don't miss the **King Kamehameha V Judiciary History Center**, where you can browse thought-provoking historical displays about martial law during WWII, the overthrow of the monarchy and the reign of Kamehameha I.

Kamehameha the Great Statue   Statue

(Map p56; 447 S King St) Standing before the Ali'iolani Hale, a bronze statue of Kamehameha the Great faces 'Iolani Palace. Often ceremonially draped with layers of flower lei, the statue was cast in 1880 in Florence, Italy, by American sculptor Thomas Gould. The current statue is a recast,

Downtown Honolulu & Chinatown

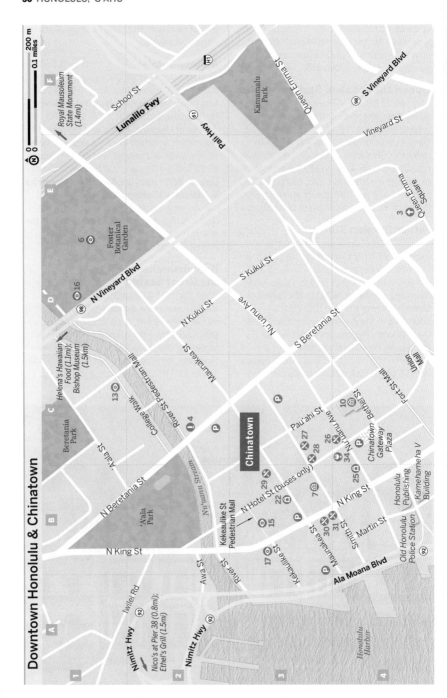

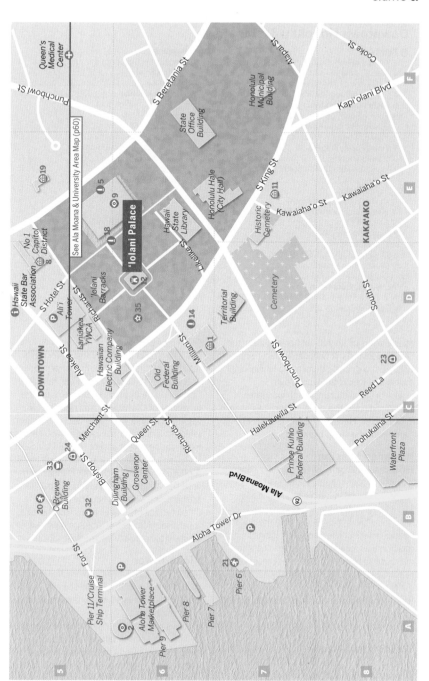

Downtown Honolulu & Chinatown

as the first statue was lost at sea near the Falkland Islands. It was dedicated here in 1883, just a decade before the Hawaiian monarchy would be overthrown.

The original statue, which was later recovered from the ocean floor, now stands in Kohala on Hawai'i, the Big Island, where Kamehameha I was born.

Hawaiian Mission Houses Historic Site
Museum

(Map p56; ☏808-447-3910; www.missionhouses. org; 553 S King St; 1hr guided tour adult/child $12/6; ☺10am-4pm Tue-Sat, guided tours 11am, noon, 1pm, 2pm & 3pm) Occupying the original headquarters of the Sandwich Islands mission that forever changed the course of Hawaiian history, this modest museum is authentically furnished with handmade quilts on the beds and iron cooking pots in the stone fireplaces. It's free to explore the grounds, but you'll need to take a guided tour to see inside any of the buildings.

Washington Place
Historic Building

(Map p56; ☏tour reservations 808-586-0248; www.washingtonplacefoundation.org; 320 S Beretania St; ☺tours by reservation only, usually 10am Thu) **FREE** Formerly the governor's residence, this colonial-style mansion was built in 1846 by US sea captain John Dominis. The captain's son became the governor of O'ahu and married the Hawaiian princess who later became Queen Lili'uokalani. After the queen was released from house arrest inside 'Iolani Palace in 1896, she lived here until her death in 1917. A plaque near the sidewalk is inscribed with the lyrics to 'Aloha 'Oe,' the patriotic anthem she composed. The building is still used for official events. To reserve a tour, phone or visit http://ags.hawaii.gov/ washingtonplace/visitor-information.

Aloha Tower
Landmark

(Map p56; ☏808-544-1453; www.alohatower. com; 1 Aloha Tower Dr; ☺9am-5pm; **P**) **FREE** Built in 1926, this 10-story landmark was once the city's tallest building. In the golden days when all tourists to Hawaii arrived by ship, this pre-WWII waterfront icon – with its four-sided clock tower inscribed with 'Aloha' – greeted every visitor. These days, Hawaii Pacific University occupies the mostly defunct Aloha Tower Marketplace, which was meant to lure in people arriving at the nearby cruise ship docks. Take the elevator to the top-floor observation deck for fabulous 360-degree views of Honolulu and the waterfront.

Cathedral of St Andrew Church

(Map p56; ☑808-524-2822; www.thecathedral ofstandrew.org; 229 Queen Emma Sq; ⊙usually 9am-5pm Tue-Fri, services 11:30am Wed, 5:30pm Sat, 7am, 8am & 10:30am Sun; P) FREE King Kamehameha IV, attracted to the royal Church of England, decided to build his own cathedral and founded the Anglican Church in Hawaii in 1861. The cathedral's cornerstone was laid in 1867, four years after his death on St Andrew's Day – hence the building's name. The architecture is French Gothic, utilizing stone and stained glass shipped from England.

Royal Mausoleum
State Monument Mausoleum

(Mauna 'Ala; http://dlnr.hawaii.gov/dsp/parks/ oahu/royal-mausoleum-state-monument; 2261 Nuuanu Ave; ⊙8am-4pm Mon-Fri) FREE Known as Mauna 'Ala, or Fragrant Hills, in Hawaiian, this is the final resting place of Hawaii's two prominent royal families, the Kamehamehas and the Kalakauas. Completed in 1865 for Prince Albert, it's adjacent to the public O'ahu Cemetery. The mausoleum is home to the remains of almost all of Hawaii's monarchs, their consorts, and various princes and princesses. A sacred place to all Hawaiians, the manicured grounds are peaceful and the Gothic Revival chapel is on the National Register of Historic Places.

◎ Ala Moana & Around

Ala Moana means 'Path to the Sea' and its namesake road, Ala Moana Blvd (Hwy 92), connects the coast between Waikiki and Honolulu. Although many people think of Ala Moana only for its shopping mall, Ala Moana Regional Park, which is O'ahu's biggest beach park, makes a relaxing alternative to crowded Waikiki.

A wave of development continues to transform the area with hip loft-style condos and faux-industrial commercial developments.

Ala Moana Regional Park Beach

(Map p60; ☑808-768-4616; 1201 Ala Moana Blvd; P♨) Opposite the Ala Moana Center mall, this city park boasts a broad, golden-sand beach nearly a mile long, buffered from passing traffic by shady trees. Ala Moana is hugely popular, yet big enough that it never feels too crowded. This is where Honolulu residents come to go running after work, play beach volleyball and enjoy weekend picnics.

The park has numerous facilities, including lit **tennis courts**, ball fields, picnic tables, drinking water, restrooms, outdoor showers and lifeguard towers.

Honolulu Museum of Art Museum

(Map p60; ☑808-532-8700; www.honolulu museum.org; 900 S Beretania St; adult/child $20/free, 1st Wed & 3rd Sun each month free; ⊙10am-4:30pm Tue-Sun, tours 10am-noon Tue-Sat, 1-2:30pm Wed & Fri-Sun; P♨) This exceptional fine-arts museum is among the best of its kind anywhere in the world. The collection is effectively a 'best of' summary of major art movements globally over the last several centuries (eg the Impressionist room includes a Van Gogh, a Monet, two Gauguins etc).

Plan on spending a couple of hours at the museum, possibly combining a visit with lunch at the Honolulu Museum of Art Café (p69).

Water Giver Statue Statue

(Map p60; 1801 Kalakaua Ave, Hawaii Convention Center) Fronting the Honolulu Convention Center, this magnificent statue was created by local artist Shige Yamada. It symbolically acknowledges the Hawaiian people for their generosity and expressions of goodwill to newcomers. Its sister statue is the **Storyteller** (p83) in Waikiki.

Ala Moana & University Area

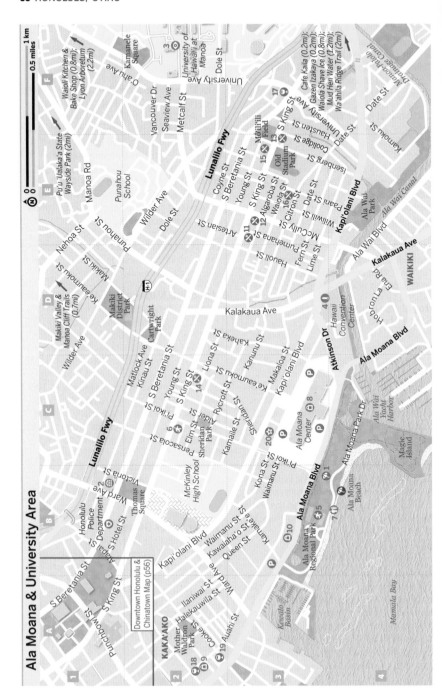

Ala Moana & University Area

◎ University Area

At the entrance to the lovely Manoa Valley, the neighborhood surrounding the University of Hawai'i (UH) Manoa campus (also known as Moiliili) has a vibrant feel, with a collection of cafes, eclectic restaurants and one-of-a-kind shops. There's plenty of action around the University Ave and S King St intersection.

University of Hawai'i at Manoa
University

(Map p60; UH Manoa; Map p60; ☎808-956-8111; http://manoa.hawaii.edu; 2500 Campus Rd; Ⓟ) About 2 miles northeast of Waikiki, the main campus of the statewide university system has a contemporary feel offset by towering, ancient trees. Today, its breezy, tree-shaded campus is crowded with students from islands throughout Polynesia and Micronesia. The university has strong programs in astronomy, oceanography and marine biology, as well as Hawaiian, Pacific and Asian studies.

From Waikiki or downtown Honolulu, take bus 4 or 13; from Ala Moana, it's bus 6 or 18.

◎ Upper Manoa Valley & Makiki

Welcome to Honolulu's gardens. Roads into the verdant upper Manoa Valley wind north of the University of Hawaii Manoa campus, passing historic homes and entering forest reserve land in the hills above downtown's high-rises. It can be pouring with rain up here while beachgoers are basking in the sunshine at Waikiki. Rainbows are frequent and provide the inspiration for names of the UH sports teams. Further west lies Makiki Heights, the neighborhood where former US president Barack Obama spent much of his boyhood.

Lyon Arboretum
Gardens

(☎808-988-0456; http://manoa.hawaii.edu/lyon arboretum; 3860 Manoa Rd; donation $5, guided tour $10; ◷8am-4pm Mon-Fri, 9am-3pm Sat, tours 10am Mon-Sat; Ⓟ🚼) ✈ Beautiful walking trails wind through this highly regarded 200-acre arboretum managed by the University of Hawai'i. It was originally founded in 1918 by a group of sugar planters growing native and exotic flora species to restore Honolulu's watershed and test their economic benefit. This is not your typical overly manicured tropical flower garden, but a mature and largely wooded arboretum, where related species cluster in a seminatural state. For a guided tour, call at least 24 hours in advance.

Pu'u 'Ualaka'a State Wayside Park
Viewpoint

(www.hawaiistateparks.org; 2760 Round Top Dr; ◷7am-7:45pm Apr-Aug, to 6:45pm Sep-Mar; Ⓟ) **FREE** The best free view in Honolulu! At this hillside park, sweeping views extend from

Diamond Head on the left, across Waikiki and downtown Honolulu, to the Waiʻanae Range on the right. The airport is visible on the coast and Pearl Harbor beyond that. The blue Pacific is a backdrop to everything. It's less than 2.5 miles up Round Top Dr from Makiki St to the park entrance. Signs detail the area's history as a macadamia nut farm.

🌀 ACTIVITIES

The beaches and the mountains help define Honolulu, meaning that outdoor activities are available for all. Think surfing, bodyboarding, stand-up paddleboarding (SUP), swimming in the sea and hiking the inland mountains. Free lit tennis courts dot the city and an abundance of golf courses are close at hand. It's an outdoor activities paradise.

Atlantis Cruises   Wildlife

(Map p56; ☏800-381-0237; http://atlantisadventures.com; Pier 6, Aloha Tower Dr; 2½hr whale-watching cruise adult/child from $48/24; ⊙whale-watching cruise 11:30am Jan-Mar) Atlantis runs whale-watching cruises with an onboard naturalist on a high-tech boat

designed to minimize rolling. Reservations are essential; book online for discounts. There is a 'whale watch guarantee' and transportation is available from select Waikiki hotels ($12). Atlantis also runs a **submarine tour** (Map p84; ☏800-548-6262; www.atlantissubmarines.com; 252 Paoa Pl, Hilton Hawaiian Village; ⊙60min tour adult $120, child taller than 36in $60) from Waikiki.

Blue Hawaiian Helicopters   Scenic Flights

(☏808-871-8844; www.bluehawaiian.com; 99 Kaulele Pl; tours from $230) Soar over Oʻahu. The 45-minute Blue Skies of Oʻahu flight takes in Honolulu, Waikiki, Diamond Head, Hanauma Bay and the whole of the Windward Coast, then the North Shore, central Oʻahu and Pearl Harbor. Everything you need to know, including video clips, is on the website. Book well ahead.

Makiki Valley & Manoa Cliff Trails   Hiking

(http://hawaiitrails.ehawaii.gov) A favorite workout for city dwellers, the 2.5-mile Makiki Valley Loop links three Puʻuohiʻa-area

Atlantis Cruises submarine tour

trails. These paths are usually muddy, so wear stout shoes and pick up a walking stick. The loop cuts through a lush tropical forest, primarily composed of non-native species introduced to reforest an area stripped by Hawaii's 19th-century *'iliahi* (sandalwood) industry.

Nā Mea Hawaii   Arts & Crafts

(Map p60; ☎808-596-8885; www.namea hawaii.com; Ward Centre, 1200 Ala Moana Blvd; ⊘class times vary) This highly recommended community-oriented bookstore (p65), art gallery and gift shop hosts free classes, workshops and demonstrations in hula dancing, Hawaiian language, traditional feather lei making and *lauhala* weaving, ukulele playing and more. Check the website for schedules and if preregistration is required. There's at least one cultural class each day.

Bike Shop   Cycling

(Map p60; ☎808-596-0588; www.bikeshop hawaii.com; 1149 S King St; bicycle rental per day from $20, car rack $5, delivery from $35; ⊘9am-8pm Mon-Fri, 9am-5pm Sat, 10am-5pm Sun) This place rents a variety of high-quality bicycles, including electric-assist, road, racing and mountain bikes, and can give you advice and maps of cycling routes to match your skill level. Road cyclists looking for an athletic workout should pedal the Tantalus–Round Top scenic loop. The Bike Shop also has clothing and accessories, and does maintenance.

Surf HNL   Surfing

(Map p60; ☎808-371-8917; http://surfhnl. com; 1hr lesson from $100, SUP sets rental per hr/day $30/60; ⊘8am-6pm) Surf and SUP lessons are on offer in Ala Moana Regional Park and Poka'i Bay on Leeward O'ahu. Transportation between Waikiki hotels and Ala Moana is included. For surfboard, bodyboard and SUP rentals, delivery to Ala Moana Beach costs $15, Ko Olina is $20. Reserve by phone or online.

Wa'ahila Ridge Trail   Hiking

(http://hawaiitrails.ehawaii.gov) Popular even with novice hikers, this boulder-strewn trail offers a cool retreat amid Norfolk pines and

 Pu'uohi'a–Round Top Scenic Drive

Offering skyline views to drivers and cyclists alike, the Pu'uohi'a–Round Top Scenic Drive climbs almost to the top of Pu'uohi'a (2014ft), aka Mt Tantalus. Bamboo, ginger, elephant-eared taro and eucalyptus trees make up the roadside profusion of tropical plants, as vines climb to the tops of telephone poles and twist their way across the wires. Starting above downtown Honolulu and the H-1 Fwy, this 10-mile circuit is a two-way loop called Tantalus Dr on its western side and Round Top Dr to the east. Many hiking trails branch off the loop, which passes by the unmissable Pu'u 'Ualaka'a State Wayside Park (p61) with its magnificent views.

Tantalus Lookout
WESTEND61/GETTY IMAGES ©

endemic plants, with ridgetop views of Honolulu and Waikiki. Rolling up and down a series of small saddles and knobs before reaching a grassy clearing, the 4.8-mile round-trip trail covers a variety of terrain in a short time, making an enjoyable afternoon's walk.

TOURS

Just west of Ala Moana Regional Park, fishing boats, sunset sails, dinner cruises and party boats leave daily from Kewalo Basin. More expensive guided tours may include transportation to/from Waikiki and they advertise various specials in the free tourist magazines available at the airport and around town. Many, such as helicopter flights and food

The Lovely Tradition of Lei

The tradition of lei dates back to the Polynesians, who wore garlands of everyday objects such as flowers and feathers for status, honor, and beauty. Giving lei to visitors to Hawaii dates to the 19th-century ships that first brought tourists. Passengers were greeted by local vendors who would toss garlands around the necks of *malihini* (newcomers or foreigners).

This continued during the golden era of steamship travel to the islands from the mainland in the mid-20th century. In the 1970s, when United Airlines led the way in promoting jet tourism to Hawaii, passengers could order their lei in advance, assured that a winsome local would be waiting in the terminal to place it around their necks.

Today the tradition continues. There is still a signposted row of drive-up lei shops at the airport. Better hotels still honor arriving guests with a lei and a few traditional lei-makers such as Cindy's Lei Shoppe (p64) are still going strong.

Given that you can get good lei for as little as $10, why not succumb to the gentle caress of the flower petals on your skin while the fragrant floral scent envelopes you? And, yes, they look great in selfies.

tours, may be cheaper if booked directly online, instead of through a third party such as a hotel concierge.

For a deep dive into Chinatown, check with the **Hawai'i Heritage Center** (Map p56; ☑808-521-2749; www.hawaiiheritagecenter.org; 1040 Smith St; admission $1; ☺9am-1:30pm Mon-Sat, tours 9:30am & 11:30am Wed & Fri) for details of its neighborhood walking tours.

Architectural Walking Tour Walking (Map p56; ☑808-628-7243; www.aiahonolulu. org; 828 Fort Street Mall; tours $15; ☺usually 9-11:30am Sat) Led by professional architects, these historically-minded walking tours will literally change your perspective on downtown Honolulu's capitol district. The state's business center and financial district also harbors some of Hawaii's most significant and cherished architectural treasures. Reservations are required – check the calendar and register online. The printed walking guides ($5) are excellent.

🛍 SHOPPING

Honolulu has unique shops and multiple malls offering plenty of local flavor, from traditional flower lei stands and ukulele factories to Hawaiiana souvenir shops, and from contemporary island-style clothing boutiques to vintage and antiques stores. The Ala Moana Center alone has over 340 stores and restaurants in the world's largest open-air shopping center.

Cindy's Lei Shoppe Arts & Crafts (Map p56; ☑808-536-6538; www.cindyslei shoppe.com; 1034 Maunakea St, Chinatown; ☺6am-6pm Mon-Sat, to 5pm Sun) At this inviting Chinatown landmark, you can watch aunties craft flower lei made of orchids, plumeria, twining maile, lantern 'ilima (flowering ground-cover) and ginger for all occasions ($8-10). Several other lei shops clustered nearby will also pack lei for you to carry back home. If worried about parking, you can order online and arrange curbside pickup.

PHILLIP B. ESPINASSE/SHUTTERSTOCK ©

Honolulu Museum of Art Shop

Honolulu Museum
of Art Shop
Arts & Crafts

(Map p60; ☑808-532-8703; http://honolulu
museum.org; 900 S Beretania St; ⊗10am-4:30pm
Tue-Sun) The shop at the Honolulu Museum
of Art provides an opportunity to purchase
superb Hawaiian artworks and crafts. On
offer are publications, stationery, prints,
posters, and works by Hawaii artisans and
designers that won't be found outside the
islands. No ticket is needed to visit the shop.

Kamaka Hawaii
Musical Instruments

(Map p56; ☑808-531-3165; www.kamaka
hawaii.com; 550 South St, Kaka'ako; ⊗8am-
4pm Mon-Fri) ✔ Kamaka specializes in gorgeous handcrafted ukuleles made on O'ahu
since 1916, with prices starting at around
$1000. Call ahead for free 30-minute
factory tours, usually starting at 10:30am
Tuesday through Friday. There are no retail
sales on site, but they can tell you where
to purchase both new and secondhand
Kamaka ukuleles.

Lonohana
Estate Chocolate
Chocolate

(Map p60; ☑808-286-8531; www.lonohana.com;
Salt at Our Kaka'ako, 324 Coral St, Kaka'ako;
⊗11am-6pm Sun-Thu, to 8pm Fri & Sat) ✔ All the
cocoa beans used for the chocolate sold in
this exquisite little shop are grown on a 14-
acre plot on O'ahu's North Shore. The brains
behind the operation is Seneca Klassen,
who grows the beans, manufactures the
chocolate and creates the treats sold here.
Sustainability is a core tenet of the company.

Nā Mea Hawaii
Books

(Map p60; ☑808-596-8885; www.nameahawaii.
com; Ward Centre, 1200 Ala Moana Blvd, Ala
Moana; ⊗10am-9pm Mon-Sat, to 6pm Sun) So
much more than just a bookstore stock-
ing Hawaiiana tomes, CDs and DVDs, this
cultural gathering spot also sells beautiful
silk-screened fabrics, koa-wood bowls,
Hawaiian quilts, fish-hook jewelry and hula
supplies. Check for special events, including
author readings, live local music and cultural
classes (p63).

Tin Can Mailman
Vintage

(Map p56; 📞808-524-3009; http://tincan mailman.net; 1026 Nu'uanu Ave, Chinatown; ⏰11am-5pm Mon-Fri, to 4pm Sat) If you're a big fan of vintage tiki wares and 20th-century Hawaiiana books, you'll fall in love with this little Chinatown vintage collectibles shop. Thoughtfully curated treasures include jewelry and ukuleles, silk aloha shirts, tropical-wood furnishings, vinyl records, rare prints and tourist brochures from the post-WWII tourism boom. There's an excellent selection of hard-to-find books too.

Salt at Our Kaka'ako
Mall

(Map p60; 📞808-260-5692; http://saltat kakaako.com; 691 Auahi St) This block-sized open-air mall mixes local shops and restaurants with national chains. It has the neighborhood's post-industrial vibe and has numerous interesting outlets, as well as the hip Bevy (p72) bar. There's also a large, mural-covered parking garage buried in the complex.

Kiholo Kai
Clothing

(Map p56; 📞808-936-9407; http://kiholokai. com; 125 Merchant St, Downtown; ⏰9am-4:30pm) Home to O'ahu's finest Hawaii shirts for men, this elegant shop is filled with refined patterns that will work nicely for an afternoon soiree at your waterfront estate. There's a wide range of natural fabrics and sizes – and you can get your shirt (they start at $100) in traditional or tailored fit.

✦ EATING

Honolulu has some of the best places to eat in the US, and its multicutural vibe extends to the restaurants. You'll find superb restaurants with influences from across Asia, the Pacific, the Americas and even Europe. Best of all, the city is the heart of Hawaii Regional Cuisine, with scores of talented chefs interpreting local flavors and produce.

Restaurants range from simple takeout joints to small storefronts to complex, designer destinations. Generally you'll find prices lower and quality much better than in Waikiki. Really, Honolulu's food scene is reason enough to visit the city.

From left: Kamaka Hawaii (p65); Pig & the Lady (p69); Waiola Shave Ice (p68)

Cafe Kaila

Cafe $

(☏808-732-3330; www.cafe-kaila-hawaii.com; Market City Shopping Center, 2919 Kapi'olani Blvd, Kaimuki; mains $8-12; ☉7am-6pm Mon-Fri, 7am-3:30pm Sat & Sun) This place at the top of Kapi'olani Blvd racks up best breakfast gold medals in local culinary awards. Expect to queue to get in for the legendary lineup of incredibly well presented breakfast specials. All the beauty is on the plate (the pancakes!) – the dining room is pure utility.

Ethel's Grill

Japanese $

(☏808-847-6467; 232 Kalihi St, Kalihi; mains $8-12; ☉8am-2pm Tue-Sat) One of Honolulu's greatest hole-in-the-wall restaurants, Ethel's serves Japanese diner fare with an Okinawan bent and an overlay of Hawaii. This bustling, cash-only place has 24 seats and six parking spots, and all are usually full when Ethel's is open. Ponder photos of sumo wrestlers on the walls while you tuck into garlic ahi, *mochiko* (batter-fried) chicken and miso soup.

Kahai Street Kitchen

Hawaiian $

(Map p60; ☏808-845-0320; www.kahaistreet-kitchen.com; 946 Coolidge St, University area;

plate lunches $11-15; ☉10:30am-7:30pm Tue-Fri, to 2:30pm Sat) This smart-looking corner place has a curving front and is hugely popular with locals. There are four sizable tables out front on Coolidge St, or you can head inside for more seating. The kitchen specializes in gourmet plate lunches, salads and sandwiches. The burgers are great, as is the pork *katsu* (deep-fried fillets), and breakfast includes eggs Benedict.

Maguro Brothers

Seafood $

(Map p56; ☏808-259-7100; Kekaulike Market, 1039 Kekaulike St, Chinatown; mains $9-16; ☉9am-3pm Mon-Sat) Wind your way around vegetable and seafood vendors to this little stall buried at the back of Kekaulike Market. Everything is spare and sparkling, especially the fish, which could not be fresher. Sashimi comes in many forms atop rice bowls, or opt for the perfectly grilled garlic ahi or teriyaki salmon.

Sweet Home Café

Taiwanese $

(Map p60; ☏808-947-3707; 2334 S King St, University area; shared dishes $3-18; ☉4-11pm) Expect lines of locals waiting outside this

cafe's tiny strip-mall location. On wooden family-style tables sit steaming-hot pots; pick your broth, then choose from countless options, including all kinds of vegetables, tofu, lamb, chicken or tender beef tongue. Besides the great food and good fun, there is complimentary shave ice for dessert.

Waioli Kitchen & Bake Shop   Cafe $

(☑888-744-1619; 2950 Manoa Rd, Manoa Valley; mains $8-12; ⊙7:30am-2pm Tue-Sun) Set in a vintage compound amidst enormous trees, this little cafe cooks up superb breakfasts and lunches. Sit out on the gracious Craftsman-style 1920s veranda of what was once a girls' orphanage. Today, many of the staffers are troubled locals learning a trade, serving up fantastic macadamia nut pancakes, excellent scones, burgers and more. Great coffee too.

Waiola Shave Ice   Desserts $

(☑808-949-2269; www.waiolashaveice.com; 3113 Mokihana St; shave ice $3-5; ⊙11am-5:30pm; Ⓟⓐ) This clapboard corner shop has been making the same super-fine shave ice since 1940, and we'd argue that it's got the formula exactly right. Get yours doused

with 20-plus flavors of syrup and topped by azuki beans, *liliko'i* (passion fruit) cream, condensed milk, Hershey's chocolate syrup or spicy-sweet *li hing mui* (crack seed). Go all Hawaii and get yours POG-flavored (passion-orange-guava).

There's an even older location in **Honolulu** (Map p60; ☑808-949-2269; www.waiola shaveice.com; 2135 Waiola St; treats $3-6; ⊙10am-6pm).

Artizen by MW   Hawaiian $

(Map p56; ☑808-524-0499; www.artizenbymw. com; 250 S Hotel St, Hawai'i State Art Museum; mains $8-16; ⊙7:30am-2:30pm Mon-Fri) This impressive cafe at the Hawai'i State Art Museum is the perfect spot for breakfast or lunch, or just for a coffee break while perusing the museum's stunning collections. There are ready-made grab-and-go *bentōs*, or sit and try the avocado toast, Artizen burger or seared ahi salad. After a walking tour, the mango-peach iced tea is a joy.

Helena's Hawaiian Food   Hawaiian $

(☑808-845-8044; http://helenashawaiian food.com; 1240 N School St, Greater Honolulu; mains $6-18; ⊙10am-7:30pm Tue-Fri) Walking

Macadamia nut pancakes with pineapple

through the door is like stepping into another era at this legendary institution. Although longtime owner Helena Chock has passed away, her relatives still command the family kitchen, which opened in 1946. Most people order à la carte; cash only. A few blocks southeast of the Bishop Museum, Helena's received a James Beard Award for 'America's Classics.'

Fête   Hawaii Regional $$

(Map p56; ☑808-369-1390; http://fetehawaii. com; 2 N Hotel St, Chinatown; mains $11-30; ◷11am-10pm Mon-Thu, to 11pm Fri & Sat) One-page and ever-changing, the lunch, dinner and dessert menus reflect the intensely local farm-to-table ethos at Fête, which is run by a talented couple. The food menus may be simple, offering up a good range of takes on seasonal island cuisine, but the cocktails, wine and 'after dessert' menus are extensive. A giant living plant wall adds to the natural charm.

Pig & the Lady   Vietnamese $$

(Map p56; ☑808-585-8255; http://thepigand thelady.com; 83 N King St, Chinatown; mains $10-30; ◷11am-3pm, 5:30-9:30pm Tue-Sat) An award-winning Vietnamese fusion restaurant, the Pig & the Lady is hugely popular. Book well in advance. Imaginative lunch *banh mi* (sandwiches) come with shrimp chips or prime-rib *pho* broth; delicious dinner options include Laotian fried chicken. Can't get a table? There's takeout and you'll spot these guys at Honolulu farmers markets. The tropical-flavored soft-serve ice cream is a dream.

Mud Hen Water   Fusion $$

(☑808-737-6000; www.mudhenwater.com; 3452 Wai'alae Ave, Kaimuki; mains $10-28; ◷5:30-10pm Tue-Fri, 9:30am-2pm & 5:30-10pm Sat & Sun) Chef Ed Kenney has pulled off a real trick at this comfy corner bistro: he's created a menu of comfort foods drawn from Honolulu's many cultures and he's harmonized it. One of the city's most lauded restaurants, Mud Hen Water has seating inside or at picnic tables in a cute little side yard.

Honolulu Museum of Art Café   American $$

(Map p60; ☑808-532-8734; http://honolulu museum.org; Honolulu Museum of Art, 900 S Be-retania St, Ala Moana; mains $17-26; ◷11am-2pm Tue-Sun) Market-fresh salads and sandwiches made with O'ahu-grown ingredients, a decent selection of wines by the glass and tropically infused desserts make this an indulgent way to support the arts. Open-air tables face the courtyard and soothing fountain with spectacular sculptures by Jun Kaneko. Reservations recommended; last seating at 1:45pm. There is no museum admission charge to dine at the cafe.

Lucky Belly   Asian, Fusion $$

(Map p56; ☑808-531-1888; www.luckybellyhi. com; 50 N Hotel St, Chinatown; mains $10-25; ◷11am-2pm & 5pm-midnight Mon-Sat) Sleek bistro tables are packed elbows-to-shoulders at this arts-district noodle bar, which crafts hot and spicy Asian-fusion bites, knockout artisanal cocktails and amazingly fresh, almost architectural salads that the whole table can share. A 'Belly Bowl' of ramen soup topped with three kinds of pork is superb, as is the Korean-style brisket.

Little Village Noodle House   Chinese $$

(Map p56; ☑808-545-3008; www.littlevillage hawaii.com; 1113 Smith St, Chinatown; mains $11-20; ◷10:30am-9:30pm Wed-Mon) If you live for anything fishy in black-bean sauce, this is Honolulu's gold standard. On the eclectic pan-Chinese menu, regional dishes are served up garlicky, fiery or with just the right dose of saltiness. For a cross-cultural combo, fork into sizzling black cod steak or roasted pork with island-grown taro. Reservations recommended for dinner; BYOB.

Nico's at Pier 38   Seafood $$

(☑808-540-1377; www.nicospier38.com; 1129 N Nimitz Hwy, Kalihi; breakfast & lunch mains $8-16, dinner mains $15-30; ◷6:30am-9pm Mon-Sat, 10am-9pm Sun) Inside, the dining room is classy, outside, the seating is near the waterfront and Honolulu's fish auction. Chef Nico was inspired by the island-cuisine

From left: Blue Hawaii cocktail; Shaved Ice; Charred cabbage

scene to merge his classical French training with Hawaii's humble plate lunch. Daily seafood specials are listed alongside market-fresh fish sandwiches and local faves, such as *furikake*-crusted ahi and hoisin BBQ chicken. Good bar.

Gazen Izakaya
Japanese $$

(☑808-737-0230; www.e-k-c.co.jp/gazen/honolulu; 2836 Kapi'olani Blvd, Kaimuki; mains $12-25; ⊙4:30-11pm) It might look nondescript from the outside, but Gazen Izakaya seems like little Japan when you walk through the door. There's an authentic and refined yet casual feel, and the menu features everything from fresh sashimi and sushi to flaming teppanyaki and silky smooth homemade tofu (try the sampler for $13). Opt for the sweet-potato *mochi* for dessert. Plenty of parking.

Senia
Hawaii Regional $$$

(Map p56; ☑808-200-5412; www.restaurant senia.com; 75 N King St, Chinatown; mains $20-35; ⊙11am-2pm Tue-Fri, 5:30-9:30pm Mon-Sat) Electricity, buzz, whatever, you'll feel the energy as you enter one of the city's most innovative restaurants. It's not

big, so book. Once seated you'll get the ever-changing one-sided menu. The food is local, fresh and defines creative. Don't miss seemingly mundane fare such as charred cabbage. The service, cocktails and wine list all excel.

Alan Wong's
Hawaii Regional $$$

(Map p60; ☑808-949-2526; www.alanwongs. com; 1857 S King St, Ala Moana; mains $35-45; ⊙5-10pm) ✔ One of O'ahu's big-gun chefs, Alan Wong offers his creative interpretations of Hawaii Regional Cuisine with a menu inspired by the state's diverse ethnic cultures. Emphasis in the open kitchen is on fresh seafood and local produce. Order Wong's time-tested signature dishes, such as ginger-crusted *onaga* (red snapper), steamed shellfish bowl, and twice-cooked *kalbi* (short ribs). Reserve in advance.

Sushi Izakaya Gaku
Japanese $$$

(Map p60; ☑808-589-1329; 1329 S King St, Ala Moana; shared plates $7-40; ⊙5-10:30pm Mon-Sat) Known mostly by word of mouth, this insiders' *izakaya* (Japanese gastropub) beats the competition with adherence to tradition and supremely fresh sushi and

sashimi – no fusion novelty rolls named after caterpillars or California here. A spread of savory and sweet, hot and cold dishes include hard-to-find specialties such as *chazuke* (tea-soaked rice porridge) and *natto* (fermented soybeans).

Chef Mavro
Fusion $$$

(Map p60; ☎808-944-4714; www.chefmavro. com; 1969 S King St, Ala Moana; multicourse tasting menus from $120; ☺6-8:30pm Tue-Sat) After a high-profile solo run, maverick chef (and namesake) George Mavrothalassitis has paired up with chef Jeremy Shigekane to continue creating avant-garde dishes, all paired with Old and New World wines. The award-winning kitchen matches the produce and flavors of Hawaii with chef Mavro's homeland of Provence and beyond. Choose between four- and six-course tasting menus. Reserve ahead.

🍷 DRINKING & NIGHTLIFE

Every self-respecting bar in Honolulu has a *pupu* menu to complement the liquid sustenance, and some bars are as famous for their

appetizers as their good-times atmosphere. A key term to know is *pau hana* (literally 'stop work'), Hawaiian for 'happy hour.'

Gastropubs – mixing craft beers and clever cocktails with excellent casual food – are popular, especially in Kaka'ako and Kaimuki. For the widest assortment of bars with sunset views, head to Waikiki.

Beer Lab Hawaii
Brewery

(Map p60; ☎808-888-0913; www.beerlabhi. com; 1010 University Ave, University area; ☺11am-10pm Mon-Thu, 11am-midnight Fri & Sat, 11am-7pm Sun) Three nuclear engineers working at Pearl Harbor, who were also beer geeks, opened this brewpub, where they brought a mad-scientist ethos to the beer. The ever-changing tap list easily has Hawaii's most experimental brews – they try all sorts of things with hops, flavorings, malts and techniques. You're welcome to bring in your own food.

Bar Leather Apron
Cocktail Bar

(Map p56; ☎808-524-0808; www.barleather apron.com; 745 Fort St, Downtown; ☺5pm-midnight Tue-Sat) An old-school bar with serious cocktails crafted by a new school of wizards. It's a casual yet elegant place to try one of four clever takes on the venerable old fashioned (trying all four is *not* recommended). The house mai tai arrives in a tiki-shaped box that's actually smoking. Ingredients include raisin-Infused El Dorado Rum, spiced orgeat and ohia blossom honey. It's located on the mezzanine level of the Topa Financial Center.

Honolulu Beerworks Microbrewery

(Map p60; ☑808-589-2337; www.honolulu beerworks.com; 328 Cooke St, Kaka'ako; ⊙11am-10pm Mon-Thu, 11am-midnight Fri & Sat) This corrugated-metal-fronted warehouse microbrewery is one of O'ahu's best brewers. The inside is a cavernous mix of distressed wood and concrete, while outside there's a sweet little beer garden. Besides an ongoing mix of seasonal beers, try the regulars such as the lemony Pia Mahi 'Ai Honey Citrus Saison. Creative pub chow soaks up the suds.

La Mariana Sailing Club Bar

(☑808-848-2800; www.lamarianasailingclub. com; 50 Sand Island Access Rd, Kalihi; ⊙11am-9pm) Time warp! Who says all the great tiki bars are gone? Irreverent and kitschy, this thatch-walled 1950s joint on the harbor is filled with modern-day sailors and bemused locals. Classic mai tais are as killer as the other tropical potions, complete with tiki-head swizzle sticks and tiny umbrellas. Grab a waterfront table and dream of sailing the South Pacific.

Brue Bar Coffee

(Map p56; ☑808-441-4470; www.bruebar.com; 119 Merchant St, Downtown; ⊙7am-4pm Mon-Fri) In a gorgeous old building on Merchant St, Brue Bar's passion for quality is keeping both tea lovers and coffee aficionados happy. Order a *cortado,* an uncommon coffee drink created with aplomb here: the shot of espresso and steamed milk is served just right. Find a seat and plan out your day.

Smith's Union Bar Bar

(Smitty's; Map p56; ☑808-538-9145; 19 N Hotel St, Chinatown; ⊙8am-2am) Every year, Smith's is a gathering spot for people

remembering the Pearl Harbor attack, as it was the chosen bar of the crew of the USS *Arizona* before December 7, 1941. The rest of the time it's a dive bar in the best sense, with cheap cold beer (even a few craft brews) and a genial crowd of locals, office workers, students and the odd tourist.

Bevy Bar

(Map p60; ☑808-594-7445; www.bevyhawaii. com; 675 Auahi St, Kaka'ako; ⊙4pm-midnight Mon-Thu, to 2am Fri & Sat) ☞ The old industrial area of Kaka'ako has become trendy and Bevy is one of the trendiest, offering inventive and classic cocktails in artsy surrounds. There's tasty small-plate food, served on wine-box tables on concrete floors under dangling exposed light bulbs, and an airy terrace.

⭐ ENTERTAINMENT

The local events calendar is fairly busy. Good online sources for what's on include *Honolulu Star-Advertiser* (www.staradvertiser. com/calendar) and *Honolulu Magazine* (www.honolulumagazine.com), but you're best off checking with specific venues.

Hawaii Theatre Center Performing Arts

(Map p56; ☑box office 808-528-0506; www. hawaiitheatre.com; 1130 Bethel St, Chinatown) Beautifully restored, this architecturally significant historic theater is a major venue for dance, music and theater. Performances include top Hawaii musicians, contemporary plays, international touring acts and film festivals. The theater also hosts the annual Ka Himeni Ana competition of singers in the traditional *nahenahe* style.

Republik Live Music

(Map p60; ☑808-941-7469; http://jointhe republik.com; 1349 Kapi'olani Blvd, Ala Moana; ⊙lounge 6pm-2am on performance nights) Honolulu's most intimate concert hall for touring and local acts – indie rockers, punk and metal bands, even ukulele players – has a graffiti-bomb vibe and backlit black walls that trippily light up. Adjoining the concert space is the Safehouse, a sleek lounge that's a vision in white.

Hawaii Theatre Center

Royal Hawaiian Band
Live Music

(Map p56; ☎808-922-5331; www.rhb-music. com) Founded in 1836 by King Kamehameha III, the Royal Hawaiian Band is the only band in the US with a royal legacy, and is the only full-time municipal band in the country. The band plays all over O'ahu (check the calendar online), including a free concert most Fridays at noon at 'Iolani Palace (p44).

🅘 GETTING THERE & AWAY

When you're on O'ahu, getting to Honolulu is easy using either your own rental wheels or TheBus public transportation system.

🅘 GETTING AROUND

Just northwest of Waikiki, the **Ala Moana Center** (Map p60; ☎808-955-9517; www. alamoanacenter.com; 1450 Ala Moana Blvd, Ala Moana; ⏰9:30am-9pm Mon-Sat, 10am-7pm Sun; 🚇) mall is the central transfer point for **TheBus** (☎808-848-5555; www.thebus.org; adult $2.75; ⏰infoline 5:30am-10pm), O'ahu's public transportation system. It offers a network of handy services, but the lack of useful overall system maps makes using TheBus a lot harder than it should.

Honolulu has a shared bicycle scheme called **Biki** (https://gobiki.org). There are dozens of stations for the distinctive turquoise bikes all over Honolulu and Waikiki.

Major car-rental companies are found at Daniel K Inouye International Airport and in Waikiki.

Traffic jams up during rush hours, roughly from 7am to 9am and 3pm to 6pm weekdays. Expect heavy traffic in both directions on the H-1 Fwy during this time, as well as on the Pali and Likelike Hwys headed into Honolulu in the morning and away from the city in the late afternoon.

WAIKIKI,
O'AHU

In this chapter

Waikiki at a Glance...

Once a royal retreat, Waikiki revels in its current role as a retreat for the fun-seeking masses. In this pulsing jungle of highrises and malls, you can still hear whispers of Hawaii's past, from the swaying of hula troupes to the legacy of surfer extraordinaire Duke Kahanamoku.

Take a surfing lesson, then spend an afternoon lying on Waikiki's golden sands. Sip a sunset mai tai and head out for an island-accented meal. Then catch some live music – this is a place to exhale and relax.

Waikiki in One Day

Start your first day with an ocean-view breakfast at **LuLu's Waikiki** (p93). Stroll down to **Kuhio Beach Park** (p80), genuflect in front of the **Duke Kahanamoku Statue** (p80) and stroll the waterfront. Rent a cheap snorkel set and explore the depths off **Kapi'olani Beach Park** (p87). Then, zip across the waters off Waikiki aboard the **Holokai Catamaran** (p90). Back on land, enjoy the authentic hula and music at the free **Kuhio Beach Torchlighting & Hula Show** (p79). For dinner, you can indulge in the flavors that have made Hawaiian regional cuisine a sensation at **Roy's Waikiki** (p94).

Waikiki in Two Days

On the second day, venture up Monsarrat Ave for fine coffee and breakfast fare at **Ars Cafe and Gelato** (p97). Wander to the water across the grassy expanses of **Kapi'olani Regional Park** (p83). Follow the sand around to **Kahaloa & Ulukou Beaches** (p79), where you can arrange an impromptu surfing lesson out on the breaks where the sport began at **Canoes** (p81). While away the afternoon at uncrowded **Fort DeRussy Beach** (p87). Enjoy sunset melodies at **House Without a Key** (p100) followed by a luxurious dinner at **Hy's Steakhouse** (p95).

Previous spread: Surfing off Waikiki beaches (p80)
ANOUCHKA/GETTY IMAGES ©

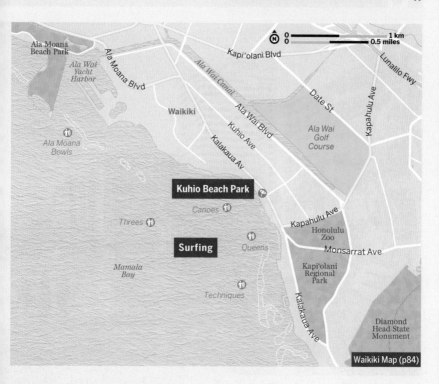

Waikiki Map (p84)

Arriving in Waikiki

Daniel K Inouye International Airport (Honolulu) About 9 miles northwest of Waikiki.

Express Shuttle Operates 24-hour door-to-door shuttle buses from the airport to Waikiki's hotels.

You can reach Waikiki via **TheBus** (p120) routes 19 or 20. Buses run every 20 minutes from 6am to 11pm daily.

Where to Stay

Waikiki's main beachfront strip, along Kalakaua Ave, is lined with hotels and sprawling resorts. Some of them are true beauties with either a historic or boutique atmosphere.

Further from the sand, look for inviting small hotels on Waikiki's backstreets. Many are quite affordable year-round. And don't forget the hundreds of condos, timeshares and apartments offered as short-term and holiday rentals, but beware that recent changes in the law have upended this sector and reduced choices.

Kuhio Beach Park

If you're the kind of person who wants it all, this beach offers everything from protected swimming to outrigger-canoe rides, and even a free sunset hula and Hawaiian-music show.

Kapahulu Groin

The beach is marked on its opposite end by Kapahulu Groin, a walled storm drain with a walkway on top that juts out into the ocean. A low stone breakwater, called the Wall, runs out from Kapahulu Groin, parallel to the beach. It was built to control sand erosion and, in the process, two nearly enclosed swimming pools were formed.

The pool closest to Kapahulu Groin is best for swimming. However, because circulation is limited, the water gets murky. Kapahulu Groin is one of Waikiki's hottest bodyboarding spots, so if the surf's right, you can find a few dozen bodyboarders riding the waves. These experienced locals ride straight for the groin's cement wall and then veer away at the last moment, thrilling the tourists watching them from the little pier above.

Great For...

☑ **Don't Miss**

The Prince Kuhio statue honors the Prince of the People.

JEFF WHYTE/SHUTTERSTOCK ©

ⓘ Need to Know

The Waikiki Beach Center (p82) has restrooms, outdoor showers, a snack bar and beach-gear-rental stand.

✕ Take a Break

Try a selection of fine mai tais and enjoy island tunes at Beach Bar (p98).

★ Top Tip

Never leave your valuables unattended on the beach.

Kahaloa & Ulukou Beaches

(Map p84) Just north of Kuhio Beach, the narrow beach between the Royal Hawaiian and Moana Surfrider hotels is Waikiki's busiest section of sand and surf. Most of the beach has a shallow bottom with a gradual slope. The only drawback for swimmers is its popularity with beginner surfers, and the occasional catamaran landing hazard.

Kuhio Beach Torchlighting & Hula Show

It all begins at the Duke Kahanamoku statue with the sounding of a conch shell and the lighting of torches after sunset. At the nearby hula mound, enjoy a truly authentic Hawaiian music and dance **show** (Map p84; ☑808-843-8002; www.waikikiimprovement.com; ☺6:30-7:30pm Tue, Thu & Sat Feb-Oct, 6-7pm Nov-Jan) **FREE**. This is no bit of tourist fluff, as top

talent regularly performs, including much-lauded hula experts from the University of Hawai'i.

Kuhio Beach Surfboard Lockers

Where most cities have bike racks or parking garages, Waikiki has a public facility that embodies the very spirit of the beach: a huge locker area for surfboards right near the sand. Located next to the police substation, this iconic storage area for local surfers is the perfect offbeat photo op. Hundreds of boards are stored here by locals in between their time out on the water.

Outrigger Canoes

Hop aboard a boat for a jaunt to see the sights above and below the water. Some surf outfits offer outrigger-canoe rides (from $100 for four people) that take off from the beach and ride the tossin' waves home – kids especially love those thrills.

WARREN BOLSTER/GETTY IMAGES ©

Surfing

Waikiki has good surfing year-round, with the largest waves rolling in during winter. Gentler summer surf breaks are best for beginners. Surfing lessons and surfboard, stand-up paddleboarding (SUP) and bodyboard rentals can be arranged at the concession stands along the sand at Kuhio Beach Park, near the bodyboarding hot spot of Kapahulu Groin.

Great For...

☑ Don't Miss

The statue of Duke Kahanamoku in Kuhio Beach Park (off Kalakaua Ave).

Duke Kahanamoku

The Duke was a true Hawaiian hero, winning numerous Olympic swimming medals, breaking the world record for the 100yd freestyle in his first competitive event, and becoming known as 'the father of modern surfing.' He even had stints as sheriff of Honolulu and as a Hollywood actor. Duke also pioneered the Waikiki 'beachboys,' teaching visitors how to surf. His statue (Map p84; off Kalakaua Ave, Kuhio Beach Park) is always draped in colorful lei.

Getting Started: Diamond Head Surfboards

One of the best Waikiki-area **shops** (Map p84; ☏808-691-9599; https://dhshi.myshopify. com; 525 Kapahulu Ave; surfboard rentals per day from $25; ◷10am-6pm Mon-Thu, to 7pm Fri-Sun) for board rentals of all kinds, it has

Waikiki Beach

MCDOW PHOTO INC/SHUTTERSTOCK ©

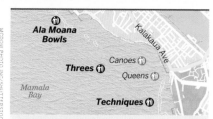

a huge range on offer. As well as renting out surfboards, stand-up paddleboards and bodyboards by the hour, day or week, it has excellent personalized surfing lessons based out of its well-stocked shop. Its Hawaii Republic T-shirts are popular.

Surf Spots for Beginners

World-famous **Canoes** (Pops; Map p84) surf break is right offshore – you can spend hours watching surfers of all types riding the curls. It is often busy with classes and is an easygoing mix of left and right breaks with a crowd from around the world enjoying long, consistent rides. When you have mastered Canoes, try **Queens** (Map p84), which is an all-round great wave. It's a longboard dream and is usually crowded, especially when any of the many surf contests are on.

Threes

Very reliable at low tide, **Threes** (Map p84) has a big following with locals, who appreciate its picture-perfect shape in almost all conditions (when highest, it forms small barrels). It's a half-mile out, so be ready for a long paddle.

Ala Moana Bowls

Literally known for its 'bowls,' this break has barrels you can stand up in when conditions are right. It's near the entrance to Ala Wai Harbor and is a fast hollow left. There's usually a serious crew of locals here.

Techniques

The name of this **break** (Map p84) dates to the 1930s, when surfers developed hollow boards in order to execute the maneuvers needed to surf these breaks. Previously the cumbersome heavy redwood boards couldn't be used here.

⊙ SIGHTS

Yes, the beach is the main sight, but Waikiki also has historic hotels, evocative public art, amazing artifacts of Hawaiian history and even a zoo and aquarium.

Stones of Life of Kapaemahu and Kapuni   Statue
(Na Pohaku Ola Kapaemahu a Kapuni; Map p84; off Kalakaua Ave, Kuhio Beach Park) Near the police substation at **Waikiki Beach Center**, four ordinary-looking volcanic basalt boulders are actually sacred and Hawaiian symbols. They are said to contain the *mana* (spiritual essence) of four wizards who came to O'ahu from Tahiti around 400 CE. According to ancient legend, the wizards helped the island residents by healing their maladies, and their fame became widespread. As a tribute when the wizards left, the islanders placed the four boulders where the wizards had lived.

Royal Hawaiian Hotel   Historic Building
(Map p84; ☎808-923-7311; www.royal-hawaiian. com; 2259 Kalakaua Ave; ⊗tours 1pm Tue & Thu) FREE With its Moorish-style turrets

and archways, this gorgeously restored 1927 art-deco landmark, dubbed the 'Pink Palace,' is a throwback to the era when Rudolph Valentino was *the* romantic idol and travel to Hawaii was by Matson Navigation luxury liner. Its guest list reads like a who's-who of A-list celebrities, from royalty to Rockefellers, along with luminaries such as Charlie Chaplin and Babe Ruth. Today, historic tours explore the architecture and lore of this grande dame.

Waikiki Aquarium   Aquarium
(Map p84; ☎808-923-9741; www.waikiki aquarium.org; 2777 Kalakaua Ave; adult/child $12/5; ⊗9am-5pm, last entry 4:30pm; ⊕) 🐟 Located on Waikiki's shoreline, this university-run aquarium recreates diverse tropical Pacific reef habitats. You'll see rare fish species from the Northwestern Hawaiian Islands, as well as hypnotic moon jellies and flashlight fish that host bioluminescent bacteria. Especially hypnotizing are the Palauan chambered nautiluses with their unique spiral shells – in fact, this is the world's first aquarium to breed these endangered creatures in captivity, a

Kapi'olani Regional Park

JAMES CRAWFORD/DESIGN PICS/GETTY IMAGES ©

ground-breaking achievement. It's a pleasant 15-minute walk southeast of the main Waikiki beach strip.

Moana
Surfrider Hotel
Historic Building

(Map p84; ☑808-922-3111; www.moana-surfrider.com; 2365 Kalakaua Ave; ⊘tours 11am Wed) **FREE** Christened the Moana Hotel when it opened in 1901, this beaux-arts plantation-style inn was once the haunt of Hollywood movie stars, aristocrats and business tycoons. The historic hotel embraces a seaside courtyard with large banyan trees and a wraparound veranda, where island musicians and hula dancers perform in the evenings.

Princess Kaiulani Statue
Statue

(Map p84; off Kuhio Ave) Princess Kaiulani was heir to the throne when the Kingdom of Hawaii was overthrown in 1893. This statue of the princess feeding her beloved peacocks sits in Waikiki's Kaiulani Triangle Park and was unveiled in 1999 on the 124th anniversary of her birth. Known for her beauty, intelligence and determination, the Princess visited President Grover Cleveland in Washington after the overthrow but could not prevent the annexation of Hawaii by the US. She died at the young age of 23.

Makua and Kila Statue
Statue

(Map p84; off Kalakaua Ave, Kuhio Beach Park) A bronze charmer, this warm-hearted public art sculpture shows a young surfer (Makua) sharing a moment with a monk seal (Kila). It's inspired by the children's book *Makua Lives on the Beach*, a story about Hawaiian values of love and respect.

Kapi'olani Regional Park
Park

(Map p84; ☑808-768-4623; off Kalakaua & Paki Aves) In its early days, horse racing and band concerts were the biggest attractions at Waikiki's favorite green space. Although the racetrack is long gone, this park named after Queen Kapi'olani, who once lived nearby, is still a beloved outdoor venue for live music and local community gatherings, from farmers markets and arts-and-crafts fairs

to festivals and rugby matches. On a stroll, you'll marvel at the many huge, old trees.

Queen Kapi'olani Statue
Statue

(Map p84; off Kalakaua Ave, Kap'iolani Regional Park) This bronze statue depicts Queen Kapi'olani, the wife of King David Kalakaua – his statue sits at the other end of Waikiki. The queen was a beloved philanthropist, known for her love of children. Among other accomplishments, she founded a maternity home in 1890 for disadvantaged Hawaiians and today you'll hear her name often – the park, a hospital, a major boulevard and a community college are named for her.

Surfer on a Wave Statue
Statue

(Map p84; off Kalakaua Ave) Opposite the entrance to Honolulu Zoo and right on the beach, the *Surfer on a Wave* statue celebrates surfing as a major part of the culture of Waikiki. Cast in bronze by Robert Pasby, it was unveiled in 2003.

Storyteller Statue
Statue

(Map p84; off Kalakaua Ave) This bronze statue just off Kalakaua Ave represents 'The Storytellers', the keepers of Hawaiian culture. For centuries, women have been key to the preservation of Hawaiian oral traditions, and the storytellers preserve the identity of their people and land by reciting poems, songs, chants and genealogies. The Storyteller's companion statue is the **Water Giver statue** (1801 Kalakaua) at the Hawaiian Convention Center.

US Army
Museum of Hawai'i
Museum

(Map p84; ☑808-955-9552; www.hiarmymuseumsoc.org; 2131 Kalia Rd; donations welcome, audio tour $5; ⊘10am-5pm Tue-Sat, last entry 4:15pm; **P**) **FREE** At Fort DeRussy, this museum exhibits an almost mind-numbing array of military paraphernalia as it relates to Hawaii's history, starting with the shark-tooth clubs that Kamehameha the Great used to win control of the islands more than two centuries ago. Old photographs and stories convey an understanding of the influence of the US military presence in Hawaii.

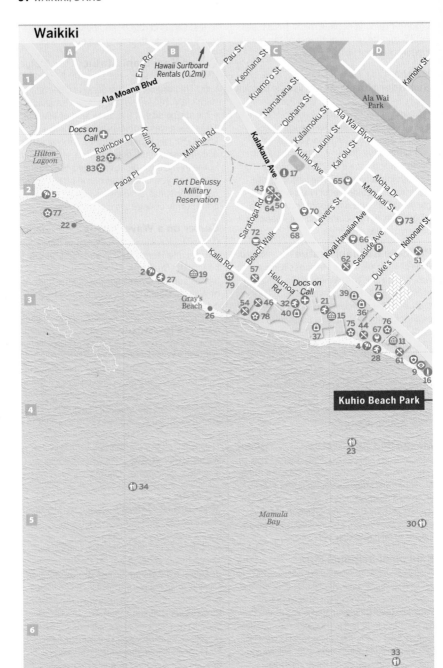

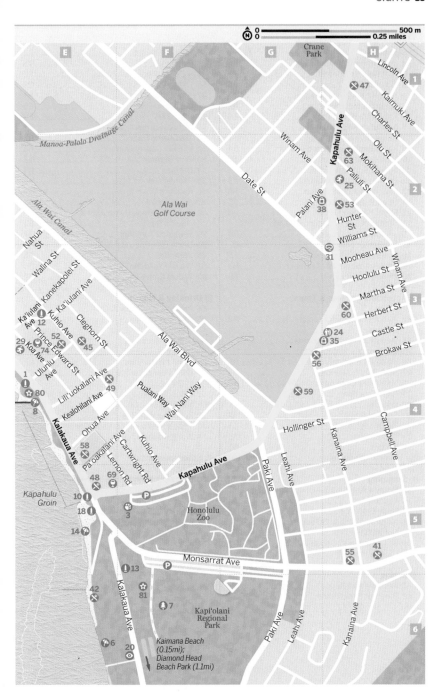

Waikiki

Honolulu Zoo   Zoo

(Map p84; ☏808-971-7171; www.honoluluzoo.
org; cnr Kapahulu & Kalakaua Aves; adult/child
$19/11; ☺9am-4:30pm; P♿) Honolulu Zoo
displays tropical species from around the
globe. There are 42 acres of tropical greenery, over 1200 animals and a petting zoo
for kids. Hawaii has no endemic land mam-
mals, but in the aviary near the entrance
you can see some native birds, including
the *nene* (Hawaiian goose) and '*apapane,*
a bright-red Hawaiian honeycreeper. Make
reservations for family-oriented twilight
tours and zoo camp-outs.

The city-run zoo has struggled through
years of challenges. In 2016 it lost its Association of Zoos and Aquariums accredita-
tion over its perennial funding woes. However,
voters approved a dedicated revenue
stream, and the zoo regained its accredi-
tation in 2020. In a positive step forward, it
welcomed three new cheetahs in 2019.

◉ BEACHES

Queen's Surf Beach   Beach

(Wall's; Map p84; off Kalakaua Ave, Kapi'olani
Beach Park; ♿) Just south of Kuhio Beach,
the namesake beach for the famous surf
break is a great place for families, as the
waves are rarely large when they reach
shore but they are still large enough for
bodyboarding, which means older kids can
frolic for hours. Also, there are lifeguards.
At the south end of the beach, the area in
front of the beach pavilion is popular with
the local gay community.

Fort DeRussy Beach   Beach

(Map p84; off Kalia Rd; ♿) Less crowded than
adjoining beaches, this often-overlooked
beauty extends along the shore of its namesake military facility. The water is usually
calm and good for swimming, but it's shallow
at low tide. When conditions are right, windsurfers, bodyboarders and board surfers all
play here. KOA Beach Service (p88) rents
bodyboards, kayaks and snorkel sets. A wide,
grassy lawn with palm trees offers some
sparse shade, and an alternative to baking
on the sand.

Kahanamoku Beach   Beach

(Map p84; Paoa Pl; ♿) Fronting the **Hilton
Hawaiian Village** (☏808-949-4321; www.
hiltonhawaiianvillage.com; 2005 Kalia Rd), large
Kahanamoku Beach is Waikiki's western-
most beach. It takes its name from Duke
Kahanamoku (1890–1968), the legendary
Waikiki surfer whose family once owned the
land where the resort now stands. Hawaii's
champion surfer and Olympic gold medal
winner learned to swim right here. The beach
offers calm swimming conditions and a gently sloping, if rocky, bottom. Public access is
at the end of Paoa Pl, off Kalia Rd, and Holo-
moana St (where there's easy parking).

Kaimana Beach   Beach

At the Diamond Head edge of Waikiki,
Kaimana is a prime triangle of sandy oceanfront that's far from the frenzied tourist
scene. It's commonly called Sans Souci
Beach for the name of the hotel that once
stood near today's **New Otani Kaimana
Beach Hotel** (☏808-923-1555; www.kaimana.
com; 2863 Kalakaua Ave). Local residents
come here for their daily swims. A shallow
reef close to shore and a breakwater make
for wave-free, protected waters and provide
good snorkeling. There are lifeguards.

Kapi'olani Beach Park Beach   Beach

(Map p84; off Kalakaua Ave, Kapi'olani Regional
Park) Where did all the tourists go? From
Kapahulu Groin south to the Natatorium, this
peaceful stretch of beach, backed by a green
space of banyan trees and grassy lawns, offers a relaxing niche with none of the frenzy
found on the beaches fronting the Waikiki
hotel strip. Facilities include restrooms and
outdoor showers. Kapi'olani Beach is a popular weekend picnicking spot for local families,
who unload the kids to splash in the ocean
while adults fire up the BBQ.

The widest northern end of Kapi'olani
Beach is nicknamed Queen's Surf Beach
(p115). On a few summer nights, classic
movies are shown for free on a huge outdoor screen (www.sunsetonthebeach.net).

Right in the middle sits the excellent
Barefoot Beach Cafe (p123), reason
enough to visit this stretch of the shore.

Diamond Head

The extinct crater of Diamond Head is now a state monument, with picnic tables and a spectacular hiking trail up to the 761ft-high summit. The trail was built in 1908 to service military observation stations located along the crater rim.

Inside the crater rim, there are information and historical displays, restrooms, drinking fountains and a picnic area. From Waikiki, catch bus 23 or 24; from the closest bus stop, it's about a 20-minute walk to the trailhead. By car, take Monsarrat Ave to Diamond Head Rd and turn right immediately after passing Kapi'olani Community College (KCC). Enter the park through Kahala Tunnel.

From the **Diamond Head Lookout** (3483 Diamond Head Rd), there are fine views over Kuilei Cliffs Beach Park and up the coast toward Kahala. On the east side of the parking area, look for the Amelia Earhart Marker, which recalls her 1935 flight from Hawaii to California. It's an enjoyable 1.4-mile walk beyond Kaimana Beach in Waikiki.

NORBERT TURI/SHUTTERSTOCK ©

🏃 ACTIVITIES

Waikiki is good for swimming, bodyboarding, surfing, sailing and other watersports most of the year, and there are lifeguards, restrooms and outdoor showers scattered along the beachfront. Between May and September, summer swells make the water a little rough for swimming, but great for surfing.

WATER SPORTS

Hawaii Surfboard Rentals
Surfing, SUP

(☑808-689-8989; www.hawaiisurfboardrentals. com; surfboard rental minimum 2 days $60; ⊗7am-8pm) This outfit has a huge variety of boards to rent. Free surfboard, SUP, bodyboard and car-rack delivery and pickup across Waikiki and much of O'ahu; weekly rates are an especially good deal.

KOA Beach Service
Beach

(Map p84; ☑808-944-1962; https://koabeach service.com; Fort DeRussy Beach; umbrella & 2 beach loungers all day $50; ⊗9am-6pm Jun-Aug, to 5pm Sep-May) Right on the sand, this well-run stand has everything you might want for a fun-filled day on uncrowded Fort DeRussy Beach. Rentals include several types of chairs and loungers, lockers, SUPs (all day $75), surfboards (all day $50), one-person kayaks (per hour $15) and snorkel sets (all day $20).

SNORKELING & SCUBA DIVING

Waikiki's crowded central beaches are not particularly good for snorkeling. Two top choices are Kaimana Beach (p87) and Queen's Surf Beach (p87), where you'll find some live coral and a decent variety of tropical fish. But to really see the gorgeous stuff – coral gardens, manta rays and more exotic fish – head out on a boat. You can easily rent snorkel sets and scuba-diving equipment, or book ahead for boat trips and PADI open-water certification courses.

Snorkel Bob's
Snorkeling

(Map p84; ☑808-735-7944; www.snorkelbob. com; 700 Kapahulu Ave; snorkel set rental per week from $9; ⊗8am-5pm) A top spot to get your gear. Rates vary depending on the quality of the snorkeling gear and accessories packages, but excellent weekly discounts are available and online reservations taken. You can even rent gear on O'ahu, then return it to a Snorkel Bob's location on another island. It also rents beach gear and wetsuits.

O'ahu Diving
Diving

(☑808-721-4210; www.oahudiving.com; 2-dive trips for beginners $145) This place specializes in first-time experiences for beginner divers without certification, as well as deepwater boat dives offshore and PADI refresher classes if you're already certified and have some experience under your belt. Trips depart from various locations near Waikiki.

KAYAKING

Fort DeRussy Beach has fewer swimmers and catamarans to share the water with than Waikiki's central beaches, which makes it a good spot for kayaking.

Go Bananas Watersports
Water Sports

(Map p84; ☑808-737-9514; https://gobananas kayaks.com; 799 Kapahulu Ave; 1-/2-person kayak per day $35/50; ☺9am-7pm) Everything you need to kayak in the waters off O'ahu is available at this fully stocked shop, including great advice. Rates include everything you need for your adventure, even roof racks for rental cars. It also rents SUPs.

SPAS

Abhasa Spa
Spa

(Map p84; ☑808-922-8200; www.abhasa.com; 2259 Kalakaua Ave, Royal Hawaiian Hotel; 50min massage from $165; ☺9am-9pm) Locally inspired experiences include traditional Hawaiian-style *lomilomi* ('loving hands') and *pohaku* (hot stone) massage, sea-salt scrubs, as well as *kukui* (candlenut), coconut and coffee-oil body treatments.

A sister spa to **Spa Khakara** (Map p84; ☑808-685-7600; www.khakara.com; 2255 Kalakaua Ave, Sheraton Waikiki; 50min massage from $140; ☺9am-9pm).

Na Ho'ola Spa
Spa

(Map p84; ☑808-237-6330; www.nahoolaspa waikiki.com; 2424 Kalakaua Ave, Hyatt Regency Waikiki; 50min massage from $200; ☺8:30am-9pm) At this bi-level spa, *limu* (seaweed) wraps detoxify, *kele-kele* (mud) wraps soothe sore muscles and *ti*-leaf wraps heal sun-ravaged skin, while macadamia-nut oil and fresh pineapple scrubs exfoliate. Ocean views are blissful.

Duke Kahanamoku Statue (p80)

 TOURS

Several catamaran cruises leave right from Waikiki Beach – just walk down to the sand, step into the surf and hop aboard. There is the option of a 90-minute, all-you-can-drink 'booze cruise.' Reservations are recommended for sunset sails, which sell out quickly.

Na Hoku II Catamaran   Cruise

(Map p84; ☎808-336-7422; https://nahoku2. com; near Outrigger Waikiki Beach Resort; 90min catamaran trips $40-45) With its unmistakable yellow-and-red striped sails, this catamaran is a local icon. These hard-drinkin' tours (drinks included in ticket price) set sail four times daily, shoving off from in front of Duke's Waikiki (p99) bar. The sunset sail usually sells out, so book early.

Holokai Catamaran   Cruise

(Map p84; ☎808-922-2210; https://sailholokai. com; near Outrigger Reef Waikiki Beach Resort, Gray's Beach; catamaran trips $40-80; 👪)

Sporting tall orange and white sails and a white body, this custom-built catamaran offers windy but thrilling high-speed cruises, more relaxed snorkel trips and, of course, a sunset booze cruise departing from Gray's Beach between the **Halekulani** (☎800-367-2343; www.halekulani.com; 2199 Kalia Rd;) resort and the Outrigger Reef Waikiki Beach Resort.

SHOPPING

Amidst the chains dotting Waikiki's upscale malls and resorts, you can find excellent local boutiques with island designs and creations.

For mundane needs, you won't be able to miss the ubiquitous **ABC Stores**, convenient places to pick up essentials such as beach mats, sunblock, snacks, cold beer, macadamia-nut candy and sundries, not to mention 'I got lei'd in Hawaii' T-shirts and bobbing, grass-skirted hula girls for the dashboard of your car.

Catamaran, Waikiki Beach

Bailey's Antiques & Aloha Shirts
Clothing, Antiques

(Map p84; ☏808-734-7628; http://aloha shirts.com; 517 Kapahulu Ave; ⊙10am-6pm) Unremarkable outside, Bailey's has the finest aloha-shirt collection on O'ahu, possibly the world! Racks are crammed with thousands of collector-worthy vintage aloha shirts in every conceivable color and style, from 1920s kimono-silk classics to 1970s polyester specials to modern offerings. Prices vary from 10 bucks to several thousand dollars.

Na Lima Mili Hulu No'eau
Arts & Crafts

(Map p84; ☏808-732-0865; www.featherlegacy. com; 762 Kapahulu Ave; ⊙usually 9am-4pm Mon-Sat) ⚑ The late Aunty Mary Louise Kaleonahenahe Kekuewa's daughter and granddaughter keep alive the ancient craft of feather lei-making at this small storefront, whose name means 'the skilled hands that touch the feathers.' It can take days to produce a single feather lei, prized by collectors. Call ahead to check opening hours or make an appointment for a personalized lesson.

Fighting Eel
Clothing

(Map p84; ☏808-738-9295; www.fightingeel. com; 2233 Kalakaua Ave, building B, Royal Hawaiian Center; ⊙10am-10pm) Hawaii-designed fashionable wear is the hallmark of local designers Rona Bennett and Lan Chung. It also has swimsuits, children's clothing, jewelry and accessories.

Malie Organics
Cosmetics

(Map p84; ☏808-922-2216; www.malie.com; 2259 Kalakaua Ave, Royal Hawaiian Resort; ⊙9am-9pm) Beauty oils, creams, perfumes and more are sold in this shop that looks as good as it smells. Everything is locally made from organic and natural ingredients, mostly derived from native Hawaii plants and flowers.

Nohea Gallery
Arts & Crafts

(Map p84; ☏808-596-0074; www.noheagal lery.com; 2424 Kalakaua Ave, Hyatt Regency Waikiki Beach Resort; ⊙9am-10pm) This

 LGBTQ+ Waikiki

Waikiki's LGBTQ+ community is tightly knit, but full of aloha for visitors. Start off at friendly, open-air Hula's Bar & Lei Stand (p98), which has ocean views of Diamond Head to meet a variety of new faces, play pool and boogie. More stylish and classy, **Bacchus Waikiki** (Map p84; ☏808-926-4167; www.bacchus-waikiki.com; 408 Lewers St, 2nd fl; ⊙noon-2am) is a wine bar and cocktail lounge with happy-hour specials, shirtless bartenders and Sunday-afternoon parties on the terrace. For nonstop singalongs, hit Wang Chung's (p100), a living-room-sized karaoke bar.

Tiki-themed **Tapa's Restaurant & Lanai Bar** (Map p84; ☏808-921-2288; www.tapaswaikiki.com; 407 Seaside Ave, 2nd fl; ⊙2pm-2am Mon-Fri, from 9am Sat & Sun; 🛜) is a bigger chill-out spot with bartenders, pool tables, a jukebox and karaoke nights. Hidden up an alley a few blocks away, **In Between** (Map p84; ☏808-926-7060; www.inbetweenwaikiki.com; 2155 Lau'ula St; ⊙noon-2am) attracts an older crowd for 'the happiest of happy hours.'

By day, have fun in the sun at Queen's Surf Beach (p87) and (illegally clothing optional) **Diamond Head Beach Park** (3300 Diamond Head Rd).

October is a good reason to visit O'ahu as it's **Honolulu Pride** (https://hawaiilgbtlegacyfoundation.com; Kapi'olani Regional Park), with weeks of parties and events culminating in a huge parade followed by concerts.

Honolulu Pride
IMPASSIONED IMAGES/SHUTTERSTOCK ©

From left: ABC Stores (p90); Aloha Shirts; Garden courtyard at the Royal Hawaiian Center

ANOUCHKA/GETTY IMAGES ©

RUSTY426/SHUTTERSTOCK ©

high-end gallery sells original paintings, *gyotaku* fish prints (rubbings of freshly caught fish), handcrafted jewelry, glassware, pottery and woodwork, all of it made in Hawaii. Local artisans occasionally give demonstrations of their crafts on the sidewalk outside.

Ukulele PuaPua   Musical Instruments
(Map p84; ☎808-923-9977; www.hawaiian
ukuleleonline.com; 2255 Kalakaua Ave #13,
Sheraton Waikiki; ☉8am-10:30pm) Avoid
those flimsy souvenir ukuleles and head
to this serious little shop to find the real
thing. Try a free group beginner lesson
(4pm daily).

Royal Hawaiian Center   Mall
(Map p84; ☎808-922-2299; www.royalhawaiian
center.com; 2201 Kalakaua Ave; ☉10am-10pm;
☏) Not to be confused with the Royal
Hawaiian Resort hotel next door, this
upscale shopping center has four levels
and houses more than 80 top-end stores;
some local such as Fighting Eel (p91),
some chains such as Apple. It hosts many
free activities and performances.

 EATING

Waikiki has a lot of restaurants aimed
at the vacationing masses, but amidst
the over-priced under-whelmers you can
find some gems, including a few where a
beach view doesn't equal dull food.

Waikiki is close to Honolulu neighborhoods with excellent restaurants – the
Ala Moana area is just west. Kapahulu
Ave stretches north from the east end
and offers a string of great dining options
while the casual enclave of Monsarrat Ave
is just a short walk.

 Waikiki Beach Area

You can have a good meal and a view along
Waikiki Beach. Just inland, there are many
more decent options. Along Kalakaua Ave,
chains overflow with hungry tourists –
most of whom can probably find the same
chains in their hometowns.

Barefoot Beach Cafe   Cafe $
(Map p84; ☎808-924-2233; https://barefoot
beachcafe.com; 2699 Kalakaua Ave, Queen's Surf
Beach; mains $8-15; ☉7am-8:30pm) Waikiki's

JEFF WHITE/SHUTTERSTOCK ©

best beach cafe is just south of the sand at Queen's Beach. Order at the window and grab a shady table close to the water and tuck into island-accented breakfasts, snacks and lunches. The kitchen shows great attention to details, whether it's eggs Benedict, garlic fries or a plate lunch. There's live music nightly (5:30pm).

Eggs 'n' Things   Breakfast $

(Map p84; ☑808-923-3447; www.eggsnthings. com; 343 Saratoga Rd; mains $9-18; ☺6am-10pm; ☻) This bustling diner dishes straight-up comfort food: banana macadamia-nut pancakes with tropical syrups (guava, honey or coconut), sugary crepes topped with fresh fruit, or fluffy omelets scrambled with Portuguese sausage. You'll fit right in with the early-morning crowd of jet-lagged tourists lined up outside the door.

Waikiki Yokocho   Japanese $$

(Map p84; ☑808-926-8093; www.waikiki-yokocho.com; 2250 Kalakaua Ave; mains $7-30; ☺11am-midnight) Ride an escalator down to a perfectly authentic Japanese food court. Try to choose between 16 different stalls and restaurants. Your options range from

organic *o-musubi* (rice cakes) to bento boxes to tempura and more. Some places are self-serve, while others offer table service. Kids are delighted by the rows of free vintage arcade games.

LuLu's Waikiki   American $$

(Map p84; ☑808-926-5222; www.luluswaikiki. com; 2586 Kalakaua Ave, Park Shore Waikiki; mains $7-25; ☺7am-2am; ☻) Surfboards on the wall and an awesome ocean view set the mood at this cheery open-air restaurant, bar and nightclub. LuLu's filling breakfasts, complete with 'dawn patrol' omelets, eggs Benedict, stuffed French toast, *loco moco* (a dish of rice, fried egg and hamburger patty topped with gravy or other condiments) and fruit bowls, are always a hit. Sunset happy hour runs from 3pm to 5pm.

La Mer   French $$$

(Map p84; ☑808-923-2311; www.halekulani. com; 2199 Kalia Rd, Halekulani; 3-/4-course prix-fixe dinner menu $125/155; ☺5:30-9:30pm; ℗) At the luxury Halekulani (p90) resort, La Mer is rated by traditionalists as Waikiki's top fine-dining destination. A neoclassical

French menu puts the emphasis on Provençal cuisine with the addition of fresh Hawaii-grown ingredients, such as seafood, including abalone. Wines are perfectly paired; diners are required to have jackets. The beach views are superb.

Orchids   Buffet $$$

(Map p84; ✆808-923-2311; www.halekulani. com; 2199 Kalia Rd, Halekulani; brunch buffet adult/child $76/34, mains other times $16-64; ⏰7:30am-9:30pm Mon-Sat, 9am-2:30pm Sun) O'ahu's most elegant Sunday brunch spread covers all the bases, with a made-to-order omelet station; a buffet of *poke*, sashimi, sushi and salads; and a decadent dessert bar with coconut pie and homemade Kona coffee ice cream. This indulgence draws acolytes from across O'ahu, so reserve ahead.

Roy's Waikiki   Hawaii Regional $$$

(Map p84; ✆808-923-7697; www.royshawaii. com; 226 Lewers St; mains $24-53; ⏰light menu 11am-5pm, dinner 5pm-9:30pm Mon-Thu, to 10pm Fri-Sun) This contemporary incarnation of Roy Yamaguchi's island-born chain is perfect for a flirty date or just celebrating the good life. The ground-breaking chef's signature *misoyaki* butterfish, blackened ahi (yellowfin tuna) and macadamia-nut-crusted mahimahi are always on the menu. The famous hot chocolate soufflé for dessert is a must.

The bar makes great cocktails and there's seating outside under tiki torches.

Veranda   Cafe $$$

(Map p84; ✆808-921-4600; www.moana-surf rider.com; Moana Surfrider, 2365 Kalakaua Ave; afternoon tea from $34; ⏰6-11am, noon-3pm & 5:30-9:30pm; P) For colonial atmosphere that harks back to early-20th-century tourist traditions, enjoy afternoon tea here. It comes complete with finger sandwiches, scones with pillowy Devonshire cream and tropically flavored pastries. Portions are small, but the oceanfront setting and house-blended teas are memorable. Make

reservations and come prepared to shoo away pesky birds. It's also a fine place for a waterfront breakfast.

Kuhio Ave Area

Along Kuhio Ave, and the many nearby streets and alleys, are all manner of places to eat, from humble to superb; many are just holes in the wall.

Musubi Cafe Iyasume   Japanese $

(Map p84; ✆808-921-0168; https://iyasume hawaii.com; 2427 Kuhio Ave, Aqua Monarch Hotel; mains $5-9; ⏰6:30am-9pm) This hole-in-the-wall keeps busy making fresh *onigiri* (rice balls) stuffed with seaweed, salmon roe and sour plums. Other specialties include salmon-roe rice bowls, Japanese curry and island-style *mochiko* fried chicken. In a hurry? Grab a bentō box to go. The namesake *musubi* is a definitive version with grilled Spam atop a block of white rice wrapped in nori (seaweed sheet).

Marukame Udon   Japanese $

(Map p84; ✆808-931-6000; www.facebook. com/marukameudon; 2310 Kuhio Ave; mains $4-12; ⏰7am-10pm; 🍴) Everybody loves this reconstructed Japanese noodle shop, which is so popular there is often a line stretching down the sidewalk. Watch those thick udon noodles get rolled, cut and boiled fresh right in front of you, then stack mini plates of giant tempura and *musubi* (rice balls) stuffed with salmon or a sour plum on your cafeteria tray.

Mahiku Farmer's Market   Market $

(Map p84; ✆808-225-4002; https://mahiku farmersmarket.com; 2155 Kalakaua Ave, Bank of Hawaii Waikiki Center; snacks from $1.50; ⏰4-8pm Mon-Tue & Thu) Wrapping around a glassy commercial building, this farmers market attracts dozens of vendors selling produce, prepared foods, artworks and crafts. Sample your way around the myriad mostly Asian-flavored snacks; the fresh banana lumpias are extraordinary.

MAC 24/7 American $$

(Map p84; ☑808-921-5564; www.mac247
waikiki.com; 2500 Kuhio Ave, Hilton Waikiki
Beach; mains $9-32; ⊘24hr; 🖼) If it's 3am
and you're famished, skip the temptation
for a cold $25 burger from room service
(*if* you have room service) and drop by
Waikiki's best all-night diner (their slogan:
'We don't close unless it snows.'). The
dining room has a bold style palette and
by day it has a lovely garden view. Food
(and prices) are a cut above.

Hy's Steakhouse Steak $$$

(Map p84; ☑808-922-5555; www.hyswaikiki.
com; 2440 Kuhio Ave; mains $40-110; ⊘5-10pm)
Hy's is so old-school that you expect to
find inkwells on the tables. This traditional
steakhouse has a timeless old leather
and wood interior. But ultimately, it's not
whether you expect to see Frank and Dean
at a back table; rather, it's the steak at Hy's
that is the main drawcard.

🍽 Kapahulu Ave

On the outskirts of Waikiki, Kapahulu Ave
is one of the most interesting streets for
dining across Honolulu. The sheer number
creative bistros and cafes will delight any
hungry person out for a stroll. It's an easy
walk from Waikiki Beach. Look for standout
neighborhood eateries, drive-ins and bak-
eries, cooking up fare from Hawaiian soul
food to Japanese country cuisine.

Waiola Shave Ice Desserts $

(Map p84; ☑808-949-2269; www.waiolashave
ice.com; 3113 Mokihana St; shave ice $3-5; ⊘11am-
5:30pm; 🅿🖼) This clapboard corner shop
has been making the same super-fine shave
ice since 1940, and we'd argue that it's got
the formula exactly right. Get yours doused
with 20-plus flavors of syrup and topped by
azuki beans, *liliko'i* (passion fruit) cream,
condensed milk, spicy-sweet *li hing mui*
(crack seed) or go all Hawaii and have POG
flavor (passion-orange-guava). There's an
older location in **Honolulu** (p68).

Roy's Waikiki

Rainbow Drive-In   Hawaiian $

(Map p84; ☑808-737-0177; www.rainbowdrive in.com; 3308 Kanaina Ave; meals $4-10; ⏰7am-9pm; P🚹) This plate-lunch legend draws legions of locals and tourists from Waikiki. Wrapped in rainbow-colored neon, it's a throwback to another era. Construction workers, surfers and gangly teens order down-home favorites such as mixed-plate lunches, *loco moco* and Portuguese sweet-bread French toast.

Everything's fresh, although there are better plate lunch places, such as **Kahai Street Kitchen** (p67) over by the University of Hawaii.

Ono Seafood   Seafood $

(Map p84; ☑808-732-4806; 747 Kapahulu Ave; mains $7-12; ⏰9am-6pm Tue-Sat) Arrive early at this addictive, made-to-order *poke* shop before it runs out of fresh fish marinated in *shōyu* (soy sauce), house-smoked *tako* (octopus), spicy ahi rice bowls or boiled peanuts spiked with star anise. The *shōyu* ahi is beloved by regulars. There are a couple of humble tables outside. Very limited parking.

Leonard's   Bakery $

(Map p84; ☑808-737-5591; www.leonards hawaii.com; 933 Kapahulu Ave; snacks from $1.30; ⏰5:30am-10pm Sun-Thu, to 11pm Fri & Sat; P🚹) It's almost impossible to drive by the Leonard's eye-catching vintage 1950s neon sign without seeing a crowd of tourists. This bakery is famous for its *malasadas* (sweet deep-fried dough rolled in sugar) Portuguese-style – like a dough-nut without the hole. Order variations with *haupia* (coconut cream) or guava filling for more flavor. Be sure to get yours hot from the fryer.

Tonkatsu Tamafuji   Japanese $$

(Map p84; ☑808-922-1212; www.facebook. com/tamafujihonolulu; 449 Kapahulu Ave; mains $16-30; ⏰4-9:30pm Mon & Wed-Fri, 5-9:30pm Sat & Sun) Katsu, the deep-fried Japanese cooking method that coats meats like pork and chicken in a perfectly crispy exterior made from panko bread crumbs. This

Rainbow Drive-In

bright and cheerful place packs in crowds for some of O'ahu's best. Choose your cut of pork and soon you'll be enjoying fabulous katsu with unlimited shredded cabbage and rice. Meat options include oysters, chicken and shrimp.

Sansei Seafood Restaurant & Sushi Bar
Japanese $$

(Map p84; ☑808-931-6286; www.sanseihawaii. com; 2552 Kalakaua Ave, 3rd fl, Waikiki Beach Marriott Resort; shared plates $5-20, mains $16-38; ☺5:30-10pm Sun-Thu, to 1am Fri & Sat; ☐) From the mind of one of Hawaii's top chefs, DK Kodama, this Pacific Rim menu rolls out everything from creatively stylish sushi and sashimi to Dungeness crab ramen with black-truffle broth – all to rave reviews. Tables on the torchlit veranda equal prime sunset views. Free parking with validation.

Uncle Bo's Pupu Bar & Grill
Fusion $$

(Map p84; ☑808-735-8311; www.unclebos restaurant.com; 559 Kapahulu Ave; shared plates $8-21, mains $20-39; ☺5pm-1am, kitchen until 11:45pm) Inside this mustard-yellow storefront, boisterous groups devour the inventive chef's encyclopedic list of fusion *pupu* (appetizers) crafted with island flair, such as *kalua* pig nachos and garlicky spicy shrimp. For dinner, focus on market-fresh seafood such as baked *opah* (moonfish) or pan-roasted shellfish. Reservations recommended. There's a full bar and a cheap late-night menu.

Monsarrat Ave

Wander past the zoo and Waikiki School to reach an outcrop of great casual cafes and restaurants on mostly residential Monsarrat Ave, right in the shadow of Diamond Head.

Ars Cafe and Gelato
Cafe $

(Map p84; ☑808-734-7897; http://ars-cafe. com; 3116 Monsarrat Ave; mains $6-12; ☺6:30am-6pm Mon-Sat, 8am-6pm Sun) Avocado toast two cuts above the cliche is but one of the

Waikiki's Mystery Observer

Nobody knows his or her name, but on Instagram, **@misterver** has a huge following thanks to a steady stream of brilliant candid photos shot on Waikiki's streets and beaches. Don't look for glossy tourist moments, instead savor candid sides of a neighborhood better known for its ever-changing flood of visitors. Dogs, decrepit buildings, unguarded moments, artful snaps and idiosyncratic looks are captured anonymously and on the fly.

 @MISTERVER ©

delights at this cafe, which is also a gallery for local artists. Enjoy excellent coffee as mellow, jazzy tunes play gently.

Don't miss the ice cream by the wizard of the Mid-Late Summer creamery, Aaron Lopez. His esoteric flavors like burnt milk and marshmallow maple molasses change weekly.

Pioneer Saloon
Fusion $

(Map p84; ☑808-732-4001; www.pioneer-saloon.net; 3046 Monsarrat Ave; mains $9-16; ☺11am-8pm) The crowds are proof: people love Pioneer Saloon's Japanese-fusion plate lunches, with dozens of choices, from grilled ahi to fried baby octopus to *yakisoba* (fried noodles). The fried chicken with garlic sauce and the grilled miso salmon are tops. Look for the potted plants outside; and prepare for loads of whimsical nonsense decor inside. Don't miss the shave ice.

🍷 DRINKING & NIGHTLIFE

If you're looking for a frosty cold beer or a fruity cocktail to help you recover from a day at the beach, there are endless options in Waikiki. Sip a sunset mai tai and be hypnotized by the lilting harmonies of slack key guitars, then mingle with locals who come here to party too.

Cuckoo Coconuts   Lounge
(Map p84; 📞808-926-1620; www.cuckoo coconutswaikiki.com; 333 Royal Hawaiian Ave; ⏰11am-midnight) Mismatched wobbly tables under a canopy of canvas and ragged umbrellas, plus a menagerie of aging potted tropical plants, give this bar a carefree, unpretentious vibe. Every night there's a hard-working lineup of musicians with a familiar list of croon-worthy classics and time-tested patter. Settle back, have some sort of deep-fried treat, enjoy a cheap drink and get carried away.

Hula's Bar & Lei Stand   Gay
(Map p84; 📞808-923-0669; https://hulas. com; 134 Kapahulu Ave, 2nd fl, Waikiki Grand Hotel; ⏰10am-2am; 📶) This friendly, open-air

bar is Waikiki's legendary gay venue and a great place to make new friends, boogie and have a few drinks. Hunker down at the pool table, or gaze at the spectacular vista of Diamond Head. The breezy balcony-bar also has views of Queen's Surf Beach (p87), a prime destination for a sun-worshiping LGBTQ+ crowd.

Beach Bar   Bar
(Map p84; 📞808-922-3111; www.moana-surfrider.com; 2365 Kalakaua Ave, Moana Surfrider; ⏰10:30am-10:30pm) Waikiki's best beach bar is on an atmospheric stretch of Kahaloa & Ulukou Beaches. The atmosphere comes from the historic Moana Surfrider (p83) hotel and its vast banyan tree. The people-watching of passersby, sunbathers and surfers is captivating. On an island of mediocre mai tais, the versions here are some of O'ahu's best (the 'sunset mai tai' is the top choice).

Gorilla in the Cafe   Cafe
(Map p84; 📞808-922-2055; www.facebook. com/gorillahawaii; 2155 Kalakaua Ave; ⏰6:30am-9pm Mon-Fri, 7am-10pm Sat & Sun) Owned by Korean TV star Bae Yong-joon, this artisan

From left: Mai Tai; Leonard's (p96); Moana Surfrider Hotel (p83)

coffee bar brews Waikiki's biggest selection of 100% Hawaii-grown beans from independent farms all around the islands. Handmade pourovers are worth the extra wait, or just grab a fast, hot espresso or creamy frozen coffee concoction blended with banana. It has a little circle of tables outside.

Lulu's Waikiki   Cocktail Bar

(Map p84; ☎808-926-5222; www.luluswaikiki. com; 2586 Kalakaua Ave, Park Shore Waikiki; ⏰7am-2am) Brush off your sandy feet at Kuhio Beach, then step across Kalakaua Ave to this surf-themed open-air bar and grill with 2nd-story lanai (balcony) views of the Pacific Ocean and Diamond Head. Lap up sunset happy hours (3pm to 5pm daily), then chill out to acoustic acts and local bands later most evenings.

Punchbowl Coffee   Coffee

(Map p84; https://punchbowlcoffee.com; 234 Beach Walk; ⏰10am-8:30pm) In the back of a parking lot, this truck uses potted palms to create a minute oasis amidst the Waikiki buzz. Superb hot and cold coffee and tea drinks, plus a few snacks. Grab a spot on a bench and exhale.

Maui Brewing Co   Brewery

(Map p84; ☎808-843-2739; http://mauibrewing co.com; 2300 Kalakaua Ave, 2nd fl, Holiday Inn Resort Waikiki Beachcomber; ⏰11am-11pm) Hawaii's largest bar features over two dozen of Maui Brewing's microbrews. Under lights made from kegs, you can lounge in the vast, industrial space, enjoying classic beers like Bikini Blonde lager, Coconut Hiwa porter and Pineapple Mana wheat. The large outdoor terrace has views of the resort-filled skyline.

Duke's Waikiki   Bar

(Map p84; ☎808-922-2268; www.dukeswaikiki. com; 2335 Kalakaua Ave, Outrigger Waikiki Beach Resort; ⏰7am-midnight) It's a raucous scene, especially when weekend concerts spill onto the beach. It takes its name from Duke Kahanamoku and the surfing theme prevails throughout this carousing landmark where selfies and holiday camaraderie are encouraged. Upstairs, the tiki torchlit veranda at the **Hula**

Grill (Map p84; ☑808-923-4852; www.
hulagrillwaikiki.com; 2335 Kalakaua Ave, 2nd fl,
Outrigger Waikiki Beach Resort; mains $20-40;
☺6:30am-10pm; P ☀) has a more soothing
live Hawaiian soundtrack several nights a
week. Skip the food.

Wang Chung's   Karaoke
(Map p84; ☑808-921-9176; http://wangchungs.
com; 2424 Koa Ave, Stay Waikiki; ☺5pm-2am;
☏) Wang Chung's is a happy-go-lucky
gay-friendly karaoke bar that's found a ret-
ro-chic home in the **Stay Waikiki** (☑808-
923-7829; www.stayhotelwaikiki.com) hotel just
a block inland from Kuhio Beach.

Arnold's Beach Bar & Grill   Bar
(Map p84; ☑808-924-6887; www.facebook.
com/Arnoldswaikiki; 339 Saratoga Rd; ☺10am-
2am) The antidote to soulless hotel bars,
this grass-shack dive bar with a smoky
patio lures beach bums who knock back
cheap microbrews in the middle of a sunny afternoon. Down a stiff 'Tiki Tea' while
pretending the bar's naked mannequins
don't freak you out. It's down an alley;
follow the sounds of live music from 5pm
to 8pm.

⭐ ENTERTAINMENT

On any given night Waikiki offers first-rate
live Hawaiian music and hula dancing. You
can enjoy much of it for free or the price of
a drink.

Good online sources for what's on – especially special events – include *Honolulu
Star-Advertiser* (www.staradvertiser.com/
calendar) and *Honolulu Magazine* (www.
honolulumagazine.com). But you're best
off checking with specific venues.

House Without a Key   Live Music
(Map p84; ☑808-923-2311; www.halekulani.
com; 2199 Kalia Rd, Halekulani; ☺7-9pm)
Named after a 1925 Charlie Chan novel
set in Honolulu, this genteel open-air
hotel lounge sprawls beneath a waterfront
century-old kiawe tree (that's clearly

barely hanging on as the sea level rises).
A genteel crowd gathers here for sunset
cocktails, excellent Hawaiian music and
solo hula dancing by former Miss Hawaii
pageant winners. Panoramic ocean
views are as intoxicating as the tropical
cocktails.

Hilton Hawaiian
Village Fireworks   Fireworks
(Map p84; Kahanamoku Beach; ☺7:45pm Fri)
FREE Every Friday night, the Hilton Hawaiian
Village (p87) stages a booming 10-minute
fireworks show. Although it's done in
conjunction with a touristy luau (Hawaiian
feast) near one of the pools, the actual show
is over the water in front of Kahanamoku
Beach and can be seen from across Waikiki.
For the best views, join the locals and tourists on Fort DeRussy Beach (p87).

Kani Ka Pila Grille   Live Music
(Map p84; ☑808-924-4990; www.outrigger
reef.com; 2169 Kalia Rd, Outrigger Reef Waikiki
Beach Resort; ☺11am-10pm, live music 6-9pm)
Once happy hour ends, the Outrigger's
poolside bar sets the scene for some of
the most laid-back live-music shows of
any of Waikiki's beachfront hotels, with
traditional and contemporary Hawaiian
musicians playing familiar tunes amidst a
patter of jokes.

Tapa Bar   Live Music
(Map p84; ☑808-949-4321; www.hiltonhawaiian
village.com; 2005 Kalia Rd, ground fl, Tapa
Tower, Hilton Hawaiian Village; ☺10am-11pm,
live music from 7:30-8pm) **FREE** It's worth
navigating through the gargantuan Hilton
resort complex to this Polynesian-themed
open-air bar just to see some of the best
traditional and contemporary Hawaiian
groups performing on O'ahu today. Head
over on Friday and Saturday nights to
catch longtime favorite Olomana, an
acoustic trio. There is also live entertainment many nights in the hotel's Tropics
cafe; famed singer Henry Kapono performs
on Saturdays.

Royal Hawaiian Band   Live Music

(Map p84; ☎808-786-6677; www.rhb-music.com; Kapi'olani Park Bandstand, 2686-2882 Kalakaua Ave, Kapi'olani Regional Park; ☺2pm Sun) The Kapi'olani Park Bandstand is the perfect venue for this time-honored troupe that performs classics from the Hawaiian monarchy era. It's a quintessential island scene that caps off with the audience joining hands and singing Queen Lili'uokalani's 'Aloha 'Oe' in Hawaiian. Check their website for details on performances at special events and festivals. They also perform at **'Iolani Palace** (p44; ☎808-922-5331).

Blue Note Hawaii   Live Music

(Map p84; ☎808-777-4890; www.bluenotehawaii.com; 2335 Kalakaua Ave, Outrigger Waikiki Beach Resort; ticket price varies; ☺showtimes vary) A sophisticated music venue that draws top acts performing blues, jazz, pop, rock, reggae and Hawaiian music. There's a dinner option that includes banquet fare (mains $25 to $34).

⭐ Luau & Dinner Shows

'Aha 'Aina   Luau

(Map p84; ☎808-921-4600; http://royal-hawaiianluau.com; Royal Hawaiian Resort, 2259 Kalakaua Ave; adult/child 5-12yr from $180/100; ☺5-8pm Mon & Thu) This oceanfront dinner show is like a three-act musical play narrating the history of Hawaiian *mele* (songs) and hula. The buffet features good renditions of traditional Hawaiian and Polynesian fare, and unlimited drinks. There are cultural demonstrations, such as making cloth from bark. The highlight is the fire dancing.

Waikiki Starlight Luau   Luau

(Map p84; ☎808-947-2607; www.hiltonhawaiianvillage.com/luau; 2005 Kalia Rd, Hilton Hawaiian Village; adult/child 4-11yr from $111/71; ☺5:30-8pm Sun-Thu, weather permitting; 👪) Enthusiastic pan-Polynesian show, with buffet meal, outdoor seating at a rooftop venue, Samoan fire dancing and *hapa haole* (literally, 'half foreign') hula. Like other resort luaus, there are pricey options that allow guests to cut the long food lines.

Hilton Hawaiian Village fireworks

GETTING THERE & AWAY

Daniel K Inouye International Airport (HNL; 808-836-6411; www.airports.hawaii.gov/hnl; 300 Rodgers Blvd;) is about 9 miles northwest of Waikiki.

BUS

From the airport, reach Waikiki via **TheBus** (808-848-5555; www.thebus.org; adult $2.75; infoline 5:30am-10pm) routes 19 or 20. Buses run every 20 minutes from 6am to 11pm daily. Luggage is restricted to what you can hold on your lap or stow under the seat (maximum size 22in x 14in x 9in). Both routes run along Kuhio Ave.

AIRPORT SHUTTLE

Express Shuttle (808-439-8800; www. airportshuttlehawaii.com; fare to Waikiki 1 way $17), run by Roberts Hawaii, operates shuttle buses from Daniel K Inouye International Airport to Waikiki's hotels, departing every 20 to 60 minutes. Transport time varies depending on the number of stops. There are surcharges for large luggage like surfboards. Note that groups of three or more will save money using a taxi or rideshare.

CAR

From the airport, the easiest and most atmospheric driving route to Waikiki is via the Nimitz Hwy (Hwy 92), which becomes Ala Moana Blvd. Alternatively, take the H1 (Lunalilo) Fwy eastbound, then follow signs to Waikiki. The drive between the airport and Waikiki takes about 30 minutes without traffic; allow at least 45 minutes during weekday rush hours.

TAXI

Taxis from the airport to Waikiki cost $35 to $45.

GETTING AROUND

Major car-rental companies have branches in Waikiki.

Most stops for TheBus in Waikiki are found inland along Kuhio Ave. The Ala Moana Center mall, just northwest of Waikiki, is the island's main bus-transfer point.

Bus 13 is handy: it runs down Kuhio Ave and Kapahulu Ave and operates every 15 to 30 minutes from 5am to 11:30pm. It serves Chinatown and Downtown in the west and the University of Hawaii in the north.

Where to Stay

Waikiki's main beachfront strip, along Kalakaua Ave, is lined with hotels and sprawling resorts. Some of them are true beauties with either a historic or boutique atmosphere. Most are aimed at the masses, however.

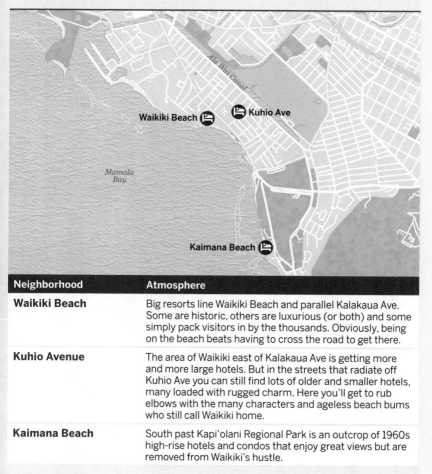

Neighborhood	Atmosphere
Waikiki Beach	Big resorts line Waikiki Beach and parallel Kalakaua Ave. Some are historic, others are luxurious (or both) and some simply pack visitors in by the thousands. Obviously, being on the beach beats having to cross the road to get there.
Kuhio Avenue	The area of Waikiki east of Kalakaua Ave is getting more and more large hotels. But in the streets that radiate off Kuhio Ave you can still find lots of older and smaller hotels, many loaded with rugged charm. Here you'll get to rub elbows with the many characters and ageless beach bums who still call Waikiki home.
Kaimana Beach	South past Kapi'olani Regional Park is an outcrop of 1960s high-rise hotels and condos that enjoy great views but are removed from Waikiki's hustle.

NA PALI COAST WILDERNESS STATE PARK, KAUA'I

Na Pali Coast Wilderness State Park at a Glance...

Kaua'i's most magnificent natural spectacle, this 17-mile stretch of soaring green-clad cliffs, white-sand beaches, turquoise coves and gushing waterfalls, is both pristine and hauntingly beautiful. Each of the five major valleys – Kalalau, Honopu, Awa'awapuhi, Nu'alolo and Miloli'i – is more stunning than the last. No road could negotiate such stark wilderness, and even the legendary Kalalau Trail is ultimately defeated by sheer buttresses of rock. While fit trekkers can at least hike as far as Kalalau Valley, it's also possible to experience the coastline by kayak, raft or catamaran.

Na Pali Coast in One Day

Take the definitive day hike along the **Kalalau Trail** (p112), trekking first to Hanakapi'ai Beach and then continuing up the valley to scenic Hanakapi'ai Falls. A demanding 8-mile round-trip, it's rewarded with stupendous views along the Na Pali Coast. Cool off after your hard work with a sunset swim at **Ke'e Beach** (p116).

Na Pali Coast in Two Days

Head out on a **boat tour** (p108) to admire the full sweep of the Na Pali cliffs from out on the ocean, snorkel just offshore and potentially enter hidden sea caves. Spare some time to visit Ha'ena's stunning **Limahuli Garden** (p120) too, or if you surf, ride the waves at **Makua (Tunnels) Beach** (p120).

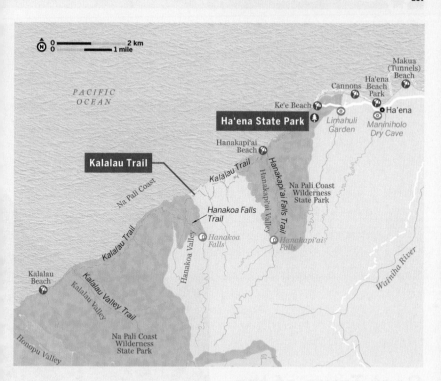

Na Pali Coast

PACIFIC OCEAN

Makua (Tunnels) Beach

Ha'ena Beach Park

Cannons

Ke'e Beach

Ha'ena State Park

Limahuli Garden

Ha'ena

Maniniholo Dry Cave

Hanakapi'ai Beach

Kalalau Trail

Kalalau Trail

Kalalau Trail

Hanakapi'ai Falls Trail

Na Pali Coast Wilderness State Park

Na Pali Coast

Hanakapi'ai Valley

Hanakoa Falls Trail

Kalalau Trail

Hanakoa Valley

Hanakoa Falls

Hanakapi'ai Falls

Waimha River

Kalalau Beach

Kalalau Valley Trail

Kalalau Valley

Honopu Valley

Na Pali Coast Wilderness State Park

Arriving at the Na Pali Coast

To park at **Ha'ena State Park**, 5 minutes' walk from the Kalalau trailhead, you must have a permit (www.gohaena.com). Available for three timed slots daily – even day hikers will likely need more than one – they're sold online a month ahead and often sell out. Overnight parking is forbidden, so campers should arrive by shuttle or contact **YMCA Camp Naue** (808-826-6419; http://ymcaofkauai.org/campnaue.html; Kuhio Hwy; tent sites $20 per person aged 3 or over), which offers parking for $5 per night.

The park is the turnaround point for the **North Shore Shuttle** (p121). The last bus back leaves at 5pm daily.

Sleeping

Hikers on the Kalalau Trail are allowed to camp for a maximum of 5 nights, with one night permitted in Hanakoa Valley in each direction, and the rest in Kalalau Valley at the far end.

Camping permits become available 90 days in advance and sell out quickly. It's also possible to camp on Miloli'i Beach, which can only be reached by sea.

Boat Tours of the Na Pali Coast

As you cruise the Pacific, luxuriating in views of the Na Pali Coast, the primordial valleys seem to offer glimpses of the Polynesian past. Boats set off from North Shore locations in summer only; winter trips start on the Westside and access the Na Pali cliffs via the less dramatic western shoreline.

Great For...

❶ Need to Know

Overnight campers require permits from **Hawaii State Parks** (http://camping. ehawaii.gov).

☑ **Don't Miss**

The procession of steepling, corrugated cliffs lined up along the shoreline.

Kayaking

Kayaking the 17-mile length of the Na Pali Coast is one of the world's great outdoor adventures. Between April and October, local operators offer full-day guided trips in two-person kayaks, requiring 12 hours' paddling. Longer expeditions include overnight camping at Kalalau Valley and/or Miloli'i. You don't need to be a triathlete, but you should be in top physical condition. Talk through the challenges in advance.

Due to prevailing currents, all long-distance kayakers start from the North Shore and take out on the Westside. Potentially deadly swells preclude making the trip in winter. While you can rent kayaks for self-guided expeditions, only consider going without a guide if you have extensive experience in ocean (not river) kayaking. Never kayak alone.

Kayaking Outfitters

Na Pali Kayak (☎808-826-6900; www.napa likayak.com; 5075 Kuhio Hwy, Hanalei; tours per person $225 plus tax & state park fees) Guided one-day trips along the full Na Pali Coast cost $250, overnight trips from $380 per person. Shorter excursions from Polihale on the Westside only cover the calmer leeward coast.

Kayak Kaua'i (☎808-826-9844, 888-596-3852; www.kayakkauai.com; Na Pali 1-day tour, late April to early Oct, $250; Na Pali camping trips, May-Sep, from $368; Blue Lagoon Tour adult/child 5-12yr $105/95; kayak rental per day with delivery $45-55) One-day ($250) and multi-day (from $368) Na Pali trips, plus kayak rentals.

Kayaking the Na Pali coast

Catamarans

The cushiest way to cruise, catamarans offer smoother rides, ample shade and restrooms, plus, potentially, crowd-pleasing amenities like water slides and unlimited food and beverages. Varying in size, some have sails, while others are entirely motorized.

Rafts

Rafts are the thrill seeker's choice, bouncing along the water (bad backs beware), enter-
ing caves (in mellower weather) and making beach landings, but most lack shade, rest-rooms or comfy seating. The best rafts are RIBs, with hard bottoms allowing smoother rides.

Booking

Book boat or kayak tours as far ahead as possible – ideally, before you arrive. High surf or foul weather may cause cancellations and repeated rescheduling.

✕ Take a Break

Pick up lunchtime snacks when you breakfast in Hanalei at **Hanalei Bread Company** (☏808-826-6717; Hanalei Center, 5-5183 Kuhio Hwy; mains $9-14; ⏰7am-5pm).

★ Top Tip

If you're prone to seasickness, opt for a catamaran and take medication before your cruise. Check conditions; mornings are generally calmer.

TED JOHN JACOBS/GETTY IMAGES ©

Kalalau Trail

Stretching for 11 amazing miles beyond the end of the North Shore highway, the Kalalau Trail is Hawaii's single greatest trail. Whether you opt for a day hike – popular round-trips last 4 or 8 miles – or a multi-night camping trip, you'll be granted a fabulous face-to-face encounter with the glorious valleys of the Na Pali Coast.

Great For...

☑ Don't Miss

Coast and jungle views on the 4-mile round-trip hike from Ke'e Beach to Hanakapi'ai Beach.

Trail Overview

The world-class Kalalau Trail inches along the oceanfront edge of the Na Pali cliffs for 11 miles, from Ke'e Beach to Kalalau Valley. It only returns to sea level when en route, 2 miles along at Hanakapi'ai Beach, from where a separate 2-mile trail climbs to towering Hanakapi'ai Falls. The 8-mile round-trip trek to the falls is the longest possible day hike, and typically takes 6 to 8 hours.

Ke'e Beach to Hanakapi'ai Beach

The Kalalau Trail begins with a steep ascent from **Ke'e Beach**. It's immediately beautiful, with lush tropical vegetation and superb views. A mile along, now 400ft above the ocean, vast coastal

PACIFIC OCEAN

Kalalau Trail 🚶 Ke'e Ha'ena Beach

Hanakapi'ai Beach

Hanakoa Valley

Hanakapi'ai Falls

Kalalau Beach

Na Pali Coast Wilderness State Park

❶ Need to Know

The day's final North Shore Shuttle, back to Hanalei or Princeville, leaves Ha'ena State Park at 5pm.

✗ Take a Break

Reward yourself with an ocean-view fish dinner at Opakapaka (p121).

★ Top Tip

Hiking to Hanakapi'ai Falls requires multiple stream crossings; you won't be sorry if you bring water shoes as well as hiking boots.

PAVEL TVRDY/SHUTTERSTOCK ©

panoramas open up ahead. The trail then winds through successive hanging valleys, curving inland to cross trickling cascades before veering back to the next headland.

It takes most hikers approaching two hours to complete the 2-mile trek to **Hanakapi'ai Beach**. As the trail drops back down to the sea, you have to cross broad Hanakapi'ai Stream; a rope is often strung between the banks. The white-sand beach at the river mouth is constantly re-configured by the waves, and may take the form of a sandbar, cut off beyond a small lagoon. Do not swim here.

Hanakapi'ai Beach to Hanakapi'ai Falls

To create an unforgettable 8-mile all-day hike, add on the spur trail that branches inland for 2 miles, parallel to Hanakapi'ai Stream, to the waterfall at the head of narrow Hanakapi'ai Valley. This valley is prone to flash flooding, so only hike in fair weather.

This was once a densely populated agricultural area, and you may spot traces of long-abandoned taro fields and coffee groves. Water shoes can be a great help for repeated stream crossings and, on the rocky upper part of the trail, clambering over slippery boulders.

Eventually you come to spectacular **Hanakapi'ai Falls**, where falling water tumbles 300ft into a wide pool that's placid enough for swimming. Directly beneath the falls, the plummeting water forces you back from the rock face – a warning from nature, as falling rocks are common.

Hanakapi'ai Beach to Hanakoa Valley

Hiking beyond Hanakapi'ai Beach is only allowed if you have camping permits. The trail switchbacks steeply out of Hanakapi'ai, climbing 840ft in just over a mile. Once again it's magnificently verdant, penetrating deep into unspoiled hanging valleys before returning to high, exposed headlands. The overlook that provides your first sight of **Hanakoa Valley** also offers the first long-range prospect of the full majesty of the Na Pali coast's pleated, cathedral-like cliffs.

At Hanakoa, 4 miles on from Hanakapi'ai, you have to cross the main valley stream, this time twice. There's another set of falls in this valley too, thundering down a colossal 2000 feet from the cliffs above. A rough trail climbs a third of a mile through the forest to the pool at the base, where swimming is forbidden.

Hanakoa Valley to Kalalau Valley

Over its final 5-mile stretch, the trail becomes drier and more exposed. With less vegetation to bind the hillsides together, it's often just a narrow ledge scraped into a denuded slope of crumbling red gravel, and you may be glad of hiking poles to spare your quivering legs.

Towards the end, the trail leads across the front of **Kalalau Valley**, where you'll feel dwarfed beneath 1000ft lava-rock cliffs, then proceeds to the campsites on idyllic Kalalau Beach, at the valley's western end. Kalalau no longer has a permanent population, and it's not the hippie hang-out it used to be either, but it remains something very close to an earthly Paradise.

Kalalau Beach

In summer only, very strong swimmers can swim another half-mile along the coast to reach Honopu Beach; wear fins, because there's a strong current against you when you try to swim back.

When you're finally ready to leave Kalalau, simply retrace your steps for the 11 miles back to Ke'e.

Kalalau Trail Safety

Although trailfinding is never difficult, the Kalalau Trail is *very* rugged, and hiking its entire length is not for everyone. Only fit, experienced hikers need apply, and with a costly helicopter rescue the only potential help in any emergency, it's essential to be prepared.

Wear the appropriate gear, and bring all the food and water you need, or purify fresh water drawn en route. The ground underfoot ranges from unforgiving rock to slimy mud, and crumbling gravel to slippery clay, so sturdy boots or shoes are crucial, but it's also worth carrying footwear suitable for stream crossings. Don't wade streams deeper than knee-high, don't swim at Hanakapi'ai Beach, and take extra care after rain.

If you're prone to vertigo, you may find some of the ocean-edge drop-offs alarming. The scariest parts come in the 5-mile stretch to Kalalau Valley at the very end, though, way beyond where you'd go on a day hike.

Mosquitoes are bloodthirsty and the sun can ravage, so always wear insect repellent and sunblock. And finally, you *must* pack out your trash.

Kalalau Trail Permits

To hike any further than Hanakapi'ai Beach – which is only advisable for hardy, experienced hikers with no fear of heights – you must obtain **camping permits** in advance. A maximum of 5 nights' camping is allowed, shared between Hanakoa Valley 4 miles further along – where you can only stop for one night in each direction – and Kalalau Valley at the far end.

Permits, available 90 days in advance and often sold out, cost $20 per person per night ($15 for Hawaii residents); for full details, see www.dlnr.hawaii.gov/dsp/hiking/kauai/kalalau-trail.

RAPHAEL RIVEST/SHUTTERSTOCK ©

❶ Trail Maps

The state parks office in Lihu'e can provide a Kalalau Trail brochure with a map. Another good source, sponsored by the county, is **Kaua'i Explorer** (www.kauaiexplorer.com).

❶ Danger: Hanakapi'ai Beach

Be warned: numerous hikers have drowned at Hanakapi'ai Beach. Swimming is prohibited, and it's never safe. Never turn your back on the ocean, especially near the river mouth.

SHANE MYERS PHOTOGRAPHY/SHUTTERSTOCK ©

Ha'ena State Park

As it nears its end, overshadowed by the looming Na Pali cliffs, Kuhio Hwy fords a flowing stream beyond wonderful Limahuli Garden to enter the beautiful and mysterious Ha'ena State Park.

Pele, the Hawaiian goddess of fire, is said to have rejected Ha'ena as a potential home on account of the water that percolates through its wet and dry caves. Now a 230-acre state park, the area is dominated by the sharp-pointed 1280ft peak popularly known as 'Bali Hai,' the moniker under which it starred in the 1959 movie musical *South Pacific*. Its real name is Makana ('Gift'). Apt, for sure.

Ke'e Beach

Long renowned as one of the North Shore's most glorious beaches, lovely Ke'e Beach, beside the Kalalau trailhead at the end of Kuhio Hwy, has been given a new lease of life by recent parking restrictions.

There's usually safe swimming in the reef-enclosed area at its western end, hard against the Na Pali cliffs, and it makes a

Great For...

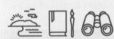

☑ **Don't Miss**

Taking in a superlative sunset at Ke'e Beach – it's an island rite of passage.

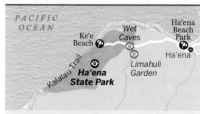

PACIFIC OCEAN

Ke'e Beach

Kalalau Trail

Ha'ena State Park

Wet Caves

Limahuli Garden

Ha'ena Beach Park

Ha'ena

ℹ **Need to Know**

There's no parking at Ke'e Beach. To park at the end-of-the-road parking lot you must book a permit in advance, via www.gohaena.com.

✗ **Take a Break**

There are no restaurants or snack bars in the state park. Pack a picnic.

★ **Top Tip**

It's easiest to visit Ha'ena State Park using the **North Shore Shuttle** (p121) leaving your car in Hanalei or Princeville.

sublime spot for a sunset dip after a hike on the Kalalau Trail. Walk eastwards along the sands, fringed by trees that seem to perch on spiders' legs since erosion exposed their roots, and you'll soon start getting sensational views along the Na Pali cliffs.

Always follow lifeguards' advice before you enter the water; Ke'e's looks can be deceptive, and vicious currents can suck swimmers through the reef and out to sea. Facilities include outdoor showers and restrooms.

Ke'e is no longer notorious for overcrowding, now that the only access is via a scenic quarter-mile boardwalk from the road's-end parking lot, for which permits have to be booked well in advance. The North Shore Shuttle stops there, and waits to pick up passengers until 5pm daily.

Kaulu o Pa'oa Heiau

Black lava walls on the headland immediately west of Ke'e Beach mark the outlines of two hugely significant ancient heiau (temples). The first, **Kaulu o Pa'oa**, was dedicated to the forest goddess Pa'oa, while **Kaulu o Laka** above it is a large platform that's celebrated in Hawaiian legend as the place where the goddess Laka may have first danced the hula. It's also said to be where the volcano goddess Pele fell in love with Lohiau.

Sadly, the trail to both sites has been closed since sustaining flood damage in 2018. Check with the lifeguards at Ke'e to see whether it has reopened.

Wet Caves

Two wet caves lie within the boundaries of Ha'ena State Park. Formed by the ceaseless pounding of the waves over countless years, the massive cavern of **Waikapala'e Wet Cave** is as enchanting as it is spooky. It's located across the highway, a short walk back from the road's-end parking lot. **Waikanaloa Wet Cave** is further back along the south side of the road.

You may be tempted to wade into the water of Waikapala'e's deep chamber to experience the blue reflected sunlight. Be warned, though, that it may be contaminated with leptospira bacteria; the rocks are slippery; and there's nothing to hold onto once you're in the water. That said, it does make one hell of an Instagram glamor shot. If you insist on risking it, make sure to have someone watching out for you, and shower immediately afterwards

Backyard Graveyards

Ancient burial sites lie underneath countless homes and hotels throughout Hawaii. Construction workers often dig up iwi (bones) and moepu (funeral objects), while locals swear by eerie stories of equipment malfunctioning until bones are properly reinterred and prayers given.

Desecration of iwi is illegal and a major affront to Native Hawaiians. Thanks to the Native American Graves Protection and Repatriation Act, passed by Congress in 1990, burial councils on each island oversee the treatment of remains and the preservation of burial sites.

One of Kaua'i's best known cases involved Naue Point in Ha'ena, the site of some 30 confirmed iwi. Starting in 2002 and lasting close to nine years, the case went through numerous phases of court hearings, public demonstrations and burial-treatment proposals and ended with the state allowing the landowner to build.

What might potentially happen? Could a landowner lose the right to build? Probably not. It's more likely for the state to approve a burial-treatment proposal to remove the iwi and reinter them off-site, an outcome that Native Hawaiians find woefully inadequate. In any case, many hotels and condos have been constructed on land with iwi now sitting in storage or remaining underground. What happens to those restless spirits?

At Po'ipu's Grand Hyatt Resort, the director of Hawaiian and community affairs performs blessings somewhere on resort grounds at least once a month to quell any 'spiritual disturbance.'

Facing page: Waikanaloa Wet Cave

Ha'ena

Remote, resplendent and idyllic, the village of Hae'na marks where the ribbon road ends amid lava rock pinnacles, lush forest and postcard-perfect beaches. In the wet season the cliffs are positively weeping with waterfalls. It's also long been the site of controversy, as many of its luxury homes were built atop *iwi kupuna* (ancient Hawaiian burial grounds).

⊙ SIGHTS

Limahuli Garden   Gardens

(📞808-826-1053; http://ntbg.org/gardens/limahuli; 5-8291 Kuhio Hwy; self-guided adult/student/child under 18yr $20/10/free; 2½hr guided tours adult/student & children 10-17yr $40/20; ⊘9:30am-4pm Tue-Sat, guided tours 10am Tue-Fri; P♿) ✿ Perhaps the most beautiful spot on an island of unsurpassed beauty, this magnificent garden is a must-see stop on any North Shore itinerary. Besides cherishing species unique to this region of Kaua'i – some to this very valley – it also displays plants brought to Hawaii from elsewhere. While guided and self-guided tours follow a three-quarter-mile trail through its landscaped front portion, the preserve's 985 acres extend back into the sheer-walled depths of the valley, where its serious conservation work takes place.

This wonderful place forms part of the National Tropical Botanical Garden, which also runs two gardens in Po'ipu. To give it the time it deserves, come as early as possible, before the day's full heat sets in. Allow 1½ hours to walk the trail, enjoying spectacular close-up views of Makana Peak (popularly known as Bali Hai). In winter, it's common to see whales breaching offshore.

The garden's driveway climbs inland just before the stream that marks the boundary of Ha'ena State Park (p116). Although you don't need a permit to drive here, you have to reserve in advance for a specific time, and you're only allowed to park here during your actual visit.

Makua (Tunnels) Beach   Beach

Yet another too-good-to-be-true North Shore beach. Named for the underwater caverns and lava tubes that pepper the near-shore reef, Tunnels ranks among Kaua'i's finest snorkel spots in summer. It's also the North Shore's most popular dive site, suitable for shore dives. In winter, however, the swell picks up and the surf can be heavy.

In the shoulder season, the snorkeling can still be decent, but always check with lifeguards before heading into the water. Beware especially of a current flowing west toward the open ocean.

Access to Makua Beach is notoriously difficult. Two short dirt roads link it with the highway, but parking is very limited, and you may attract hostility. Most beachgoers park at Ha'ena State Park (p116), then walk a half-mile along the sandy foreshore.

Ha'ena Beach Park   Beach

At this beautiful county-run beach, just under a mile before the end of the road, the sea is usually smooth and safe for swimming in summer. Ask lifeguards about conditions before going in, though, especially between October and May, when it's rendered dangerous by an endlessly pounding shore break that creates a strong undertow.

Maniniholo Dry Cave   Cave

Flat-bottomed Maniniholo Dry Cave, across from Ha'ena Beach Park, is deep, broad and fun to explore, though the further you penetrate, the lower the ceiling and the darker your surrounds. A constant seep of water from the walls keeps the interior dank. As you inch toward the rear wall, remember that you are standing below a massive monolith of Jurassic proportions.

✪ ACTIVITIES

Hanalei Day Spa   Spa

(📞808-826-6621; www.hanaleidayspa.com; Hanalei Colony Resort, 5-7130 Kuhio Hwy; massage 50/80min $110/140; ⊘9am-6pm Tue-Sat) If you're tired or need to revitalize, this friendly (if modest) spa offers comp-etitively priced massages, including Hawaiian *lomilomi*, and body treatments like an Ayurvedic body wrap.

🔒 SHOPPING

Na Pali Art Gallery
& Coffee House   Arts & Crafts

(📞808-826-1844; www.napaligallery.com; Hanalei Colony Resort, 5-7132 Kuhio Hwy; ⏱7am-6pm Mon-Sat, to 1pm Sun; 🛜) At this small gallery, you can peruse a quality array of local artists' paintings, woodwork, sculptures, ceramics, jewelry and collectibles. It's also the perfect spot to pick up an early morning coffee as you head for the Kalalau Trail.

✖ EATING & DRINKING

There is but one restaurant and one cafe in Ha'ena. The only bar is located inside the only restaurant, next door to the only coffee joint. All share the same superb ocean view.

Opakapaka   Seafood $$

(📞808-378-4425; www.opakapakagrillandbar. com; Hanalei Colony Resort, 5-7132 Kuhio Hwy; mains $15-36; ⏱11am-9pm; 🅿) The only restaurant west of Hanalei is so close to the beach that ocean breezes waft through the windows. Its well-judged menu includes everything from fresh catch to burgers to pasta – appetizers like fish tacos or the poke bowl are enough for a decent lunch – and there's a lively bar. Linger a while; as our waitress advised, 'you've got all day.'

➊ GETTING THERE & AWAY

Ha'ena is linked to Hanalei along Kuhio Hwy via several one-lane bridges. If a bridge floods, you'll be cut off.

The **North Shore Shuttle** (📞888-409-2702; https://kauainsshuttle.com; single ride/day pass/week/month $5/10/20/40) stops at Opakapaka restaurant, alongside the Hanalei Colony Resort lodging option, en route to and from the end of the highway.

 Sacred Sharks

Being attacked by a *mano* (shark) can certainly be deadly; precautions like not swimming in murky waters, especially after rain, will help you avoid them. Statistically speaking, though, you're more likely to die from a bee sting than a shark attack, and you should be more concerned about contracting leptospirosis or giardiasis in those infamous muddy waters than becoming a lunchtime snack.

Rather than letting any hardwired phobia of large predators get you down, try considering the *mano* from another perspective: as sacred. For many Hawaiian families, the *mano* is their *'aumakua* (guardian spirit). *'Aumakua* are family ancestors whose *'uhane* (spirit form) lives on in the body of an animal, watching over members of their living *'ohana*. Revered for their ocean skill, *mano* were also considered the *'aumakua* of navigators. Even today, *mano 'aumakua* are said to guide lost fishermen home, or toward areas of plentiful fish to make for a bountiful sojourn.

HANALEI BAY,
KAUA'I

Hanalei Bay at a Glance...

Precious few places can boast the natural beauty and barefoot soul of Hanalei, the jewel of Kaua'i's North Shore. The bay is the thing, of course, home to a half-dozen legendary surf breaks. Even if you haven't come for the waves, you'll love the beach, with its wide sweep of cream-colored sand and magnificent jade mountain views.

In the plantation-era buildings of the town itself, a half-mile back from the beach, you can shop for vintage treasures or chic beach gear, snack on noodles or poke, or duck into a world-class dive bar.

Hanalei Bay in One Day

Start with the steep, short climb up the **Okolehao Trail** (p130) before grabbing coffee and a pastry at **Hanalei Bread Company** (p132). Now it's time to rent a kayak or stand-up paddleboard (SUP) and paddle up the Hanalei River.

Decompress with a sunset beach walk at **Black Pot Beach** (p126), then hit the bar at **Tahiti Nui** (p133) for dinner (surprisingly good!) and drinks.

Hanalei Bay in Two Days

On day two, delve a little deeper into Hanalei's history and traditions. Learn where poi comes from on a tour of **Ho'opulapula Haraguchi Taro Farm** (p130), then visit pretty **Wai'oli Hui'ia Church** (p128), and the **Mission House** (p128) hidden away behind the farm.

Take time to sample smoothies or shave ice from Hanalei's roadside kiosks, and browse its intriguing boutiques. Cap off your day with a divine wine-splashed dinner at **Bar Acuda** (p133).

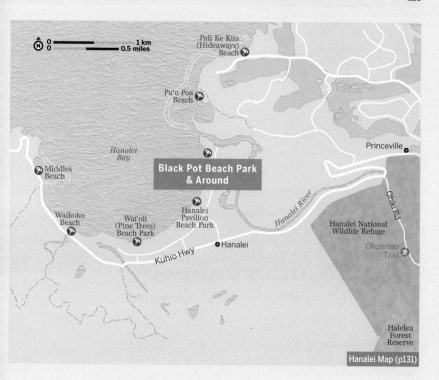

Hanalei Map (p131)

Arriving in Hanalei Bay

The North Shore is easy to reach either by public transport, or under your own steam. As always on Kaua'i, a rental car, best picked up at the airport, will give you much greater flexibility. Taxis are expensive and hard to wrangle.

Sleeping

Lodging along the North Shore is less about hotels and more about rental homes, B&Bs and farmstays. The ideal option for groups and families is to rent a condo in Princeville or a beach house in Hanalei or points west.

Hanalei itself tends to be expensive; for better value, look for accommodations in nearby Kilauea or Princeville.

Black Pot Beach Park

Black Pot Beach Park & Around

With their stunning mountain backdrop, there's no resisting the beaches of Hanalei Bay. Soon, though, you'll be dying to surf those beautiful waves. Even if you're a beginner, you're in luck. Link up with a local surf school, and head to the pier.

Great For...

☑ Don't Miss

A tropical cocktail at a Hanalei grass-shack tiki bar.

The Setting: Hanalei Bay

A perfect crescent of golden sand lines the two-mile stretch of beautiful **Hanalei Bay** that runs west from the mouth of the Hanalei River. It's divided into four named sections, though as you enjoy a beachfront walk you can't tell where one ends and the next begins. Each offers different conditions for swimming and surfing, so don't assume it's safe to enter the ocean wherever you choose along the continuous strip.

Black Pot Beach Park

The short easternmost stretch of Hanalei Bay, alongside the mouth of the Hanalei River, usually offers the calmest surf among the wild North Shore swells and is popular with novice surfers. It's also known as **Hanalei Pier** for its unmistakable

KELSEY NEUKUM/SHUTTERSTOCK ©

Black Pot
Beach Park
(Hanalei Pier)

PRINCEVILLE

Hanalei
Bay

Weke Rd

Hanalei
River

Kuhio Hwy

HANALEI

ℹ Need to Know

Restrooms, showers and lifeguards are all available at Black Pot Beach.

✕ Take a Break

For a takeout lunch, you can't beat fresh *poke* from the fish market at Hanalei Dolphin (p133).

★ Top Tip

Park along Weke Rd if you have to, as the public lots at the beach parks quickly fill up.

landmark jetty, which is perfect for a sunset stroll. In summer, swimming, snorkeling and SUP are decent – though the river itself can carry bacteria. Kayakers launch from a small boat ramp on the river.

The sandy-bottomed beach slopes gently, providing ideally safe conditions to learn to surf. **Surf lessons** run by local schools typically take place just west of the pier.

Although the beach re-opened in 2019, following a year-long closure in the wake of the 2018 floods, its camping facilities remained closed at the time of writing.

Hanalei Pavilion Beach Park

Pretty much at the center of Hanalei Bay, next around the curve from Black Pot Beach, this scenic beach park commands a white-sand crescent that's just made for walking or jogging. Waters are typically not as calm as beside the pier, but swimming and paddling are usually possible in summer. Facilities include restrooms and outdoor showers. The one downside is that there's only a small parking lot, but street-parking spaces are often available along Weke Rd.

Wai'oli (Pine Trees) Beach Park

Offering respite from the sun, this park is equipped with restrooms, outdoor showers, beach volleyball courts and picnic tables. Winter brings big swells, and locals dominate the surf spot known as **Pine Trees** in honor of the waterfront ironwoods. There's a challenging shore break here, and swimming is only possible during summer calms.

Waikoko Beach

Protected by a reef on the western bend of Hanalei Bay, sandy-bottomed Waikoko Beach – literally, 'blood water' – offers shallower and calmer waters than the middle of the bay. It's thus the safest for family swimming, but sadly it has no facilities.

Hanalei Town

Hit hard by devastating floods in April 2018, when it was deluged by an astonishing US record of 49.69 inches of rain within 24 hours, laidback little Hanalei swiftly bounced back, and remains as enchanting as ever.

The main drag, set a half-mile inland from the ocean, still looks like the plantation village it used to be, though these days its wooden buildings are entirely given over to stores, boutiques, cafes and restaurants.

Waiʻoli Huiʻia Church

The green clapboard Waiʻoli Huiʻia Church stands on a huge manicured lawn just west of central Hanalei, against a beautiful mountain backdrop. It was originally built by Hanalei's first missionaries, William and Mary Alexander, who arrived here in 1834 in a double-hulled canoe. Its current American Gothic-style incarnation, complete with graceful stained-glass windows and curving pews, dates from 1912.

Follow the path to the rear to reach the two-story **Waiʻoli Mission House**, where the Alexanders lived from 1837 onwards. Set in lush gardens, surrounded by a white picket fence, it's furnished in authentic period style. When you arrive, ring the large bell beside the outdoor chimney, and a guide will emerge to offer you a guided tour (no reservations).

Hanalei Valley Lookout

Hanalei National Wildlife Refuge

Among the largest rivers in the state, the Hanalei River winds through a fertile valley that has been a major agricultural resource ever since the first *kanaka maoli* (Native Hawaiians) planted taro here. Many taro patches became rice paddies in the 19th century to feed the Chinese laborers on the sugar plantations, and four rice mills were operating in the valley by the 1930s. Although taro production has greatly declined elsewhere in Hawaii, however, here in Hanalei it dominates once more.

The 917-acre Hanalei National Wildlife Refuge was established in 1972 to protect five endangered native waterbirds: *ae'o* (Hawaiian stilt; slender with black back, white chest and long pink legs), *'alae ke'oke'o* (Hawaiian coot; slate gray with white forehead), *'alae 'ula* (Hawaiian moorhen; dark gray with black head and distinctive red-and-yellow bill); *koloa maoli* (Hawaiian duck; mottled brown with orange legs and feet); and *nene* (Hawaiian goose; black head and striped neck), which is no longer officially considered to be endangered. A further 45 bird species are regular visitors.

The refuge is closed to the public, but the **Hanalei Valley Lookout** in Princeville offers a distant overview, and you can enter it on foot by joining the Ho'opulapula Haraguchi Taro Farm Tour (p130). It's also possible to drive into the refuge by turning left onto Ohiki Rd, immediately after the Hanalei Bridge, but parking is only permitted at the trailhead for the Okolehao Trail (p130).

NICKOLAY STANEV/SHUTTERSTOCK ©

🏃 ACTIVITIES

As well as being the summer launching point for Na Pali cruises, Hanalei Bay stands at the mouth of the Hanalei River, which offers 6 miles of tranquil scenery, ideal for kayaking or SUP.

Kayak Hanalei   Water Sports
(☎808-826-1881; http://kayakhanalei.com; 5-5070a Kuhio Hwy; rental per day surfboard $23, kayak set $35-75, SUP set $40, 2hr surfing or SUP lessons $85-130, kayak tours adult/child 5-12yr $109/99; ⊙8am-4:30pm) The only Hanalei-based outfit offering kayak rentals and local tours, this long-established, family-run outfitter also rents SUP sets and surfboards. Tours, available weekdays only, start on the river and head to Princeville and back. Beginners surfing and SUP lessons can be booked daily except Sunday.

Okolehao Trail   Hiking
(Ohiki Rd) For a dramatic overview of the taro fields of Hanalei Valley, and the crescent bay beyond, climb the gruelling but rewarding Okolehao Trail. Ascending a sharp wooded ridge, it reaches successive forest clearings where views open up east to Kilauea Lighthouse and west to the Na Pali Coast. Carry lots of water and expect plenty of mud. Most hikers turn back after 1.25 miles, but informal and very precarious pathways lead higher up towards inaccessible peaks.

Pedal 'n' Paddle   Adventure Sports
(☎808-826-9069; http://pedalnpaddle.com; Ching Young Village, 5-5190 Kuhio Hwy; ⊙9am-6pm) This full-service rental shop, conveniently located in the heart of Hanalei, offers good daily and weekly rates for renting snorkel sets, boogie boards, SUP sets, kayaks, bicycles and almost all the camping gear you could need for trekking the Na Pali Coast.

Waipa Foundation   Volunteering
(☎808-826-9969; www.waipafoundation.org; 5-5785 Kuhio Hwy) This nonprofit organization owns and manages an entire traditional Hawaiian *ahapua'a*, a fundamental land division extending from peak to shore. Volunteer opportunities include sessions on the fourth Saturday of each month, when visitors join hands-on community activities such as clearing invasive plants from waterways, or working in the taro fields. Sign up in advance and they'll prepare lunch for you.

Hawaiian Surfing
Adventures   Water Sports
(☎808-482-0749; www.hawaiiansurfing adventures.com; 5-5134 Kuhio Hwy; 90min group surfing lesson $75, SUP lesson $65, surfboard/SUP rental per day from $20/40; ⊙store 9am-3pm, last lesson starts 2pm) Surfing lessons for novices include 30 minutes on land and one hour in the water. SUP lessons could even get you doing yoga poses atop your board.

🎫 TOURS

Ho'opulapula Haraguchi
Taro Farm Tour   Food & Drink
(☎808-651-3399; www.haraguchiricemill.org; 5-5070a Kuhio Hwy; tours incl snack adult/child 5-12yr $70/50; ⊙9:45am Wed, by reservation only) 🌿 Learn about cultivating taro on Kaua'i at this sixth-generation family-run nonprofit farm. Three-hour farmer-guided tours take you out into the *lo'i kalo* (waterlogged taro fields), offering a small glimpse of the otherwise inaccessible Hanalei National Wildlife Refuge and demonstrating the processes involved in preparing the crop.

Na Pali Catamaran   Boating
(☎866-255-6853, 808-826-6853; www.napali catamaran.com; Ching Young Village, 5-5190 Kuhio Hwy; 4hr tours $250) This exceptional outfit offers morning and afternoon Na Pali cruises from Hanalei between March and October. Its 35ft power catamaran is smaller and less majestic than a sailing cat but much less exposed than a Zodiac, and doesn't feel crowded. When conditions are right, it can venture into sea caves. Minimum age five years. Check for online or phone discounts.

Captain Sundown   Boating
(☎808-826-5585; https://captainsundown. com; 3hr tours $151, 6hr $259) During the summer season – generally, late April until early October – this sailing catamaran offers

Hanalei

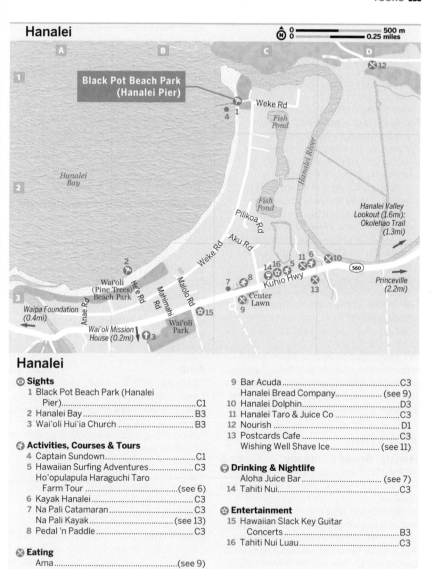

N
0 — 500 m
0 — 0.25 miles

Black Pot Beach Park
(Hanalei Pier)

Weke Rd

Fish Pond

Hanalei Bay

Fish Pond

Hanalei River

Pilikoa Rd

Aku Rd

Weke Rd

Hee Rd

Mahimahi Rd

Malolo Rd

Anae Rd

Hee Rd

Wai'oli
(Pine Trees)
Beach Park

Waipa Foundation
(0.4mi)

Wai'oli Mission
House (0.2mi)

Wai'oli
Park

Kuhio Hwy

Center
Lawn

560

Hanalei Valley
Lookout (1.6mi);
Okolehao Trail
(1.3mi)

Princeville
(2.2mi)

Hanalei

◎ Sights
1 Black Pot Beach Park (Hanalei
  Pier)..C1
2 Hanalei Bay B3
3 Wai'oli Hui'ia Church B3

✦ Activities, Courses & Tours
4 Captain Sundown.............................C1
5 Hawaiian Surfing Adventures.................C3
  Ho'opulapula Haraguchi Taro
  Farm Tour ....(see 6)
6 Kayak Hanalei....................................C3
7 Na Pali Catamaran C3
  Na Pali Kayak ....(see 13)
8 Pedal 'n Paddle...............................C3

✖ Eating
  Ama..(see 9)

9 Bar Acuda.. C3
  Hanalei Bread Company....................(see 9)
10 Hanalei Dolphin.............................. D3
11 Hanalei Taro & Juice Co C3
12 Nourish.. D1
13 Postcards Cafe C3
  Wishing Well Shave Ice ....(see 11)

🍷 Drinking & Nightlife
  Aloha Juice Bar ....(see 7)
14 Tahiti Nui..C3

✦ Entertainment
15 Hawaiian Slack Key Guitar
  Concerts B3
16 Tahiti Nui Luau..................................C3

six-hour snorkeling adventures along the Na Pali Coast, plus three-hour sunset cruises. While too large to enter sea caves, it ensures a relatively smooth ride, and the trampoline nets upfront are a joy. Captain Bob has plenty of stories. No children under seven years of age.

Na Pali Explorer
Boating

(☎808-338-9999; www.napaliexplorer.com; 4½hr tour from Hanalei $149, 6hr tour from Kikiaola $189; 🚸) Rigid-hull inflatable rafts, being hard-bottomed, give a smoother ride than all-inflatable Zodiacs. The summer-only 4½hr Na Pali tours from Hanalei are in a 48ft

¶◎¶ Homage to Kalo

Hawaiian cosmology relates that Papa (earth mother) and Wakea (sky father) gave birth to Haloa, a stillborn brother to man. Haloa was planted in the earth and from his body came the *kalo* plant, known as taro in English, a staple crop for Oceanic cultures and the major food source in pre-contact Hawaii.

Kalo is still considered sacred, hailed as the 'staff of life' and imbued with tradition and spiritual significance. Hanalei is home to the largest taro-producing farm in the state, Ho'opulapula Haraguchi (p130), growing the purple, starchy potato-like plant in *lo'i kalo* (wet taro fields). Rich in nutrients, *kalo* is usually boiled and pounded into poi, an earthy, sticky paste that serves as a basic starch.

raft, carrying up to 36 passengers, with a restroom and a canopy for shade. They also offer six-hour tours from Kikiaola Harbor on the West Coast, potentially including beach landings, in a 24ft, 14-passenger raft.

⊗ EATING

Hanalei Bread Company   Bakery $
(📞808-826-6717; Hanalei Center, 5-5183 Kuhio Hwy; mains $9-14; ⊙7am-5pm) Great coffee and breakfast specials – like bacon and onion pizzas with soft eggs cracked on top – draw morning crowds to this organic bakery and cafe in the heart of Hanalei; expect to wait in line. And eat those fresh-baked pastries and breads quick – they wilt fast in the humidity.

Wishing Well Shave Ice   Ice Cream $
(📞808-639-7828; www.wishingwellshaveice. com; 5-5080 Kuhio Hwy; shave ice from $5; ⊙9:30am-5pm) It's worth paying a few dollars extra at Hanalei's finest shave-ice stand for its organic rather than its regular syrups; the liliko'i (passion fruit) and mango flavors in particular are out of this

world. It also serves acai bowls and cold-pressed coffee, and has some well-shaded picnic tables.

Nourish   Health Food $
(📞808-346-2254; www.nourishhanalei.com; 5225 Hanalei Plantation Rd; items $9-14; ⊙11am-3pm Tue-Fri) ✔ Set on a little-known Princeville backroad, this little farm stand overlooks an amazing Hanalei panorama taking in beach, town, river and valley. It serves a simple but healthy lunchtime menu of homegrown salads, fruit bowls and smoothies.

Hanalei Taro & Juice Co   Hawaiian $
(📞808-651-3399; www.hanaleitaro.com; 5-5070a Kuhio Hwy; dishes $5-15; ⊙10am-3pm; 🖕) ✔ Find this roadside trailer near Hanalei's eastern end for a taste of poi – the traditional Hawaiian staple, prepared on the family's nearby taro farm – or other typical luau foods like *kalua* pig. Almost everything comes taro flavored, from tropical smoothies to hummus, burgers or rice cakes. They also serve wraps, sandwiches and sizeable plate lunches.

Ama   Noodles $$
(📞808-826-9452; www.amahanalei.com; Hanalei Center, 5-5161 Kuhio Hwy; mains $19; ⊙5-9pm) This no-reservations offshoot of neighboring Bar Acuda enjoys Hanalei's finest outdoor setting, facing mountains cascading with waterfalls. Treating Japanese-style ramen noodles as fine dining, it tops them with seared ahi (tuna), chicken or pork, but also offers a vegetarian version. Sides include spicy, deep-fried Brussels sprouts, while dessert is homemade donuts.

Kaua'i Ono   Hawaiian $$$
(📞808-634-3244; www.kauaiono.com; Princeville Ranch, 4520 Kapaka St; 5-course dinner $70; ⊙6:30pm Tue & Wed) ✔ For something different and delicious, join the twice-weekly crowd for this outdoor feast at Princeville Ranch. From a fancy trailer, chef Justin Smith delivers a five-course menu of fresh produce from Kaua'i farms – the likes of *kalua* pork with mashed breadfruit – to communal tables beneath a huge awning. Check schedule and reserve online; BYOB.

Postcards Cafe
Seafood $$$

(✆808-826-1191; www.postcardscafe.com; 5-5075 Kuhio Hwy; mains $28-42; ⊙5:30-9pm; 🅿) 🍃 This charming clapboard cottage, marked by a rusted anchor out front, specializes in seafood dishes with world-fusion flavors like wasabi-crusted ahi or fennel-crusted lobster tail. There's no meat on the menu, but vegetarian and vegan alternatives are available.

Bar Acuda
Mediterranean $$$

(✆808-826-7081; www.restaurantbaracuda.com; Hanalei Center, 5-5161 Kuhio Hwy; shared plates $15-25; ⊙5:30-10pm, kitchen closes 9:30pm) 🍃 Reserve in advance to dine in this smart 'tapas and wine' restaurant, which is Hanalei's most chef-driven spot. It typically takes four or five of its sharing plates including selections like fresh Hawaiian fish, Spanish meatballs and French lentils to provide a satisfying dinner for two. The excellent wine list features both new- and old-world vintners.

Hanalei Dolphin
Seafood $$$

(✆808-826-6113; www.hanaleidolphin.com; 5-5016 Kuhio Hwy; mains lunch $12-16, dinner $26-42; ⊙restaurant 11:30am-9pm, market 10am-7pm) Arrive early at this riverside setting at Hanalei's eastern end for lunch or a sunset dinner, with fresh fish served cooked or as sushi, and steak and chicken options too. The poke and raw fish in their adjoining fish market is the best deal.

🍸 DRINKING & NIGHTLIFE

Tahiti Nui
Bar

(✆808-826-6277; http://thenui.com; 5-5134 Kuhio Hwy; ⊙11am-10pm Sun-Wed, to 1am Thu-Sat) The legendary Nui (rendered famous by its cameo role in *The Descendants*) is a tiki dive bar with heart and history, and a rather tasty dinner menu. Usually crowded from mid-afternoon onward, it gets rollicking nightly with live Hawaiian music from 6:30pm until 8:30pm. It's especially busy on weekends, when it's the only place open past 10pm.

Aloha Juice Bar
Juice Bar

(✆808-639-2826; Ching Young Village, 5-5190 Kuhio Hwy; drinks and bowls from $7; ⊙10am-

4pm) In a red shack at the west end of Ching Young Village, this irresistible juice stand is renowned for its thick fruit smoothies and fresh veggie juices; look for cut-price offers on surplus fruit. It also has acai bowls, pineapple whip, chocolate-dipped bananas, cracked coconuts and fresh and dried fruits.

☆ENTERTAINMENT

Tahiti Nui Luau
Luau

(✆808-826-6277; http://thenui.com; 5-5134 Kuhio Hwy; adult/senior/teen/under-13 $80/ $67/$47/$37; ⊙5pm Wed) The North Shore's one weekly luau is everything a Hawaiian luau should be. Housed in a separate dining room adjoining the much-loved Tahiti Nui bar, it has the feel of a genuine family party, with homespun entertainment followed by small-scale but authentic hula displays and fire dancing.

Hawaiian Slack Key Guitar Concerts
Live Music

(✆808-826-1469; www.hawaiianslackkeyguitar. com; Hanalei Community Center, Malolo Rd; adult/13-19yr/6-12yr $25/20/10; ⊙4pm Fri, 3pm Sun) Veteran musicians Doug and Sandy McMaster perform Hawaiian-style slack key guitar and ukulele in a relaxed atmosphere.

They also play at Princeville Community Center, 4334 Emmaline Drive, at 6pm on Tuesday.

ℹ GETTING THERE & AWAY

There's only one road into and out of Hanalei. During heavy rains, common in winter, the Hanalei Bridge can close due to flooding; those on the 'wrong' side are stuck until it reopens.

The North Shore Shuttle (p314) links Waipa, a half-mile west of Hanalei, with Ha'ena State Park, for access to Ke'e Beach and the Kalalau Trail.

ℹ GETTING AROUND

Pedal 'n' Paddle (p130) ents cruisers (per day/ week $15/60) and hybrid road bikes ($20/80), all including helmets and locks.

WAIMEA CANYON, KAUA'I

Waimea Canyon

Four million years ago, a colossal earthquake almost split Kaua'i in two. The resultant chasm has yawned wider ever since to form Waimea Canyon. A scenic spectacle unlike any other in Hawaii, it ranges from raw red-earth cliffs to striated peaks, and plummeting waterfalls to verdant forest. And beyond it, up on the roof of Kaua'i, remote Koke'e State Park is just as extraordinary, commanding wondrous views over the Na Pali Coast, and holding magnificent wilderness trails.

Waimea Canyon in Two Days

Follow Rte 550 right to the top, through Waimea Canyon and Koke'e state parks. Stop at the many stunning lookouts along the way, and be sure to pause at the **Koke'e Natural History Museum** (p145). Then head back down to Waimea to explore its extraordinary past.

On day two, take a cruise to see the fabulous Na Pali cliffs from the ocean, then spend the afternoon strolling the main street in artsy Hanapepe.

Waimea Canyon in Four Days

On day three, hike in **Koke'e** (p142); choose one long trail or a couple of short ones, and spend the day admiring one of nature's greatest masterpieces.

Day four provides reflection time. Contemplate eternity beneath the cliffs at **Polihale** (p146). Dine at **Wrangler's Steakhouse** (p149) because you deserve a thick steak. End with a sunset at **Kekaha Beach Park** (p146), looking out across the sea to the 'Forbidden Island' of Ni'ihau.

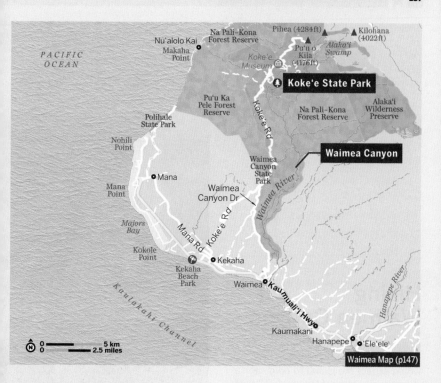

Waimea Map (p147)

Arriving in Waimea Canyon

Waimea is easily reached by rental car and served by **Kaua'i Bus** (p149). There's no public transportation up to the state parks, however.

Sleeping

Along with a rather wonderful resort-like historic hotel and a handful of cute inns in Waimea, and rough cabins up on the mountaintop, the Westside holds some pretty darned good vacation homes, several looking right onto the beach.

Far fewer tourists stay here than elsewhere on the island, though; you have to like the idea of getting away from it all.

Hiking Waimea Canyon

Of all Kaua'i's wonders, none can touch Waimea Canyon for grandeur. Few would expect the island to hold such a gargantuan abyss of lava rock, 10 miles long and over 3500ft deep.

Great For...

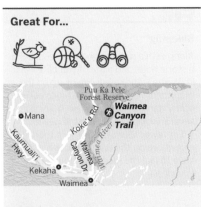

ⓘ Need to Know

Cell phones do not work here. Hike with a companion or let someone know when you expect to return.

★ **Top Tip**

Do not drink fresh water found along the trails without treating it.

MARTINM303/GETTY IMAGES ©

Geography

Known as the Grand Canyon of the Pacific, Waimea Canyon was created when Kaua'i's original shield volcano, Wai'ale'ale, slumped along an ancient fault line. The horizontal striations along its walls represent successive volcanic eruptions. The red colors indicate where water has seeped through the rocks, draining mineral rust from the iron ore inside.

Waimea River, which flows through the canyon, is Kaua'i's longest, fed by tributaries bringing reddish-brown waters from the Alaka'i Swamp.

Waimea Canyon Drive

This magnificent scenic drive traces the entire length of Waimea Canyon's western rim and continues into Koke'e State Park, climbing 19 miles from the coast to Pu'u o Kila Lookout. Starting from Waimea's visitor center as Waimea Canyon Dr, it meets Koke'e Rd after 8 miles, and takes its name.

Scenic lookouts along the way – notably the breathtaking **Waimea Canyon Lookout**, shortly after Mile 10, and **Pu'u Hinahina Lookout**, just before Mile 14 – offer superb views. The major lookouts hold restrooms and the occasional food truck, and some have short hiking trails too, but there are no gas stations.

If you're here first thing in the morning, you can beat the crowds by driving straight to the far end of the road, then visiting the lookouts in reverse order, as you descend.

Waimea Canyon Drive

Waimea Canyon Trails

Trekking to the bottom of Waimea Canyon is, thanks to the steep climb back out again, only recommended for seriously fit hikers. Start by descending the narrow, switchbacking **Kukui Trail** from the Iliau Nature Loop trailhead, just before Mile 9 on Hwy 550. In its 2.5-mile course down to the river, it drops 2000ft, but offers little in the way of sweeping panoramas. If you've only time for a short hike, just go the first mile down, to reach a bench with an astonishing view.

ⓘ Camping

All four backcountry campgrounds ($18 per night) in Waimea Canyon are on forest reserve land. They have picnic shelters and pit toilets, but no other facilities. Advance permits are required.

From the foot of the trail, the 11.5-mile **Waimea Canyon Trail** follows the river all the way down to Waimea town. Alternatively, if you hike upstream instead, you'll meet the **Koaiʻe Canyon Trail** a half-mile along. This moderate trek, measuring 3 miles each way, leads along the south side of Koaiʻe Canyon to swimming holes that are best avoided after rain, when flash floods threaten.

Hiking Tips

The rugged hiking trails of Waimea Canyon are shared with pig hunters, so be careful, and wear brightly colored clothing. They're busiest on weekends and holidays. Trail maps are available at the Kokeʻe Natural History Museum (p145). Hiking poles or a sturdy walking stick will ease the steep descent into the canyon.

Make sure you know when the sun's due to go down and aim to return long before dark, as daylight inside the canyon fades well before sunset. Beware of rain, which creates hazardous conditions: red-dirt trails quickly become slick, and river fords rise to impassable levels.

Pack light, but carry enough water for your entire trip, especially the uphill return hike. Don't drink fresh water without treating it.

MATT BOYLE/SHUTTERSTOCK ©

✕ Take a Break

Carry all your food for the day. Sometimes food stands at the lookouts sell snacks or drinks, but you can't depend on it.

Swamp Trail (p144)

MAKENA STOCK MEDIA/GETTY IMAGES ©

Hiking Koke'e State Park

Koke'e (ko-keh-eh) State Park encompasses some of Kaua'i's most precious ecosystems and extraordinary landscapes. Even a brief visit is hugely rewarding, thanks to roadside lookouts perched atop the Na Pali Coast.

Koke'e also ranks among Hawaii's greatest hiking destinations, with amazing trails that venture out to dramatic coastal overlooks and into the depths of the mysterious Alaka'i Swamp (p148).

You could easily do three separate day hikes in entirely different terrains, from swampy bogs to wet forest to knife-edge, red-dirt canyon rims. Along the way, you'll get abundant opportunities to spot endemic species like endangered rainforest birds.

Much of the park is 4000ft above sea level, so bring a fleece jacket; winter temperatures can dip below 40°F (4°C).

Getting to the Trails

Many of the best trails start along the main highway, while others set off from Halemanu Rd, which leaves Koke'e Rd just north of Mile 14. Whether it's passable in a non-4WD vehicle depends on recent

Great For...

☑ Don't Miss

Views over the Kalalau Valley from the Kalalau Lookout at mile marker 18.

Tropical flowers

SARAH LYNN MARTIN/SHUTTERSTOCK ©

Na Pali Coast
Wilderness
State Park

Kuia Natural   **Koke'e**
Area Reserve   **State Park**

Koke'e Rd

Na Pali–Kona
Forest Reserve

❶ Need to Know

For trail information, stop at the Koke'e
Museum, or visit the Na Ala Hele
website (www.hawaiitrails.hawaii.gov).

✕ Take a Break

Refuel with a bowl of Portuguese bean
soup at **Koke'e Lodge** (☏808-335-6061;
www.kokeelodge.com; Mile 15, Koke'e Rd;
mains $9-12; ☺9am-4pm).

★ Top Tip

Officially the rainy season lasts from
Octpber to May, but you'll likely need a
waterproof layer year-round.

rainfall. Many car rental agreements forbid
off-road driving.

Nu'alolo & Awa'awapuhi Trails

This stupendous full-day wilderness loop
leads to two otherwise inaccessible, utterly
unbelievable clifftop lookouts. It begins by
descending the **Nu'alolo Trail**, which starts
just downhill from Koke'e Lodge. The early
stretches are swampy, but as you descend
through thick rainforest, occasional long-
range views open up, across to parallel ridges
and out to the island of Ni'ihau. Eventually,
after 3.75 miles, you follow a narrow ledge
to reach **Lolo Vista Point**, where you're
greeted by astonishing Na Pali views.

Retrace your steps for 0.75 miles – which
entails clambering up via slick muddy
footholds – to join the **Nu'alolo Cliffs
Trail** at a conspicuous intersection. After
2.1 miles of winding through dense woods

and head-high grass, and inching above
a fearsome bare-earth abyss, this in turn
meets the **Awa'awapuhi Trail**.

Head oceanwards for 0.3 miles to reach
the magnificent **Awa'awapuhi Lookout**,
a stark headland perched 2500ft above
a sinuous valley, supposedly carved by a
slithering eel (*puhi*, in Hawaiian).

Now climb the 3.1 miles back up to
Koke'e Rd on the Awa'awapuhi Trail. The
trailhead is 1.7 miles up from Koke'e Lodge,
so you'll have to walk back down the
highway or thumb a ride.

Cliff & Canyon Trails

For some of the best family hiking in the
park, set off along the straightforward 1.8-
mile **Cliff Trail**, which includes a 0.8 miles
hike down from Halemanu Rd. Enjoy the
canyon views, then, if you don't have kids
in tow, keep going on the forested, 1.7-mile
Canyon Trail. With over 1700ft of up-and-
down elevation change as it dips into the
upper reaches of the canyon, this one's a
knee-buster.

The Canyon Trail begins with a steep descent, with truly awesome views every step of the way, then climbs to reach a vast red-dirt promontory, poised above stark cliffs. Just beyond, some huff-and-puff climbing brings you to **Waipo'o Falls**. Don't expect to see the actual falls; you're right at the top of them, but it's too dangerous to venture any lower. Instead, you'll find a pool with some small cascades running into it.

If you've had enough, turn around at the falls. Otherwise, follow the trail across the stream to the canyon rim. It ends at **Kumuwela Lookout**, where you can rest at a picnic table before backtracking to Halemanu Rd.

For an alternate return route, make a right at the signed intersection with the **Black Pipe Trail** at the top of the switchback where you leave the canyon rim. This half-mile route ends at the 4WD road, where you turn left (downhill) and walk back to where you started.

If you have a 4WD, you can skip the steep bits by accessing the trail system from the end of Kumuwela Ridge.

Pihea Trail to Alaka'i Swamp Trail

For sheer scenic splendor, you can't beat the first mile of the Pihea Trail. Setting off from **Pu'u o Kila Lookout**, at road's end, it follows a bare ridge, slick with mud, with panoramic views over Kalalau Valley to one side and dense rainforest to the other. The trail grows ever more challenging, with steep sections where you effectively have to climb miniature waterfalls. Persist to reach **Pihea Lookout**, perched atop the highest peak (4284ft).

View of Kalalau Valley from Pu'u o Kila Lookout

To create a strenuous 7.5-mile round-trip trek, drop down inland on the Pihea Trail shortly before the lookout to enter a magical, moss-laden mountaintop forest.

Head left onto the Alaka'i Swamp Trail 0.75 miles along. This descends a rickety stairway to a small stream, which you cross by either wading or rock-scrambling. A 4-mile round-trip hike, mostly along an unstable wooden boardwalk, then leads across eerie, misty boglands to breathtaking **Kilohana Lookout**.

Koke'e Natural History Museum

This two-room museum (☎808-335-3353; www.kokee.org; Mile 15, Koke'e Rd; donation $3; ⊕9am-4pm; 👤) holds detailed topographical maps, exhibits on flora and fauna, and historical photographs. It also has botanical sketches of endemic plants and taxidermic representations of some of the wildlife that calls Koke'e home. Helpful staff can provide detailed current advice on hiking, and sell a map of the trails.

Koke'e Resource Conservation Program

If you want to contribute your time and energy into keeping Koke'e beautiful, get into the backcountry with this **ecological restoration organization** (☎808-335-0045; www.krcp.org) 🌿. It's backbreaking work, but think of it as a hike with some weed-whacking in between.

★ **Eo e Emalani I Alaka'i**

Commemorating Queen Emma's 1871 expedition to the Alaka'i Swamp, this outdoor festival takes over Koke'e's meadows in mid-October.

◉ SIGHTS

Polihale State Park State Park

(https://hawaiistateparks.org/kauai; 🚻) The endless expanse of Polihale Beach is as mystical as it is enchanting. The long slow drive here, along a rutted 5-mile dirt road, brings you to the edge of eternity. The wide virgin beach curls into dunes that climb into bluffs, while the foothills of the Na Pali cliffs rise to the north. Families come here to camp and picnic, surf and watch sunsets.

Kekaha Beach Park Beach

The Westside is renowned for its unrelenting sun and vast beaches. At the west end of Kekaha town, this long stretch of sand is best for beachcombing and catching sunsets. It lacks lacks reef protection so check with a lifeguard whether it's OK to swim before you jump in. Under the right conditions it's good for surfing and bodyboarding. Facilities include outdoor showers, restrooms and picnic tables.

Russian Fort Elizabeth State Historical Park Historic Site

(www.fortelizabeth.org; off Kaumuali'i Hwy; ⊘dawn-dusk) FREE A Russian fort in Hawaii? Yes, really. Constructed in 1817 above the southern bank of the mouth of Waimea River on the site of an ancient *heiau* (temple), Fort Elizabeth was named after the Empress of Russia. Only its impressive outer walls, some 20ft high, are still standing. It once harbored a Russian Orthodox chapel and a cannon.

Follow the trail 100 yards beyond the fort to reach a pretty riverfront beach. Not suitable for swimming.

Menehune Ditch Archaeological Site

(Kikiaola; Menehune Rd) Little is now visible of Hawaii's most remarkable example of pre-contact cut-and-dressed stonework, supposedly constructed within a single night by the *menehune*, or 'little people.' A seven-mile aqueduct that channeled water from the Waimea River to ancient agricultural sites, it was described by Captain George Vancouver in 1793 as standing 24ft tall, with its top serving as a pathway into Waimea Canyon. Only a short masonry wall survives; the rest is said to remain intact beneath the modern road.

To get here, follow Menehune Rd inland from Kaumuali'i Hwy for almost 1.5 miles to a footbridge across the Waimea River, and look for the interpretive signboard opposite.

West Kaua'i Technology & Visitor Center Museum

(☑808-338-1332; www.westkauaivisitorcenter. org; 9565 Kaumuali'i Hwy; ⊘10am-4pm Mon, Tue, Thu & Fri) FREE Waimea's visitor center holds modest but interesting exhibits on Hawaiian culture, Captain James Cook, sugar plantations and the US military. Its gift shop sells local artisan crafts, including rare Ni'ihau shell lei.

Waimea Town Center Architecture

Waimea's plantation-era center offers some interesting architecture. Admire the 1929 neoclassical **First Hawaiian Bank** (☑808-338-1611; www.fhb.com; 4525 Panako Rd; ⊘8:30am-4pm Mon-Thu, to 6pm Fri), the art deco Waimea Theater (1938; p149) and the historic, restored **Waimea United Church of Christ** (☑808-338-9962; www.waimea church.org; 4080 Makeke Rd; ⊘Sunday service 10am) with its distinctive covering of coral.

Captain Cook Monument Monument

(Hofgaard Park, cnr Waimea Rd & Kaumuali'i Hwy) A statue of Captain Cook stands on Waimea's central green space. When his ships *Resolution* and *Discovery* sailed into Waimea Bay in January 1778, Cook changed the course of world history. This likeness is a replica of an original by Sir John Tweed in his home town of Whitby, England.

✦ ACTIVITIES

Taking a Na Pali Coast cruise from Kikiaola Small Boat Harbor, north of Waimea, should spare exposure to the rougher seas you may encounter if you sail from Port Allen.

Hike Kaua'i Adventures Hiking

(☑808-639-9709; www.hikekauaiadventures.com; half-/full day for 2 people $280/380) Longtime resident Jeffrey Courson has hiked every trail on Kaua'i and will tailor an ideal bespoke

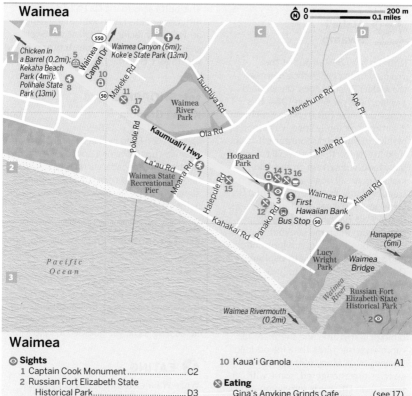

Waimea

itinerary to meet your needs. An expert on local flora, fauna and history, he includes door-to-door service too. You'll have a blast.

Na Pali Riders Boating
(☑808-742-6331; www.napaliriders.com; 9600 Kaumuali'i Hwy; 4hr tour adult/child 5-12yr

$149/129) Get a first-hand peek at sea caves (weather permitting) on Captain Chris Turner's Zodiac raft tour. Warning: it's a high-speed, no-shade, bumpy ride that's not for the faint of heart. Morning and afternoon departures available. Cash discounts.

Alaka'i Swamp

Nothing provides an out-of-the-ordinary hiking experience quite like the Alaka'i Swamp does. Designated a wilderness preserve in 1964, this soggy paradise has a hiking trail that is almost comletely lined with wooden planks, mainly to discourage off-trail trekking. Nevertheless, you'll traverse truly fantastic terrain on this hike, including misty bogs with knee-high trees and tiny, carniverous plants. On a clear day, you'll get outstanding views of the Wainiha Valley and the distant ocean from Kilohana Lookout. If it's raining, don't fret: search for rainbows and soak up the eerie atmosphere. Queen Emma was said to have been so moved by tales from this spirutual place that she sojourned here while chanting in reverence.

The swamp has its own unique biological rhythms and there are far more endemic birds than introduced species here. Many of these avian species are endagered, some with fewer than 100 birds remaining today.

Na Pali Explorer — Boating

(☑808-338-9999; www.napaliexplorer.com; 9814 Kaumuali'i Hwy; standard tour adult/child $149/129, beach landing $187/175) This Westside shop does it right, with small raft tours. You can choose whether to beach and hike to an ancient village, or go for the rip-roaring experience aboard a rigid-hull inflatable which at least has a canopy.

Waimea Rivermouth — Surfing

This river break surf site takes you both right and left; southern swells work best. Expect it to be crowded. And since it's a river break, expect the water to be dirty.

Liko Kaua'i Cruises — Boating

(☑808-338-0333; www.liko-kauai.com; 4516 Alawai Rd; 5hr cruise adult/child 4-12yr $149/109)

This outfit sails to the Na Pali Coast in a 49ft power catamaran with shade canopy and forward-facing padded seats. Snorkel gear is provided. In summer, tours go all the way to Ke'e Beach.

🔒 SHOPPING

Kaua'i Granola — Food

(☑808-338-0121; 9633 Kaumuali'i Hwy; ⊙10am-5pm Mon-Sat) Drop by this island bakery on your way up to Waimea Canyon, for snacks like trail mix, macadamia nut cookies or chocolate-dipped coconut macaroons; its signature tropically flavored granola is sold across the island.

Aunty Lilikoi Passion Fruit Products — Food, Gifts

(☑866-545-4564, 808-338-1296; www.aunty lilikoi.com; 9875 Waimea Rd; ⊙10am-6pm) Discover award-winning passion fruit–wasabi mustard, passion fruit syrup (great for banana pancakes), or massage oil (the choice for honeymooners), all made with at least a kiss of, you guessed it, *liliko'i*.

🍴 EATING

While Waimea may not have any fancy restaurants – that's not the Westside way – you can certainly sample pretty much any local cuisine here.

Ishihara Market — Supermarket, Deli $

(☑808-338-1751; 9894 Kaumuali'i Hwy; ⊙6am-7:30pm Mon-Thu, to 8pm Fri & Sat, to 7pm Sun) The deli counter at this famed Japanese supermarket is guaranteed to revive even the most jaded palate. With local favorites like kim chee sea snails or seasoned *iidako* (disconcertingly complete baby octopus), you're free to try before you buy. Daily specials usually include spicy ahi *poke* and smoked marlin, while marinated ready-to-barbecue meat and fish are always available.

Porky's — Barbecue $

(☑808-631-3071; www.porkyskauai.com; 9899 Waimea Rd; mains $11; ⊙11am-4pm Mon-Fri, to 3pm Sat) Promising 'aloha in a bun,' this much-loved little diner keeps things simple. Everyone's here for the juicy pulled pork, and you can have it on rice, in a grilled-cheese sandwich or on the signature bun.

Chicken in a Barrel
Barbecue $

(☎808-320-8397; www.chickeninabarrel.com; Waimea Plantation Cottages, 9400 Kaumuali'i Hwy; meals $11-18; ☺8am-9pm; ☎) The roomy and lovely wood-built bar/restaurant at the Waimea Plantation Cottages makes a classy venue for this popular local chain, which sells tacos, burritos and barbecue chicken.

G's Juicebar
Health Food $

(☎808-639-8785; 9691 Kaumuali'i Hwy; snacks from $8; ☺9am-4:30pm Mon-Fri, 9am-3pm Sat; ☎) Your quest for Kaua'i's top acai bowl might reach the finish line right here. A Marley Bowl comes with hemp seed, kale and bee pollen, and the Avatar with rice milk, blueberries and shaved coconut. Fresh tropical fruit smoothies and yerba mate tea will quench your thirst.

Gina's Anykine Grinds Cafe
Diner $

(☎808-338-1731; http://ginasanykinegrinds cafehi.com; 9691 Kaumuali'i Hwy; mains $5-10; ☺7am-2:30pm Tue-Thu, 7am-1pm & 6-8pm Fri, 8am-1pm Sat) 'Friendly, filling and reasonably priced' sums up this local institution, formerly known as Yumi's, where you can get a plate lunch with chicken katsu or teriyaki beef, a burger, a mini *loco moco* or special saimin.

Jo-Jo's Anuenue Shave Ice & Treats
Desserts $

(www.facebook.com/jojos.anuenue; 9899 Waimea Rd; snacks from $3; ☺10am-5:30pm; ☻) This shack delivers icy flavor: all syrups are homemade without additives. The superstar item is the *halo halo* (Filipino-style mixed fruit) with coconut.

Wrangler's Steakhouse
Steak $$

(☎808-338-1218; www.wranglerssteakhousehi. com; 9852 Kaumuali'i Hwy; mains lunch $10-17, dinner $18-35; ☺11am-8:30pm Mon-Thu, 11am-

9pm Fri, 5-9pm Sat; ☻) Yes, it's touristy, but this Western-style saloon dishes up plantation lunches in authentic *kaukau* (food) tins full of shrimp and vegetable tempura, teriyaki steak, rice and kim chee. Sizzling dinner steaks are decent – the seafood and soup-and-salad bar less so. Opt for atmospheric seating on the front lanai or back porch.

🍸 DRINKING & NIGHTLIFE

Aloha-n-Paradise
Coffee

(☎808-338-1522; www.aloha-n-paradise.com; 9905 Waimea Rd; ☺7am-noon Mon-Sat; ☎) Watch Waimea's world go by from the front porch of this ramshackle plantation-era building. Inside, a large gallery-lounge has island art on the walls and comfy sofas; the espresso bar, tucked in the back, sells coffee, muffins and a $5 cereal bar. The wifi remains on when the cafe is closed.

🎭 ENTERTAINMENT

Waimea Theater
Cinema

(☎808-338-0282; www.waimeatheater.com; 9691 Kaumuali'i Hwy; adult/child 5-10yr $9/7) This art-deco movie theater is a little behind with new releases and schedules are erratic, but there are only two cinemas on the island (the other is in Lihu'e), so no one's complaining.

ℹ️ GETTING THERE & AWAY

Waimea is easily reached by rental car, and served by **Kaua'i Bus** (☎808-246-8110; www. kauai.gov/bus; 3220 Ho'olako St, Lihu'e; one-way fare adult/senior & child 7-18yr $2/1).

There's no public transportation up to the state parks.

ℹ️ GETTING AROUND

To explore the area, you're way better off with a rental car, but bear in mind that some rental agencies forbid users to drive the dirt road to Polihale or the backroads inland.

MOLOKA'I

Moloka'i at a Glance...

Feisty and independent, while not taking life too seriously, the 'Friendly Isle' slows the pace way down.

Moloka'i is often cited as the 'most Hawaiian' of the islands. In terms of bloodlines this is true – more than 50% of residents are part Native Hawaiian. But if your idea of Hawaii includes great tourist facilities, forget it. Instead, visitors can enjoy the islands' geography and indigenous culture, see the protected ancient Hawaiian sites in the tropical east and unwind on beautiful empty beaches in the west.

Moloka'i in Two Days

After checking out Kaunakakai (p163), drive the gorgeous 27 miles east to the Halawa Valley and hike out to the waterfalls. Stop at Puko'o for lunch from the tasty counter at **Mana'e Goods & Grindz** (p166), then snorkel at **Twenty Mile Beach** (p166).

Wander around Kaunakakai gathering vittles for a dinner under the stars at your rental pad. On your last day, let the sure-footed mules give you the ride of your life to **Kalaupapa Peninsula** (p159) and crack open some fun at **Purdy's Macadamia Nut Farm** (p163).

Moloka'i in Four Days

Spend your third day in the ancient rainforests of Kamakou Preserve, followed by dinner at **Kualapu'u Cookhouse** (p167). On the morning of day four, stop by Kaunakakai and pick up some island books at **Kalele Bookstore** (p167), then head northwest to the beautiful West End beaches, before finding the ultimate souvenir at Maunaloa's **Big Wind Kite Factory** (p167).

Previous page: Halawa Valley and Hipuapua Falls (p157)
BOB POOL/SHUTTERSTOCK ©

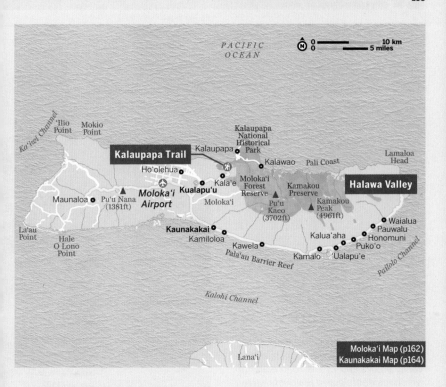

PACIFIC
OCEAN

N 0 — 10 km
0 — 5 miles

'Ilio Point
Mokio Point
Ka'iwi Channel

Kalaupapa National Historical Park
Kalaupapa
Kalaupapa Trail
Ho'olehua
Kala'e
Kalawao
Pali Coast
Lamaloa Head

Moloka'i Forest Reserve
Kualapu'u
Moloka'i
Kamakou Preserve
Halawa Valley

Moloka'i Airport
Maunaloa
Pu'u Nana (1381ft)
Pu'u Kaeo (3702ft)
Kamakou Peak (4961ft)
Waialua
Pauwalu
Honomuni
Puko'o

La'au Point
Hale O Lono Point
Kaunakakai
Kamiloloa
Kawela
Pala'au Barrier Reef
Kamalo
'Ualapu'e
Kalua'aha
Pailolo Channel

Kalohi Channel

Lana'i

Moloka'i Map (p162)
Kaunakakai Map (p164)

Arriving in Moloka'i

The Maui ferry no longer runs.

Moloka'i Airport (p314) is small; single-engine planes are the norm.

Makani Kai Air (📞808-834-1111; http://makanikaiair.com) offers scheduled and charter flights to Kalaupapa and Honolulu.

Mokulele Airlines (📞866-260-7070; www.mokuleleairlines.com) has frequent services to Honolulu and Maui.

Ohana (📞800-367-5320; www.hawaiianairlines.com) , the commuter carrier of Hawaiian Airlines, serves Honolulu, Lana'i and Maui from Moloka'i.

Sleeping

Moloka'i's one hotel is in Kaunakakai. Almost everybody stays in a B&B, cottage, condo or house. Good local sources of rental and accommodations information and reservations include www.visitmolokai.com and www.molokai.com. Quality ranges from rustic to swanky. The best have private grounds on the ocean. The nicest are usually in the verdant and coastal east. There are no hostels; camping is limited to state and county parks.

Halawa Beach Park (p156)

Halawa Valley

With stunningly gorgeous scenery, the pristine and deeply spiritual Halawa Valley enjoys end-of-the-road isolation, which residents guard jealously with gates and 'no trespassing' signs.

Great For...

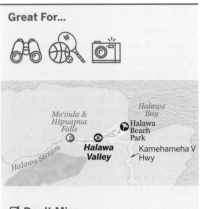

☑ Don't Miss

Cool off at the falls with a swim in the inviting pool; bring swimwear and a towel.

★ **Top Tip**

Mosquitoes are voracious on the trail.
Use insect repellent.

Halawa Beach Park

Halawa Beach was a favored surfing spot for Moloka'i chiefs and remains so today for local kids, although often you won't see a soul. The beach has double coves separated by a rocky outcrop, with the north side a bit more protected than the south.

When the water is calm, there's good swimming and folks launch sea kayaks here, but both coves are subject to dangerous rip currents when the surf is heavy.

Up from the beach, **Halawa Beach Park** (Map p162; 14777 Hwy 450/Kamehameha V Hwy) has picnic pavilions, restrooms and non-drinkable running water. Throughout the valley, there's an eerie feeling that you can't quite shake, as if the generations that came before aren't sure what to make of it all. Some locals aren't entirely welcoming of visitors.

Guides

Visiting Mo'oula and Hipuapua Falls requires a guide and several locals offer this services up the valley. Rates are usually around $60 per person depending on how long you wish to spend in the valley. You usually meet your guide near Halawa Beach Park.

Halawa Valley Molokai (📲808-542-1855; http://halawavalleymolokai.com; hikes per person $60; ⊘hikes usually begin 9am) tours are highly recommended guiding services into the valley and can be booked online; they usually include a stop at a local farm.

Halawa Beach Park

Mo'oula & Hipuapua Falls

(Map p162) The hike and spectacle of the twin 250ft Mo'oula and Hipuapua Falls, which cascade down the back of the valley, are a highlight of many Moloka'i visits. The falls are reached via a straightforward 2-mile trail lined with historical sites. To protect these sites, and because the trail crosses private property, visiting the falls requires a hike with a local guide.

❶ Local Church

Sunday services are still occasionally held in Hawaiian at the saintly little 1948 green-and-white church, where visitors are welcome any time (the door remains open).

There are numerous cultural sites along the path, which passes through lush tropical foliage. Look for the bright-orange blossoms of African tulip trees and the brilliant green of beach heliotrope trees. Among the sites is a burial ground that may date to 650 CE and a seven-tier stone temple.

Walks can easily take three to five hours with narration. Expect muddy conditions, and wear stout shoes so that you can navigate over river boulders. Some of the river crossings may be especially perilous.

Bring water and lunch and use plenty of sunscreen. Most people thrill to a bracing plunge into the pools at the bottom of the falls. Avoid days when small cruise ships visit Moloka'i, as crowds can lessen the experience. Rates start at $60 per person.

JUERGEN_WALLSTABE/SHUTTERSTOCK ©

ⓘ Kayaking

Kayaking from Halawa Beach is a popular way to see the northeastern shore and the world's tallest sea cliffs along the Pali Coast, although the logistics can be intimidating.

✗ Take a Break

After the hike, stop by Mana'e Goods & Grindz (p166) for a superb budget *katsu* plate lunch.

GERLACH PHOTOS/SHUTTERSTOCK ©

Hiking Kalaupapa Trail

A twisting trail down the steep pali (sea cliff), the world's highest, drops to the remote but spectacularly beautiful Kalaupapa Peninsula. Here, Hansen's disease (leprosy) patients were forced into isolation.

Great For...

☑ **Don't Miss**

The amazing view of Moloka'i's dramatic Pali Coast from Kalawao.

Kalaupapa Peninsula

The spectacularly beautiful Kalaupapa Peninsula is the most remote part of Hawaii's most isolated island. The only way to reach this lush green peninsula, edged with long, white-sand beaches, is on a twisting trail down the steep *pali* – the world's highest – or by plane. This remoteness is the reason that it was, for more than a century, where Hansen's disease (leprosy) patients were forced into isolation.

From the colony's inception until separation ended in 1969, 8000 patients were forced onto Kalaupapa. Less than a dozen patients (known as called 'residents') remain. They have chosen to stay in the only home they have ever known and have resisted efforts to move them away.

The peninsula has been designated a national historical park and is managed

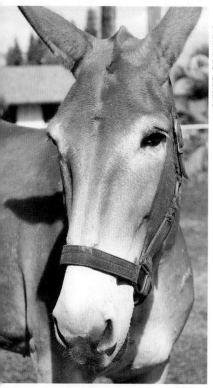

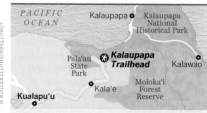

ℹ Need to Know

Since visitor numbers are limited each day, you must have a reservation with a local tour agency, such as Kalaupapa Rare Adventures (p165).

✗ Take a Break

After you climb the steep trail, order a steak at **Kualapu'u Cookhouse** (p167).

by the Hawaii State Department of Health and the **National Park Service** (☎808-567-6802; www.nps.gov/kala).

Hitting the Trail

The Kalaupapa trailhead is on the east side of Hwy 470, just north of the mule stables, and marked by the Pala'au park sign and parked Kalaupapa employee cars. The 3-mile trail has 26 switchbacks, 1400 steps and drops 1664ft in elevation from start to finish.

It's best to begin hiking by 8am, before the mules start to go down, to avoid walking in fresh dung, though you have no choice on the return trip. Allow an hour and a half to descend comfortably. It can be quite an adventure after a lot of rain, though the rocks keep it from getting impossibly muddy. Many find walking sticks a huge help.

At the bottom of the park's near-vertical *pali* is a deserted beach with stunning views of the steep cliffs you've just descended. Hikers should proceed past a parking area and wait at a row of benches near the mule stable for the mandatory bus tour.

Compulsory Tours

Everyone who comes to the Kalaupapa Peninsula is required to visit the settlement with a local tour. Reservations must be made in advance with an outfit such as Kalaupapa Rare Adventures (p165). Tours last most of the day and are done on foot or by mule, accompanied by lots of stories about life in years past. If you're not on the mule ride or another packaged tour, bring your own lunch and a bottle of water. Those not up for the adventure of traveling down a steep mountain can fly in (again, they must be on a tour). Hikes and mule rides start at 8am and finish at 3pm.

Hansen's Disease & the Peninsula

Ancient Hawaiians used Kalaupapa as a refuge when they were caught in storms at sea. The peninsula held a large settlement at the time of early Western contact and the area is rich in archaeological sites. A discovery in 2004 indicated that Kalaupapa heiau (temple) may have ritual significance and possible astronomical purposes.

In 1835 doctors in Hawaii diagnosed the state's first case of leprosy, one of many diseases introduced by foreigners. Before modern medicine, leprosy manifested itself in horrible sores. Eventually patients experienced loss of sensation and tissue degeneration that could lead to small extremities becoming deformed. Blindness was common. Alarmed by the spread of the disease, Kamehameha V signed a law that banished people with the illness to Kalaupapa Peninsula, beginning in 1866.

Hawaiian names for leprosy include *mai pake* (Chinese sickness) and *mai ho'oka'awale*, which means 'separating sickness,' a reference to how the disease tore families apart. All patients arrived at the peninsula in boats. There's no evidence that disease-fearing captains threw patients overboard to swim to land.

When the afflicted arrived on Kalaupapa Peninsula, there was no way out, not even in a casket. The original settlement was in Kalawao, at the wetter eastern end of the peninsula. Early conditions were unspeakably horrible, with the strong stealing rations from the weak, and women forced into prostitution. Life spans were invariably short and desperate.

Kalaupapa settlement

Father Damien arrived at Kalaupapa in 1873. He wasn't the first missionary to come, but he was the first to stay. What Damien provided, most of all, was a sense of hope and inspiration to others. Army vet Joseph Dutton arrived in 1886 and stayed 44 years.

In addition to his work with the sick (he was often called 'Brother Joseph,' although he never took orders), he was a prolific writer who kept the outside world informed about what was happening in Moloka'i. Sister Marianne Cope arrived a year before Damien died. She stayed 30 years, helping to establish a girls' home

and encouraging patients to live life to the fullest.

The same year that Damien arrived, a Norwegian scientist named Dr Gerhard Hansen discovered *Mycobacterium leprae,* the bacteria that causes leprosy, thus proving that the disease was not hereditary, as was previously thought. Indeed, Hansen's disease is one of the least contagious of all communicable diseases: only 4% of human beings are even susceptible to it.

In 1909 the US Leprosy Investigation Station opened at Kalawao. However, the fancy hospital was out of touch – it required patients to live in seclusion for two years, for example – so it attracted only a handful of patients and soon closed.

Since 1946 sulfa antibiotics have successfully treated and controlled leprosy, but the isolation policies in Kalaupapa weren't abandoned until 1969, when there were still 300 patients here.

The last arrived in 1965, and today the few remaining residents are all in their late 70s or older.

While the state of Hawaii officially uses the term 'Hansen's disease' for leprosy, many Kalaupapa residents consider that to be a euphemism that fails to reflect the stigma they have suffered, and continue to use the old term 'leprosy.' The degrading appellation 'leper,' however, is offensive to all. 'Resident' is preferred.

★ **Top Tip**
Stash containers of water behind rocks at the numbered switchbacks to drink on your return.

YINYANG/GETTY IMAGES ©

Moloka'i

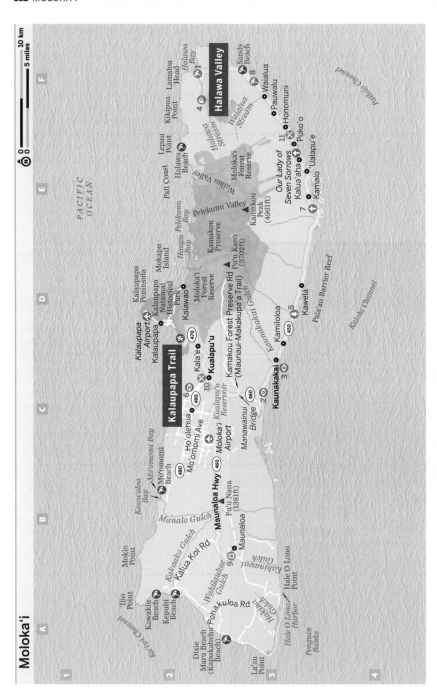

Moloka'i

Kaunakakai

◎ SIGHTS

View a photo of Moloka'i's biggest town from 50 years ago and the main drag won't look much different. Worn wood-fronted buildings with tin roofs that roar in the rain seem like refugees from a Clint Eastwood Western. But there's no artifice to Kaunakakai: it's the real deal. All of the island's commercial activities are here, and you'll visit often – if nothing else, for its shops and services.

Walking around the town can occupy a couple of hours if you take the time to get into the rhythm of things and do a little exploring. While there are stop signs, there are no stoplights. Try to visit on Saturday morning, when the street market draws crowds.

Purdy's Macadamia Nut Farm
Farm

(Map p162; 808-567-6601, 808-658-0445; www.molokai-aloha.com/macnuts; 4 Lihi Pali Ave; ⏰10am-2pm Tue-Sat) FREE Enthusiastic nut farmer Tuddie Purdy takes you on a free tour of his more-than-80-year-old orchard, explains how the nuts grow without pesticides, herbicides or fertilizers, and then lets you sample them. Everything is done in quaint Moloka'i style: you can crack open macadamia nuts on a stone with a hammer and then try macadamia-blossom honey scooped up with slices of fresh coconut.The awesomely flavorsome nuts and honey are for sale at the farm. The farm is 0.3 miles off Hwy 490.

St Joseph's Church
Church

(Map p162; http://damienchurchmolokai.org; Hwy 450/ Kamehameha V Hwy) Only two of the four Moloka'i churches that missionary saint Fr Damien (who selflessly comforted leprosy patients for 16 years) built outside the Kalaupapa Peninsula are still standing. One of them is this quaint white-wood building; the other is Our Lady of Seven Sorrows further east. This simple one-room church, dating from 1876, has a steeple, a bell, five rows of pews and some of the original wavy-glass panes. It's just past mile marker 10. The door is usually open. There's also a lei-draped statue of Fr Damien and a little cemetery beside the church.

Kapua'iwa Coconut Grove
Historic Site

(Map p162; 30 Maunaloa Hwy) Moloka'i was the favorite island playground of Kamehameha V. He had the royal 10-acre Kapua'iwa Coconut Grove planted near his sacred bathing pools in the 1860s. About a mile west of downtown, the grove makes a wonderful place to enjoy the sunset. Its name means 'mysterious taboo.' Be careful where you walk (or park): coconuts frequently plunge silently to the ground. At research time the facilities were under refurbishment and the park was closed to the public.

Kaunakakai Wharf
Port

(Map p162; Kaunakakai Pl) Come here to witness Moloka'i's busy commercial lifeline. OK, it's not that busy... a freight barge occasionally chugs in, skippers unload their catch of the day, and a local boat club practices for a canoe race. A roped-off area

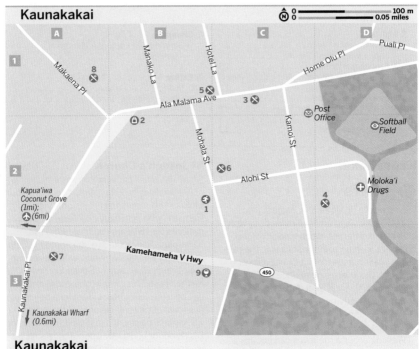

Kaunakakai

with a floating dock provides a place for kids to swim. Some of Moloka'i's fishing and ocean-based tours leave from here.

One Ali'i Beach Park   Park
(Map p162; Maunaloa Hwy) Three miles east of town, this park is split into two areas. One side has a coconut-palm-lined shore, a playing field, a children's playground, a rundown picnic pavilion and bathrooms, and although not especially attractive it's very popular with local families for huge weekend barbecues. The other side is a greener and more attractive picnic area. The water is shallow and murky.

ACTIVITIES

Moloka'i has wild ocean waters, rough trails, remote rainforests and the most dramatic oceanside cliffs in Hawaii. It's a perfect destination for adventure – just don't expect to be spoon fed.

If you're considering action at sea, note that conditions are seasonal. During summer you'll find that waters are calm on the north and west shores, and made rough by the persistent trade winds on the south shore outside of the Pala'au Barrier Reef. Plan on getting out early, before the winds pick up. Winter storms make waters rough all around the island (outside of the reef, which runs the length of the south side of the island), but even so the calm days between winter storms can be the best times to get out on the water.

Moloka'i has plenty of wind – advanced windsurfers can harness it in the Pailolo and Ka'iwi Channels, but you'll need your own gear. Among the activities operators and outfitters, there are a few that pretty much handle every activity on the island and at times loosely work together.

Kalaupapa Rare Adventures   Tours

(Molokai Mule Ride; ☑808-567-6088; www.mule ride.com; Hwy 470/Kalae Hwy; mule ride $210, hike $79; ☺8am-3pm Mon-Sat) A mule ride is the only way down the *pali* (cliff) into Kalaupapa apart from hiking (which the outfit also offers), but be prepared: this is not an easy ride. You'll be sore afterward even if you're an experienced rider – and it's a safe bet that you've never experienced a ride like this one. Make reservations well ahead.

Moloka'i Bicycle   Cycling

(Map p164; ☑808-553-5740; www.mauimolokai bicycle.com; 80 Mohala St; bike rental per day/ week from $25/75; ☺3-6pm Wed, 9am-2pm Sat & by appointment) Owner Phillip Kikukawa has great knowledge about cycling across the island. He'll do pickups and drop-offs outside opening hours. Repairs, parts and sales are available, and there's a wide selection of bikes to rent, including mountain bikes. Prices include helmet, lock, pump and maps.

Moloka'i Outdoors   Outdoors

(☑877-553-4477, 808-633-8700; www.molokai-outdoors.com; SUP or kayak tour adult/child from $90/47, 7-8hr island tour $166/87) Moloka'i Outdoors can custom design adventures and can arrange activities. It's known for paddling and stand-up paddleboard (SUP) experiences, plus day tours across the island. It offers kayak and SUP rentals (from $67 per day). It can arrange whale-watching and scuba diving, mule rides and hiking to Kalaupapa Peninsula, and transport and pickups across the island.

Snorkeling Twenty Mile Beach

Snorkeling is fantastic at **Twenty Mile Beach** (Map p162; Murphy's Beach; Hwy 450/Kamehameha V Hwy) near Waialua in East Moloka'i. Well protected by a reef, the curve of fine sand fronts a large lagoon. Near shore there are rocks and the water can be very shallow, but work your way out and you'll be rewarded with schools of fish, living sponges, octopuses and much more.

Walter Naki   Boat Tour

(Molokai Action Adventures; ☑808-558-8184, 808-213-5655; 4hr tours from $150) Walter Naki, who is also known for his cultural tours and treks, offers deep-sea fishing, whale-watching and highly recommended north-shore boat tours that include the Pali Coast. Prices are negotiable; minimum of four people.

Moloka'i Ocean Tours   Boat Tour, Fishing

(☑808-553-3290; www.molokaioceantours. com; whale-watching adult/child $75/60) Offers all types of fishing charters plus coastal tours, whale-watching and snorkeling trips.

EATING

The Saturday-morning market along Ala Malama Ave is a good source for local produce and prepared foods.

Maka's Korner   Cafe $

(Map p164; ☑808-553-8058; 35 Mohala St; meals $5-10; ☺7am-9pm Mon-Fri, 8am-2pm Sat & Sun) A dead-simple corner location belies the fine yet basic fare here. Moloka'i's best burgers come with excellent fries, although many patrons are simply addicted to the grilled mahi-mahi sandwich (go nuts and order it dressed with two shrimp tempura). Pancakes are served throughout the day. Sit at the tiny counter or at a picnic table outside.

Moloka'i Ka Hula Piko

Hawaiian oral history hails Moloka'i as the birthplace of hula. In May or early June, this free three-day **hula festival** (www.kahulapiko.com) FREE draws huge crowds to sacred hula performances. It opens with a solemn ceremony at 3am at Pu'u Nana, the site of Hawaii's first hula school.

Hula performance, Ka Hula Piko Festival
PHOTO RESOURCE HAWAII/ALAMY STOCK PHOTO ©

Mana'e Goods & Grindz
Hawaiian $

(Map p162; 808-558-8186; 8615 Hwy 450/Kamehameha V Hwy; meals $5-13; ⊙kitchen 8am-3pm Thu-Tue, store 6:30am-5.30pm Mon-Fri, 8am to 4:30pm Sat & Sun; ⓦ) Even if it wasn't your only option, you'd still want to stop here. The plate lunches are something of a local legend: tender yet crispy chicken *katsu* (deep-fried fillets), specials, such as pork stew, and standards, such as excellent teriyaki burgers and fresh fish sandwiches served on perfectly grilled buns.

Ono Fish N' Shrimp
Seafood $

(Map p164; 808-553-8187; 53 Ala Malama Ave; lunches $10-14; ⊙10:30am-2pm Mon-Fri) For some of the best seafood plates (or should that be takeout boxes?) in town, this white food truck offers up seared mahi-mahi, fish and chips, steak and shrimp combos, plus fish tacos and shrimp plates. The preparations are creative and the fish is über-fresh.

Moloka'i Burger
Burgers $

(Map p164; 808-553-3533; 20 Kamehameha V Hwy; mains $6.50-18; ⊙7am-9pm Mon-Sat; ⓦ) Moloka'i's only drive-through restaurant is a slick operation. The burgers come in many forms but are all thick and juicy. There are also sandwiches, fried chicken, and Hawaiian plates such as *loco moco*, salmon and teriyaki chicken. The dining room is pleasant enough, with a sophisticated tiled floor, while the front terrace is peacefully shady. Soft-serve ice cream is a treat.

Friendly Market Center
Supermarket $

(Map p164; 808-553-5595; 90 Ala Malama Ave; ⊙8am-8pm Mon-Fri, to 6:30pm Sat) The best selection of any supermarket on the island. In the afternoon fresh seafood from the wharf often appears.

Kamo'i Snack-N-Go
Desserts $

(Map p164; Moloka'i Professional Bldg, 28 Kamoi St; ice-cream scoops $2; ⊙10am-9pm Mon-Fri, 9am-9pm Sat, 11am-9pm Sun; ⓦ) This candy store is loaded with sweets and, more importantly, delicious Honolulu-made Dave's Hawaiian Ice Cream. The banana fudge is truly a treat. *Ube* (purple yam) is subtle and the ice cream is a beautiful purple color. Other choices include Hawaiian mud pie, toasted macadamia nut, and *liliko'i* (passion fruit). Ask to try before you buy.

Kanemitsu Bakery
Bakery $

(Map p164; 808-553-5855; 79 Ala Malama Ave; loaf of bread $5; ⊙7am-5pm Wed-Mon) Every night but Monday, slip down the alley to the town's 80-year-old bakery to join the locals at the back door buying seductively sweet and tasty hot loaves. The taciturn baker will split open your loaf and slather it with one of five spreads that include cream cheese and strawberry jelly.

Show your real inside knowledge and ask for a fresh-glazed doughnut.

Kualapu'u Cookhouse   Hawaiian $$

(Map p162; Kamuela Cookhouse; ☑808-567-9655; 102 Farrington Ave; mains $6-33; ⊗7am-8pm Tue-Sat, 9am-2pm Sun, 7am-2pm Mon) This kitsch old roadhouse serves the best meals on the island. Portions are generous – breakfasts feature huge omelets – and plate-lunch options include excellent pork *tonkatsu* (breaded and fried cutlets). The dinner menu is more ambitious; try the tasty sautéed *ono* with *liliko'i*–white wine butter. Cash only. Beer and wine can be purchased at the grocery across the street.

DRINKING & NIGHTLIFE

Bring games, books and a gift for the gab, as nighttime fun is mostly DIY on Moloka'i.

Paddler's Inn   Pub

(Map p164; ☑808-553-3300; www.paddlers restaurant.com; 10 Mohala St; ⊗8am-1am Mon-Sat; ☏) The island's only real pub has a dive feel, with a large terrace that makes up in cheer for what it lacks in charm. The long menu is served between 10am and 9pm. Items include deep-fried pub grub, burgers, steaks and pastas. There are regular live performances by local musicians. Happy hour, with discounted selected drinks, runs 2pm to 5pm daily.

🔒 SHOPPING

Kalele Bookstore & Divine Expressions   Books

(Map p164; ☑808-553-5112; http://molokai spirit.com; 64 Ala Malama Ave; ⊗10am-5pm Mon-Fri, 9am-2pm Sat; ☏) A community treasure.

Besides books, get free maps or enjoy a coffee and meet some locals out back on the shady terrace. Owner Teri Waros is a fount of info on all things Moloka'i. Make this one of your first stops.

Big Wind Kite Factory & Plantation Gallery   Arts & Crafts

(Map p162; ☑808-552-2364; www.bigwind kites.com; 120 Maunaloa Hwy; ⊗8:30am-5pm Mon-Sat, 10am-2pm Sun) Big Wind custom makes kites for high fliers of all ages. It has hundreds ready to go in stock or you can choose a design and watch production begin. Lessons are available; enquire within. There's a range of other goods to browse as well, including an excellent selection of Hawaii-themed books, artwork, clothing and crafts originating from all over.

ℹ GETTING THERE & AROUND

Renting a car is essential if you intend to explore the island or if you're renting a house or condo and will need to shop. All of Moloka'i's highways and primary routes are good, paved roads. The free tourist map, widely available on the island, is useful. James A Bier's *Map of Moloka'i & Lana'i* (from $5) has an excellent index.

A taxi from the airport costs $28 to $32 to Kaunakakai, depending on where in town you need to go. **Hele Mai Taxi** (☑808-336-0967; www.molokaitaxi.com; ⊗Mon-Sat) services the island. Many accommodations can arrange transfers.

Kaunakakai is a walking town.

The Garden of the Gods

GEOSTOCK/GETTY IMAGES ©

A Day on Lana'i

Lana'i is the most central of the Hawaii islands, but it's also the least 'Hawaiian'. Pineapple plantations are its main historic legacy, and the locals are descended from immigrant field workers from around the world, mostly the Philippines.

Great For...

☑ Don't Miss

Cathedrals, the island's most spectacular dive site, with arches, grottoes and a large lava tube.

Ferry from Maui

Expeditions Maui-Lana'i Ferry (📞800-695-2624; www.go-lanai.com; Manele Harbor; adult/child 1 way $30/20) links Lahaina Harbor on Maui with Manele Bay Harbor on Lana'i (one hour) several times daily.

Itinerary

Take the early-morning ferry from Lahaina. Keep an eye out for schools of dolphins as the boat approaches Manele Bay. Catch the shuttle into Lana'i City and pour your own coffee for breakfast at **Blue Ginger Café** (📞808-565-6363; www.bluegingercafelanai.com; 409 7th St; mains $7.50-20; ⊙6am-8pm Thu-Mon, to 2pm Tue & Wed) before browsing the town's shops and visiting the superb **Culture & Heritage Center** (www.lanaichc.org; 730 Lanai Ave; ⊙8:30am-3:30pm Mon-Fri) `FREE`.

Hulopo'e Beach (p170)

RON DAHLQUIST/DESIGN PICS/GETTY IMAGES ©

ⓘ Need to Know

Air service is limited to several flights daily to neighboring islands.

★ Top Tip

Lana'i City is laid out in a simple grid pattern, and almost all of the shops and services border **Dole Park.**

In the afternoon, snorkel at Hulopo'e Beach or dive at Manele Bay before heading back to Maui on the sunset ferry.

Larry Ellison's Lana'i

Decades of sleepy seclusion for Lana'i were interrupted in 2012 when Larry Ellison, the fabulously wealthy cofounder of software developer Oracle, bought out the island's longtime owner Castle & Cooke (which once ran the ubiquitous pineapple plantations under the Dole name). For his estimated $600-million purchase price, Ellison got 98% of Lana'i (the rest is private homes or government land) and a bevy of businesses, such as the resorts.

The Garden of the Gods

Strange rock formations, views that would overexcite a condo developer and more

deserted beaches are the highlights of northwestern Lana'i. Reached via the unpaved Polihua Rd, the stretch leading to Kanepu'u Preserve and Keahiakawelo (also called the Garden of the Gods) is fairly good, though often dusty. It generally takes about 30 minutes from town. To travel onward to Polihua Beach, though, is another matter: depending on when the road was last graded, the trip could take anywhere from 20 minutes to an hour, as you descend 1800ft down to the coast.

Journey Through an Ancient Village

Perched around the highest sea cliffs on the island (at 1080ft above sea level) is the vast Keālia Kapu and Kaunolū archaeological site, home to the largest collection of ruins on Lana'i. It's easy to get goosebumps wandering the structures of this ancient Hawaiian village, complete with houses, shrines, petroglyphs and ceremonial sites. In the 1790s Kamehameha V used it as a vacation spot between battles. He enjoyed fishing for *kawakawa* (bonito) here and famously took leaps into the ocean from a 60ft platform to prove his righteousness.

A highlight of the area is the Halulu Heiau (Temple of Halulu). Those who broke *kapu* (ancient Hawaiian law) could opt for self-imprisonment here, in a bid to be absolved of their wrongdoing.

The well-marked Keālia Kapu-Kaunolū Heritage Trail, with information boards throughout, runs for 0.5 miles around the archaeological sites and structures, including a fisherman's shrine and a canoe longhouse. You'll likely have the place to yourself. Private tours are possible.

Lana'i for Children

The kids will love **Hulopo'e Beach**, where there are some cool tide pools filled with colorful critters that will thrill the little ones; older kids will enjoy the great snorkeling or **snuba** (☑808-874-5649; www.sailtrilogy.com; tours from $220) and the **Cat Sanctuary** (☑808-215-9066; http://lanaicatsanctuary. org; 1 Kaupili Rd; ⏱10am-3pm) **FREE** home to hundreds of felines and plenty of petting opportunities.

Pu'u Pehe & Cathedrals

From Hulopo'e Beach, a path (of around 0.75 miles) leads south to the end of Manele Point, which separates Hulopo'e and Manele Bays. The point is actually a volcanic cinder cone that's sharply eroded on its seaward edge. The lava here has

From left: Pineapple plantation; Racoon Butterflyfish, Cathedrals of Lana'i

rich rust-red colors with swirls of gray and black, and its texture is bubbly and brittle – so much so that huge chunks of the point have broken off and fallen onto the coastal shelf below.

Diving in and around the bay is excellent. Coral is abundant near the cliffs, where the bottom quickly slopes off to about 40ft. Beyond the bay's western edge, near Pu'u Pehe (Sweetheart Rock), is Cathedrals, the island's most spectacular dive site, featuring arches and grottoes amid a large lava tube that is 100ft in length.

Explore Lana'i City

Lana'i City's main square, Dole Park, is surrounded by tin-roofed houses and shops, with not a chain store in sight. The architecture is little changed since the plantation days of the 1920s, although the gardening is much improved thanks to the efforts of Larry Ellison's island-management company, Pulama Lana'i. (Pulama means to care for or cherish.)

Wander between the small but delightfully varied collection of eateries and shops, all with a low-key feel not found in more touristy places.

✕ Take a Break

Enjoy top-notch sushi at **Nobu** (☑808-565-2832; www.noburestaurants.com/lanai; Four Seasons Resort Lana'i, 1 Manele Bay Rd; sashimi per piece from $6, meals $50-200; ⊙dinner 6-9:30pm, bar 4:30-10:30pm) in the Four Seasons hotel.

ROAD TO HANA, MAUI

Road to Hana at a Glance...

There's a sense of suspense you just can't shake when driving the Road to Hana, a serpentine road lined with tumbling waterfalls, lush slopes, and rugged coasts – and serious hairpin turns. Spanning the northeast shore of Maui, the legendary Hana Hwy ribbons tightly between jungle valleys, towering cliffs and powerful waterfalls. The drive is ravishingly gorgeous, but it's certainly not easy. As for rental cars, Jeeps and Mustangs are the ride of choice.

Road to Hana in One Day

Grab coffee early at the fruit stand at the **Huelo Lookout** (p189), then look for **Honomanu Bay**. Next, climb to **Wailua Valley State Wayside** (p185) for a mountain-to-sea view. Continue to **Three Bears Falls** (p184), the best in a magnificent run of roadside cascades. Slip into Hana for lunch at **Thai Food by Pranee** (p189). Visit **Pi'ilanihale Heiau & Kahanu Garden** (p176), home to the largest heiau (temple) in Polynesia. Stay overnight in Hana.

Road to Hana in Two Days

On day two, explore the underground wonders of the **Hana Lava Tube** (p178), then drive to Wai'anapanapa State Park to see its beautiful black-sand beach and walk in the footsteps of early Hawaiians on the ancient coastal **Pi'ilani Trail** (p180), which leads across a high shelf of lava with wild coastal vistas. End with a meal at **Hana Farms Grill** (p189).

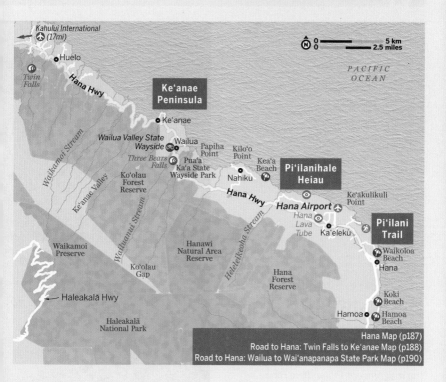

Hana Map (p187)
Road to Hana: Twin Falls to Ke'anae Map (p188)
Road to Hana: Wailua to Wai'anapanapa State Park Map (p190)

Arriving at the Road to Hana

Tours are possible along the Road to Hana, but to enjoy all it has to offer properly, and go at your own speed, rent a car. The drive begins around the eastern edge of Ha'iku, near Huelo, and finishes in Hana, or continues through Hana and along the scenic Pi'ilani Hwy (back road) towards Keokea.

Many tour companies shuttle visitors along the scenic road. There are no public buses to Hana.

Sleeping

There's only a handful of places to stay on the Road to Hana. To get an early start on the drive, spend the night in Huelo or Ha'iku. You'll find hotel rooms, condo units and rental cottages in and around Hana. There are campgrounds in Ke'anae and **Wai'anapanapa State Park** (☏808-984-8109; https://camping. ehawaii.gov/camping; campsites for up to 6 people $18).

Piʻilanihale Heiau

This site is the most significant stop on the entire Road to Hana and combines a 294-acre ethnobotanical garden with the magnificent Piʻilanihale Heiau.

Great For...

Piʻilanihale Heiau ◉
Kahanu Garden ◉
ʻUlaʻino Rd
Hana Hwy
Kaʻeleku
PACIFIC OCEAN

❶ Need to Know

☑️808-248-8912; www.ntbg.org; 650 ʻUlaʻino Rd; adult/child under 13yr $10/free, guided tour $25/free; ⊘9am-3pm Mon-Fri, to 2pm Sat, tours by appointment 11am Mon-Fri.

☑ **Don't Miss**

Tours provide fascinating details of the relationship between the ancient Hawaiians and their environment.

Touring the heiau is perhaps the best opportunity in all of Hawaii to really understand what traditional Hawaiian culture was like prior to contact with the West. Amazingly, very few people visit.

The History

Pi'ilanihale Heiau is an immense lava-stone platform with a length of 450ft. This astounding temple is shrouded in mystery, but there's no doubt that it was an important religious site. Archaeologists believe that construction began around AD 1200 and continued in phases. The grand finale was the work of Pi'ilani (the heiau's name means House of Pi'ilani), the 16th-century Maui chief credited with creating many of the coastal fishponds in the area.

Kahanu Garden

The temple occupies one corner of Kahanu Garden, near the sea. An outpost of the National Tropical Botanical Garden, Kahanu Garden contains the largest collection of breadfruit species in the world, with more than 100 varieties.

Hana Lava Tube

(Map p190) This mammoth cave was formed by ancient lava flows. It once served as a slaughter-house – 17,000lb of cow bones had to be removed before it was opened to visitors! The extensive cave reaches heights of up to 40ft, and has many stalactites and stalagmites. The journey is well signed, takes about 45 minutes, and is a perfect rainy-day activity. Admission includes a

Wai'anapanapa State Park

flashlight (torch). Kids will love the adjoining botanical maze, included in the ticket price.

Wai'anapanapa State Park

'Wai'anapanapa' means 'glistening waters,' and the clear mineral waters in the cave pools here will leave you feeling squeaky clean. Two impressive lava-tube caves are just a five-minute walk from the parking lot (808-248-4843; http://dlnr.hawaii.gov/dsp/parks/maui;).

Guided Tour

The best way to unlock the relationship between the heiau, the plants and their beautiful surroundings is to take a guided tour. These last one to two hours and take place Monday to Saturday at 11am. Reserve at www.ntbg.org.

Take a Break

Savor a scoop of chili-chocolate ice cream, served in a coconut, from **Coconut Glen's** (Map p190; 808-248-4876; www.coconutglens.com; Hana Hwy, Mile 27.5; scoop of ice cream $7; 10.30am-5pm;).

★ Top Tip

The heiau and garden are near the **Hana Lava Tube** (Ka'eleku Caverns; 808-248-7308; www.mauicave.com; 305 'Ula'ino Rd; self-guided tour adult/child under 5yr $12.50/free; 10:30am-4pm;), and it's easy to visit both in one trip.

Honokalani black-sand beach, Wai'anapanapa State Park

VICTORIA LIPOV/SHUTTERSTOCK ©

Pi'ilani Trail

This gem of a coastal trail – dating back centuries – offers a private, reflective walk with refreshing views on top of a raw lava field several meters above the sea.

Great For...

☑ **Don't Miss**

The black-sand beach in **Wai'anapanapa State Park**.

The History

More than 300 years ago, King Pi'ilani (of heiau fame) led the construction of a path around the entire island of Maui in an effort to improve commerce between its far-flung regions. Today the King's Trail, or what's left of it, follows this ancient footpath, with some of the original worn stepping stones still in use. The trail offers the opportunity to see the island in a unique and unforgettable way: by walking around it. The 200-mile trail skirts the coastline for its entire length, providing access to remote areas where traditional Hawaiian life is still practiced.

The Hike

The trail begins along the coast just below the camping area and runs parallel to the ocean along lava sea cliffs. Just a few

Hawaiian monk seal

DR. VICTOR WONG/SHUTTERSTOCK ©

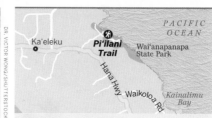

Ka'eleku

Pi'ilani Trail

Wai'anapanapa State Park

Hana Hwy

Waikoloa Rd

PACIFIC OCEAN

Kainalimu Bay

ⓘ Need to Know

For more trail details, check out the website of the **Division of State Parks** (http://dlnr.hawaii.gov/dsp/hiking/maui/ke-ala-loa-o-mauipiilani-trail).

✗ Take a Break

Bring a picnic and marvel at the staggering views along the dramatic trail.

★ Top Tip

If you plan to hike the whole trail, bring water.

minutes along you'll pass a burial ground, a natural sea arch, and a blowhole that roars to life whenever there's pounding surf. This is also the area where you're most likely to see endangered Hawaiian monk seals basking onshore.

After 0.75 miles you'll view basalt cliffs lined up all the way to Hana, and ironwood encroaching on the shoreline. Round stones continue to mark the way across lava and a grassy clearing, fading briefly on the way over a rugged sea cliff.

A dirt road comes in from the right as the trail arrives at Luahaloa, a ledge with a small fishing shack. Inland stands of ironwood heighten the beauty of the scenic last mile of cliff-top walking to Kainalimu Bay. Stepping stones hasten the approach to the bay ahead, as the trail dips down a shrubby ravine to a

quiet, black-cobble beach. Dirt roads lead another mile from here south to Hana. Alternatively, walk inland to the asphalt road, and walk or hitch back to Wai'anapanapa State Park.

Trip Planning

The trail leads 3 miles south from Wai'anapanapa State Park to Kainalimu Bay, just north of Hana Bay. The hike has a lot of payoffs up-front, so even if you just have time for the first mile, you won't regret it. In spots the loose gravel path skirts sheer, potentially fatal drops into the sea – exercise caution, and don't bring kids on this trip. Wear good hiking shoes, as it gets rougher as you go along.

Ke'anae Congregational Church

MICHAEL MARFELL/GETTY IMAGES ©

Ke'anae Peninsula

Pull off the highway to stretch your legs and enjoy a rare slice of historic Hawaii, home to an 1860s church and a wild lava coast, where families have tended stream-fed taro patches for generations.

Great For...

☑ Don't Miss

You can walk past a global cluster of tropical trees at nearby **Ke'anae Arboretum** (Map p188; https://hawaii trails.org; 13385 Hana Hwy) 🅿 **FREE**.

What awaits at the halfway point on the drive to Hana? Dramatic landscapes and the friendliest seaside village on the route. At the end of the peninsula, Ke'anae Park has a scenic coastline of jagged black lava and hypnotic white-capped waves. Plan to look but not swim: the water's rough and there's no beach. But it's oh so photogenic.

Ke'anae Congregational Church

Marking the heart of the village of Ke'anae is its **congregational church** (Lanakila 'Ihi'ihi o Iehova Ona Kaua; 325 Ke'anae Rd), built in 1860, and entered via the steps of the adjacent cottage. The church is made of lava rock and coral mortar, uncovered by whitewash. It's a welcoming place, with open doors and a guest book.

Rainbow eucalyptus tree

PAULA COBLEIGH/SHUTTERSTOCK ©

PACIFIC
OCEAN

Aunty Sandy's
Banana Bread

Ke'anae
Congregational
Church

Nua'ailua
Bay

Ke'anae
Peninsula

Hana Hwy

Ke'anae

Ko'olau
Forest
Reserve

Ke'anae
Arboretum

ⓘ Need to Know

Access the peninsula by taking Ke'anae Rd on the *makai* (seaward) side of the highway just beyond Ke'anae Arboretum.

✕ Take a Break

Craving beef jerky or ice cream? You're in luck. Continue down the highway to **Halfway to Hana** (Map p 188; www.halfway tohanamaui.com; 13710 Hana Hwy; shave ice $5.50, banana bread $6, lunch mains from $6.50; ⊙8am-4.30pm).

★ Top Tip

There are public restrooms (open 7am to 7pm) on the green, across from the small parking area.

Ke'anae Valley

Starting way up at the Ko'olau Gap in the rim of Haleakalā Crater and stretching down to the coast, the Ke'anae Valley radiates green, thanks to the 150in of rainfall it sees each year.

Ke'anae Peninsula

At the foot of the Ke'anae Valley lies the Ke'anae Peninsula, created by a late eruption of Haleakalā that sent lava gushing all the way down the valley and into the ocean. Unlike its rugged surroundings, the volcanic peninsula is perfectly flat, like a leaf floating on the water.

The rock islets you can see off the coast from Ke'anae Park – Mokuhala and Mokumana – are seabird sanctuaries.

Aunty Sandy's Banana Bread

'Da best' banana bread on the entire Road to Hana is baked fresh every morning by Aunty Sandy (☏808-248-7448; 210 Ke'anae Rd; banana bread $6, snacks $4-6, sandwiches from $6.50; ⊙8:30am-2:30pm), and it's so good that you'll find as many locals as tourists pulling up here to sample it each day. It's located in the village before Ke'anae Park.

Hana Highway bridge over Wailua Nui Stream

CHRIS CURTIS/SHUTTERSTOCK ©

Waterfalls & Swimming Holes

Along the Road to Hana, 54 one-lane bridges mark nearly as many waterfalls, some tranquil and inviting, others so sheer they kiss you with spray as you drive past.

Great For...

☑ Don't Miss

Get up close and almost personal with a waterfall on an adventure trip with **Rappel Maui** (Map p 188; ☑808-445-6407; www.rappelmaui.com; 10600 Hana Hwy; $219; ☺tours 6.45am, 8am, 9.15am, 10.30am & 11.45am).

Twin Falls

After the 2-mile marker near the start of the drive, a pool beneath the lower of the twin falls is located about a 10-minute walk in and draws flocks of local kids and tourists. If you're traveling with children or you're up for a short, pleasant hike, this is a good option. To get to the falls, follow the main trail across a stream, then turn left at the trail junction just ahead. Continue for a short distance and then climb over the aqueduct. You will have to do a bit of wading to get there. Be sure to turn around if the water is too high.

Wailua Valley State Wayside

Near the 19-mile marker, the Wailua Valley State Wayside (http:// dlnr.hawaii. gov/dsp/parks/maui; Hana Hwy; ☺6am-6pm; P) ☑ lookout comes up on the right.

Three Bears Falls

ARKANTO/SHUTTERSTOCK ©

ⓘ 8 Need to Know

Do not follow trails that cross private property without express permission from the owner.

✕ Take a Break

A handful of casual eateries, serving hearty lunch plates, cluster in the Nahiku Marketplace.

★ Top Tip

Fill up the tank in Pa'ia or Ha'iku; the next gas station isn't until Hana.

The overlook provides a broad view into verdant Ke'anae Valley, which appears to be 100 shades of green. You can see a couple of waterfalls (when they're running), and Ko'olau Gap, the break in the rim of Haleakalā crater, on a clear day. Turn towards the sea for an outstanding view of Wailua Peninsula as well – don't miss this.

A word of caution: the sign for the wayside appears at the last moment, so be on the lookout

Three Bears Falls

This beauty takes its name from the triple cascade that flows down a steep rock face on the inland side of the road, 0.5 miles past the 19-mile marker. Catch it after a rainstorm to see the cascades come together and roar as one mighty waterfall. There's limited parking up the hill to the left

after the falls. You can scramble down to the falls via a steep, ill-defined path that begins on the Hana side of the bridge. Take care: the stones are moss covered and slippery.

Pua'a Ka'a State Wayside Park

The name of this delightful park (http://dlnr.hawaii.gov/dsp/parks/maui; Hana Hwy; ⊙6am-6pm; Ⓟ) 🅿 means Rolling Pig. Cross the highway from the parking area and head inland to a pair of delicious waterfalls cascading into pools. The park is 0.5 miles after the 22-mile marker.

The best for swimming is the upper pool, visible just beyond the picnic tables. To reach it, cross the stream. Watch for falling rocks beneath the waterfall and for flash floods. To get to the lower falls, which drop into a shallow pool, walk back over the bridge and head upstream.

Hana

Heavenly Hana. Is it paradise at the end of the rainbow or something a little bit different? Due to its history and its isolated location at the end of Hawaii's most famous drive, Hana has a legendary aura. But many travelers are disappointed when they arrive to find a sleepy hamlet, population 1235. But that's because Hana takes more than an hour or two to understand.

Surprisingly, Hana doesn't try to capitalize on the influx of day trippers arriving each afternoon. This is one of the most Hawaiian communities in the state, with a timeless rural character. It's also home to many transplants willing to trade certain luxuries for a slow, thoughtful and personal way of life in a beautiful natural setting. Though 'Old Hawaii' is a cliché, it's hard not to think of Hana in such terms. Slow down, spend a night or two and enjoy the pace. There aren't many places like this left.

BEACHES

Hana Bay Beach Park is in downtown Hana. Hamoa Beach and Koki Beach sit alongside photogenic Haneo'o Rd, which loops for 1.5 miles off the Hana Hwy just south of town.

Hamoa Beach   Beach
(Haneo'o Rd; P) With its clear water, white sand and hala-tree backdrop, this famous crescent is a little gem; author James Michener once called it the only beach in the North Pacific that looked as if it belonged in the South Pacific. When the surf's up, surfers and bodyboarders flock here, though beware of rips and currents.

Hana Bay Beach Park   Beach
(Map p187; 808-248-7022; www.co.maui.hi.us/Facilities; 150 Keawa Pl; P) Croquet by the beach? Why not? Welcome to Hana's version of the town plaza, a bayside park where children splash in the surf, picnickers enjoy the view from the rocky black-sand beach and musicians strum their ukuleles – while others play croquet. When water conditions are very calm, snorkeling and diving are

good out past the pier. Currents can be strong, and snorkelers shouldn't venture beyond the headland. Surfers head to Waikoloa Beach at the northern end of the bay.

Koki Beach   Beach
(Haneo'o Rd; P) This picturesque tan beach sits at the base of red cliffs with views toward tiny 'Alau Island. Bodysurfing is excellent here, as it's shallow for quite a distance, but a rip current has been known to sweep people out to sea if they go too far. Shell picking is good at the tide pools along the edge.

SIGHTS

Hasegawa General Store   Historic Site
(Map p187; 808-248-8231; 5165 Hana Hwy; 7am-7pm Mon-Sat, 8am-6pm Sun; P) Need cash? Or maybe some screws? How about a bottle of Jim Beam? Or Ben & Jerry's Half-Baked Froyo? The narrow aisles inside this tin-roofed store are jam-packed with a little bit of everything, from hardware to produce to tourist brochures. The Hasegawa family has operated a general store in Hana since 1910, and this icon of mom-and-pop shops is frequented by locals picking up supplies, and travelers stopping for snacks and the ATM.

ACTIVITIES

Travaasa Hana resort organizes many activities for its guests, including outrigger-canoe trips and stand-up paddleboarding. Its horseback-riding tours are open to nonguests. Alternatively, have Hana imprinted in your mind by skydiving over the coast.

Skyview Soaring   Gliding
(Map p190; 808-344-9663; www.skyviewsoaring.com; Hana Airport, 700 Alalele Pl; 30min/1hr $160/300; by reservation) Haleakalā has excellent soaring conditions, and a sailplane is a unique, rewarding and safe way to see the mountain. After he cuts the engine, experienced pilot Hans Pieters will fly over the crater (weather permitting), and will let you fly too, before gliding silently back to Hana Airport.

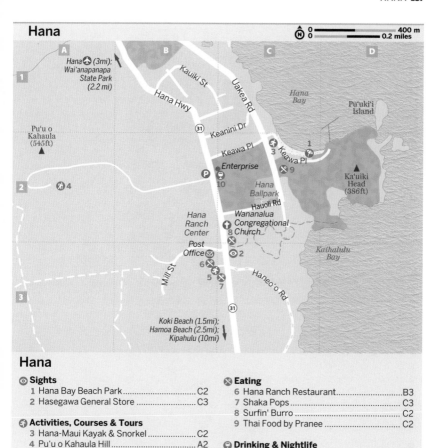

Hana

◎ Sights
1 Hana Bay Beach Park	C2
2 Hasegawa General Store	C3

✪ Activities, Courses & Tours
3 Hana-Maui Kayak & Snorkel	C2
4 Pu'u o Kahaula Hill	A2
5 Travaasa Hana Stables	B3

✪ Eating
6 Hana Ranch Restaurant	B3
7 Shaka Pops	C3
8 Surfin' Burro	C2
9 Thai Food by Pranee	C2

◎ Drinking & Nightlife
10 Preserve	C2

Maui Skydiving Skydiving
(Map p190; ☏808-379-7455; www.mauiskydiving.info; Hana Airport, 700 Alalele Pl; tandem jumps from $299) To get an adrenaline-fueled prospect of the stunning Hana coastline, jump out of a plane with Maui Skydiving. Jumps include a free fall for around 20 seconds from 10,000ft before the instructor pulls the chute and you both drift to ground level. It's a view you'll never forget. Special-deal standby jumps go for $250 per person.

Pu'u o Kahaula Hill Hiking
(Map p187; Lyon's Hill; Hana Hwy) This paved walkway up Pu'u o Kahaula Hill, behind Travaasa Hana resort's parking lot (use the gate in the left corner), makes for a fine 30-minute walk (roughly 1.5 miles round trip). It leads to Hana's most dominant landmark, a memorial to former Hana Ranch owner Paul Fagan. It's like a mountaintop heiau (stone temple), with a huge cross. Hana is laid out below.

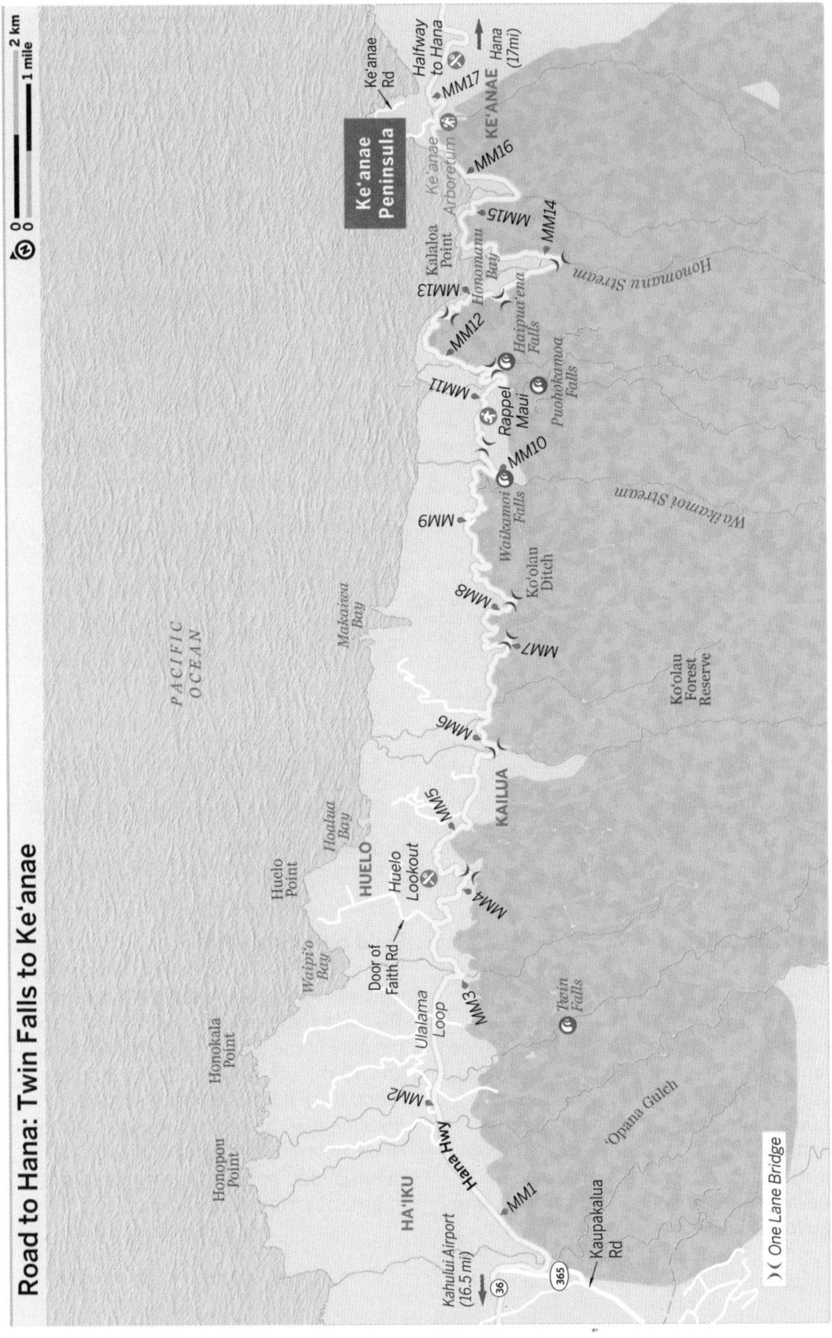

Road to Hana: Twin Falls to Ke'anae

Halfway to Hana

Hana (17mi)

MM17

KE'ANAE

Ke'anae Rd

Ke'anae Peninsula

Ke'anae Arboretum

MM16

Kailaloa Point

MM15

MM14

Honomanu Bay

Honomanu Stream

MM13

MM12

Haipua'ena Falls

Puohokamoa Falls

MM11

Rappel Maui

MM10

Waikamoi Falls

MM9

Ko'olau Ditch

Waikamoi Stream

MM8

MM7

Ko'olau Forest Reserve

MM6

Makaiwa Bay

MM5

KAILUA

PACIFIC OCEAN

Honopou Point

Homokala Point

Waipi'o Bay

Huelo Point

Ho'olua Bay

HUELO

Huelo Lookout

Door of Faith Rd

MM4

Ulalama Loop

MM3

Twin Falls

Ha'IKU

MM2

Hana Hwy

MM1

Kahului Airport (16.5 mi)

36

365

Kaupakalua Rd

'Opana Gulch

)(One Lane Bridge

2 km
1 mile

Travaasa Hana Stables
Horseback Riding

(Map p187; ☑808-270-5276, reservations 808-359-2401; www.travaasa.com; Travaasa Hana, 5031 Hana Hwy; 1hr ride $74; ☉tours 9am & 10:30am) Enjoy a trail ride through pastures and along Hana's black-lava coastline. Riders must be at least nine years old. Rides depart from stables just south of Travaasa Hana resort. Open to nonguests; book at the front desk.

EATING

To the frustration of many visitors, there are only two restaurants in town that are open for dinner (at Hana Ranch and Travaasa Hana resort), and both are pricey. Grocery stores are also limited and expensive. So load up on food in Kahului before coming to Hana, and eat a big lunch at the many excellent stalls and food trucks.

Huelo Lookout
Health Food $

Map p187; ☑808-280-4791; 7600 Hana Hwy; smoothies $5-7; ☉8am-5:30pm) ☀The fruit stand itself is tempting enough: drinking coconuts, pineapples, smoothies, acai bowls, banana bread and French crepes. But it doesn't stop there: take your goodies down the steps, where there's a shack selling waffles and sugarcane juice, and a table with a coastal panorama. Find it at mile 4.5

Thai Food by Pranee
Thai $

(Map p187; 5050 Uakea Rd; meals $10-15; ☉10:30am-4pm) Hana's ever-popular Thai lunch is served from an oversize food truck surrounded by picnic tables. Step up to the counter for a large and tasty meal, including fiery curries with mahi-mahi and fresh stir-fried dishes. The crispy *'opakapaka* (pink snapper) with green-mango salad is out of this world. Get here early for the best selection. Located opposite Hana Ball Park.

Shaka Pops
Ice Cream $

(Map p187; www.shakapopsmaui.com; ice pops $4.75; ☉11am-4pm Sun-Fri) A friendly *shaka* wave greets travelers passing this happy mobile tricycle, where frozen treats-on-a-stick come in fresh, tropical flavors from Liliko'i Cheesecake to Pineapple Ginger.

Wailua Falls

Beyond Hana but before you reach Kipahulu you'll see orchids growing out of the rocks, and jungles of breadfruit and coconut trees. Around 0.3 miles after the 45-mile marker you'll come upon the spectacular Wailua Falls, which plunge a mighty 100ft just beyond the road. There are usually plenty of people lined up snapping photos.

Locally made, the pops use seasonal produce and are definitely worth a lick. Life is a little brighter while slurping a Cocoa Hana Banana popsicle. Look for the cart by Hana Gas.

Surfin' Burro
Mexican $

(Map p187; ☑808-269-9775; Hana Hwy; mains $4-10; ☉8am-7pm Wed-Mon) Tacos? In Hana? Yep, and they're darn good too. Also serves quesadillas, breakfast burritos and fresh-made salsa. Look for the orange food truck parked between the Hotel Travaasa and Hasegawa General Store. Dishes can be made vegan if requested.

Hana Farms Grill
Grill $$

(Map p187; ☑808-248-7553; www.hanafarms online.com; 2910 Hana Hwy; mains $14-18; ☉11am-3pm Sat-Thu, 5-8pm Fri) ☀ Behind the Hana Farms stand, this little gem is *the* local choice for a lunch stop. It serves fresh seafood plates – with *liliko'i* (passion fruit) butter, turmeric-lemongrass rice, and two sides – plus slow-cooked pork-shoulder sandwiches, tacos, and juicy Maui beef burgers. Gas lamps light the colorful picnic tables beneath the thatched roofs on Friday nights.

Hana Ranch Restaurant
American $$

(Map p187; ☑808-270-5280; https://hanaranch restaurant.com; Hana Ranch Center, Mill St; mains $17-32; ☉11am-8:30pm) The wall of ukuleles is perfect for an Instagram photo at this revamped restaurant, one of a handful of

Road to Hana: Wailua to Wai'anapanapa State Park

PACIFIC OCEAN

Hana Forest Reserve

Hanawi Natural Area Reserve

Ko'olau Forest Reserve

Ke'akulikuli Point

Hana Airport

Hana (3.5mi)

Alalele Rd

Hana Farms Grill

Skyview Soaring

Maui Skydiving

Uwala Rd

KA'ELEKU

MM31

Hana Lava Tube

360

Ula'ino Rd

MM30

MM29

Kahanu Point

Pi'ilanihale Heiau

Mokupupu Point

ULA'INO

Hana Hwy

Coconut Glen's

MM28

Heleleikeoha Stream

MM27

MM26

Kilo'o Point

NAHIKU

Nahiku Rd

Makapipi Falls

MM25

Hanawi Falls

MM24

MM23

Waiohue Bay

Papiha Point

360

MM22

MM21

Wailuaiki Bay

Pua'a Ka'a State Wayside Park

MM20

WAILUA

Wailua Rd

MM19

WAILUA

Three Bears Falls

Wailua Valley State Wayside

MM18

Waikamoi Stream

Wailua Valley State Wayside

0   2 km
0   1 mile

dinner options in Hana. Enjoy the ocean view from inside or from the patio. Serves American and Hawaiian fare, from market-fresh *poke* and Hawaiian barbecue-pork ribs to fish tacos and rib-eye steak. Located off the Hana Hwy.

DRINKING & NIGHTLIFE

Preserve Bar

(Map p187; ☑808-248-8211; www.travaasa.com; Travaasa Hana, 5031 Hana Hwy; ☻restaurant 7:30am-2pm & 5-9pm, bar till later) When it comes to Hana nightlife, this is the only game in town. Maui beers, locally inspired cocktails and farm-to-table bar fare are on offer. Local musicians perform Wednesday and Thursday nights from 6:30pm to 8.30pm, sometimes accompanied by hula dancers. Come when there's live music, as otherwise the vibe can be eerily quiet and slow paced.

❶ GETTING THERE & AWAY

To drive the Road to Hana at your own pace, rent a car. The drive kicks off on the eastern fringe of Ha'iku, near Huelo, 20 miles east of **Kahului International Airport** (OGG; ☑808-872-3830; www.airports.hawaii.gov/ogg; 1 Kahului Airport Rd).

Several tour companies run Road to Hana trips, with buses and shuttles pulling over for key waterfalls and other roadside attractions. **Valley Isle Excursions** (☑808-871-5224; www.tourmaui.com; tours adult/child 0-12yr from $156/135; ☻office 5am-9pm), which includes breakfast and lunch on its Road to Hana tours, leaves Hana via the Pi'ilani Hwy (back road to Hana).

There is no public bus service to Hana or anywhere along the Road to Hana.

Read the **Road to Hana Code of Conduct** (most of which is common sense) before you set off. Don't cross private property, don't leave trash behind you, and don't park

Tips for Driving the Road to Hana

o Hundreds of cars are making the journey each day. To beat the crowd, get a sunrise start.

o Fill up your tank in Pa'ia or Ha'iku; the next gas station isn't until Hana, and the station there sometimes runs dry.

o Bring snacks and plenty to drink.

o Wear a bathing suit under your clothes so you're ready for impromptu swims.

o Bring shoes that are good for hiking as well as scrambling over slick rocks.

o Pull over to let local drivers pass – they're moving at a different pace.

o The drive can feel a bit rushed at times. If you want to slow down, consider spending one or two nights in Hana – you can visit the attractions you missed on the way back the next day.

o Leave valuables at your hotel or carry them with you. Smash-and-grab thefts do occur.

with your car protruding into the road or you will be subject to towing. Read the full code here: www.hawaiipublicradio.org/post/hana-highway-code-conduct#stream/0.

❶ GETTING AROUND

The branch of the car rental firm **Enterprise** (☑808-871-1511; www.enterprise.com; Travaasa Hana, 5031 Hana Hwy; ☻booking office in Kahului 7am-5pm Mon-Fri, 8am-noon Sat & Sun) at Travaasa Hana resort has a very small fleet available for rent.

KIHEI & WAILEA, MAUI

Kihei & Wailea at a Glance...

Everyone stops for the sunset in South Maui – just look at the throngs crowding the beach wall at Kamaʻole Beach Park II in the late afternoon. It's a scene repeated up and down the coast here every day. Across Kihei and Wailea you'll find a mixed plate of scenery and adventure that's truly unique. You can snorkel reefs teeming with turtles, kayak to remote bays or paddle an outrigger canoe. The coral gardens are so rich you can dive from the shore. And the beaches? Undeniably glorious. With reliably sunny weather, quiet coastal trails and a diverse dining scene, South Maui's an irresistible place to land.

Kihei & Wailea in One Day

The doors open early at **Kihei Caffe** (p203), a good place to fuel up before a morning of snorkeling at **Ulua Beach** (p202). Enjoy fresh fish at **Cafe O'Lei** (p204) then head to **Hawaiian Islands Humpback Whale National Marine Sanctuary Headquarters** (p196) to learn about the leviathans, who breed here in winter. Grab a craft beer at **Maui Brewing Co** (p205) and watch the sunset at **Keawakapu Beach** (p202).

Kihei & Wailea in Two Days

The next morning, take an outrigger canoe trip with **Hawaiian Sailing Canoe Adventures** (p203) for a taste of old Hawaii, before enjoying wood-fired pizza at **Monkeypod Kitchen** (p204). Stretch your legs on a stroll along the **Wailea Beach Walk** (p203), then spend the afternoon relaxing and enjoying the surf on **Wailea Beach** (p202). Make your way to the lofty **Restaurant at Hotel Wailea** (p204) for a fine dinner and a gorgeous sunset.

Previous page: Big Beach, Makena State Park (p202)
JENNA SZERLAG/DESIGN PICS/GETTY IMAGES ©

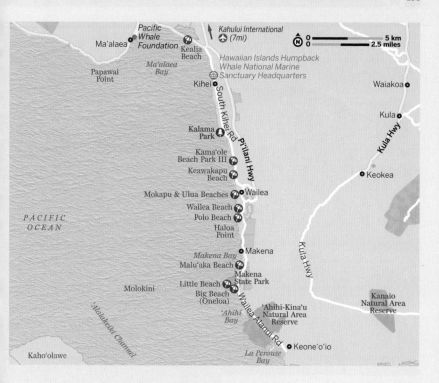

Arriving in South Maui

The airport in Kahului is 10 miles from North Kihei, 16 miles from South Kihei and 18 miles from Wailea. Almost everyone rents a car at the airport. You can expect to pay about $18 for commercial shuttle service to Kihei, and $24 to Wailea. It's $33 to $55 for a taxi, depending on your destination in Kihei, and $57 for a taxi to Wailea.

Where to Stay

Condominiums are the most common lodging option in Kihei, and condo complexes are scattered across the city. A handful of hotels and B&Bs are the only alternative. Wailea is known for its swanky oceanfront resorts, but you'll find a few posh condo developments as well. Wailea also has two hotels, both of them a short drive from the beach.

MAUI TOPICAL IMAGES/SHUTTERSTOCK ©

Whale-Watching

Each winter, about 10,000 graceful humpback whales – two thirds of the entire North Pacific humpback whale population – come to the shallow coastal waters off the Hawaiian Islands to breed and give birth.

Great For...

☑ **Don't Miss**

The free '45-Ton Talks' at 11am on Tuesday and Thursday at Humpback Whale National Marine Sanctuary Headquarters.

Whale Hot Spots

With their tail slaps, head lunges and spy hops, humpback whales sure know how to impress a crowd.

The western coastline of the island is their chief birthing and nursing ground. Luckily for whale-watchers, humpbacks are coast-huggers, preferring shallow waters to protect their newborn calves. Along the coast there's great whale-watching at many places, especially the beach walks in Kihei and Wailea.

Hawaiian Islands Humpback Whale National Marine Sanctuary

The sanctuary's Kihei headquarters is abuzz with cool whale happenings. The oceanfront deck, which sits just north of the ancient Koʻieʻie Fishpond, is an ideal spot for viewing the humpback whales

ⓘ Need to Know

Hawaiian Islands Humpback Whale National Marine Sanctuary Headquarters (Map p 195; ☏808-879-2818; http://hawaiihumpbackwhale.noaa. gov; 726 S Kihei Rd; ⊙10am-3pm Mon-Fri; 🅿🚻) **FREE**

✕ Take a Break

Alohas are warm and the breakfast top notch at Nalu's South Shore Grill (p203).

★ Top Tip

Maui's peak whale-watching season is from January through March.

that frequent the bay during winter. Free scopes are set up for viewing. Inside, displays and videos provide background, and there are lots of informative brochures about whales and other Hawaiian wildlife. Swing by at 11am on Tuesday or Thursday for the free '45-Ton Talks' about whales. The entire sanctuary extends from the shoreline to ocean depths of 600ft in the waters surrounding the Hawaiian Islands.

Whale-Watching Tours

If you want to get within splashing distance of 40-ton leviathans acrobatically jumping out of the water, take a whale-watching cruise. No one does them better than the **Pacific Whale Foundation** (Map p195; ☏808-249-8811; www.pacificwhale.org; Ma'alaea Harbor Shops, 300 Ma'alaea Rd; cruises adult/ child over 12yr from $120/106; ⊙most tours

depart 7-8am; 🚸), a conservation group that takes pride in its green, naturalist-led whale-watching trips. Trips leave from Ma'alaea Harbor and offer snorkeling lessons and wildlife talks. Snacks are provided and kids under 12 go free on certain cruises. Half-day tours concentrate on Molokini; full-day tours add Lana'i.

World Whale Day

Organized by the Pacific Whale Foundation, this family-friendly festival (www.mauiwhale festival.org; 1900 S Kihei Rd) celebrates Maui's humpback whales with crafts, live music, food booths, and environmental displays. Going for over 40 years, it's held at **Kalama Park** (Map p195; ☏808-879-4364; www.maui county.gov/Facilities; 1900 S Kihei Rd) on a Saturday in mid-February.

Shave ice (p201)

Best Local Food

The term 'cuisine' sounds a bit pretentious for Maui, where the best pupu (snacks) and entrees, such as the plate lunch and loco moco (rice, fried egg and hamburger patty with gravy), share a tasty and simple exuberance and a no-worries embrace of foreign flavors. Even Spam musubi (rice ball) has a sassy – if salty – international charm. So join the fun, sample the unknown and savor the next bite.

Great For...

✕ Take a Break

Take your plate lunch to one of the shaded picnic tables at Kama'ole Beach Park III (p202).

★ **Top Tip**

The seafood counter at Foodland grocery store sells excellent ahi (yellowfin tuna) *poke* bowls to-go, with the ahi over rice.

Day-to-day eats reflect the state's multi-cultural heritage, with Asian, Portuguese and Native Hawaiian influences the most immediately evident. Cheap, fattening and tasty, local food is the stuff of cravings and comfort. Your best bets for local food are in Kihei, although you may find some good choices further south at the Shops at Wailea, particularly at Lineage (p204) and Island Gourmet Kitchen (p203).

Plate Lunch

The classic example of local food is the ubiquitous plate lunch. Picture this: chunky layers of tender *kalua* pork, a dollop of smooth, creamy macaroni and two hearty scoops of white rice. Yum, right? The pork can be swapped for other proteins, such as fried mahimahi (fish) or teriyaki chicken.

The plate lunch is often served on disposable plates and eaten using chopsticks. A favorite breakfast combo is fried egg and spicy Portuguese sausage (or bacon, ham, Spam etc) and, always, two scoops of rice.

Top spots for plate lunches in South Maui are Kihei Caffe (p203) and Da Kitchen Express (p203).

Poke

Raw fish marinated in *shōyu* (soy sauce), oil, chili peppers, green onions and seaweed, *poke* comes in many varieties. Sesame ahi (yellowfin tuna) is particularly delicious and goes well with beer. Top spots for trying *poke* in Kihei are **Foodland** (☏808-879-9350; www.foodland.com; 1881 S Kihei Rd, Kihei Town Center; ◷5am-1am), Eskimo Candy (p203) and Tamura's Fine Wine & Liquors (p203).

Traditional plate lunch

Pupu

The local term used for all kinds of munchies or 'grazing' foods is *pupu*. Much more than just cheese and crackers, *pupu* represent the ethnic diversity of the islands and might include boiled peanuts in the shell, edamame (boiled fresh soybeans in the pod) and universal items such as fried shrimp. Try the ahi *poke* nachos at **Sunsets Bar & Grill** ([J] 808-633-4220; www.sunsetsbarandgrill.com; 470 Lipoa Pkwy; ☉10am-8pm)

Shave Ice

Ignore those joyless cynics who'll tell you that shave ice is nothing more than a snow cone. Shave ice is not just a snow

cone. It's a tropical 21-gun salute – the most spectacular snow cone on earth. The specifics? The ice is shaved as fine as powdery snow, packed into a paper cone and drenched with sweet fruit-flavored syrups in dazzling hues. For added decadence, add Kaua'i cream, azuki beans and ice cream. Give it a try at Local Boys Shave Ice (p203).

Hawaii's Seafood

Ahi is the local favorite fish, but mahimahi and *ono* (white-fleshed wahoo) are also very popular. Browse the Hawaii Seafood website (www.hawaii-seafood.org) to find out more about wild local fish, including sustainability, fishing methods, seasonality, nutrition and cooking tips.

The free Seafood Watch (wwwseafood watch.org) guide, published by the Monterey Bay Aquarium, provides at-a-glance information about ocean-friendly seafood, including sustainability specifics for Hawaii's fish. Download the free smartphone app or print a pocket guide from the website.

☑ Don't Miss

Breakfast with the crowds and the birds at Kihei Caffe (p203).

BONCHAN/SHUTTERSTOCK ©

❶ Need to Know

If you're invited to someone's home, bring a dish – preferably homemade, but a cake from a bakery is great too.

BEACHES

The further south you travel, the better the beaches.

Big Beach
Beach

(Map p195; Oneloa Beach; www.dlnr.hawaii.gov/dsp/parks/maui; Makena Rd; parking $5; ⏲parking gates 7am-7:45pm; P) This untouched beach is arguably the finest on Maui. Golden sands stretch for the better part of a mile and the waters are a beautiful turquoise. When they're calm, you'll find kids boogie boarding here, but at other times the shore-breaks can be dangerous and suitable only for experienced bodysurfers.

Keawakapu Beach
Beach

(Map p195; 808-879-4364; www.mauicounty.gov/Facilities; P) This sparkling stretch of sand is a showstopper. Extending from south Kihei to Wailea's Mokapu Beach, Keawakapu is set back from the main road and less visible than Kihei's main roadside beaches just north. It's a great place to watch the sunset.

Wailea Beach
Beach

(Map p195; 808-879-4364; www.mauicounty.gov/Facilities; off Wailea Alanui Dr; P♿) The beach on this beautiful strand slopes gradually, making it a good swimming spot. When it's calm, there's decent snorkeling around the rocky point on the southern end. Divers entering the water at Wailea Beach can follow an offshore reef that runs down to Polo Beach.

Kama'ole Beach Park III
Beach

(Map p195; 808-879-4364; www.mauicounty.gov/Facilities; 2800 S Kihei Rd; P♿) Kama'ole Beach Park III has full facilities and life-guards, plus a playground and parking lot. Also has accessibility parking, pathways and beach access for visitors with disabilities.

Mokapu & Ulua Beaches
Beach

(Map p195; 808-879-4364; www.mauicounty.gov/Facilities; Haleali'i Place; P) The lovely **Mokapu Beach** is behind the Andaz Maui resort, on the northern side of a small point between the beaches. Snorkelers should head straight for **Ulua Beach** to the south of the point.

Wailea Beach

😊 ACTIVITIES

Hawaiian Sailing
Canoe Adventures
Canoeing

(☎808-281-9301; www.mauisailingcanoe.com; adult/child 4-14yr $179/129; ⏰tours 9am; 👶) Learn about Native Hawaiian traditions and snorkel beside sea turtles on a 2½-hour trip aboard a Hawaiian-style outrigger canoe. Tours depart from Polo Beach.

Wailea Beach Walk
Walking

For the perfect sunset stroll, take the 1.3-mile shoreline path that connects Wailea's beaches and the resort hotels that front them. The undulating path winds above jagged lava points and back down to the sandy shore. In winter this is a fantastic location for spotting humpback whales.

Aqualani Beach
& Ocean Recreation
Water Sports

(☎808-283-0384; www.aqualanibeach.com; 3850 Wailea Alanui Dr, Grand Wailea Resort; snorkel/boogie board per day $20/20, kayak/SUP per hour $55/55; ⏰7am-5pm) On the beach behind the Grand Wailea, Aqualani rents all the gear you need for ocean fun. Paddle-free aqua gliders are $75 per hour with a land lesson included.

😊 EATING

From food trucks to farm-to-table eateries to chef-driven hotspots, South Maui has it all.

Nalu's South Shore Grill
Hawaiian $

(☎808-891-8650; www.nalusmaui.com; 1280 S Kihei Rd, Azeka Makai Shopping Center; breakfast $10-14, lunch & dinner $9-17; ⏰8am-10pm; 👶👶) Breakfasts are the showstoppers, from acai bowls to three-egg omelets to the vegetarian *loco moco*. The focus? Healthy, hearty and locally grown. Good Bloody Marys too, plus live music nightly.

Kihei Caffe
Cafe $

(☎808-879-2230; www.kiheicaffe.com; 1945 S Kihei Rd, Kihei Kalama Village; mains $9-19; ⏰5am-3pm) Maybe it's the sneaky birds on the patio, or the quick-to-arrive entrees, or the hovering queue, but dining at this busy Kihei institution is not exactly relaxing – but

that's part of the quirky charm. Order at the counter, fill your coffee cup at the thermos, snag a patio table, and watch the breakfast burritos, veggie scrambles and *loco moco* flash by.

Da Kitchen Express
Hawaiian $

(☎808-875-7782; www.dakitchen.com; 2439 S Kihei Rd, Rainbow Mall; mains $11-18; ⏰11am-9pm) Come to this no-frills eatery for Hawaiian plate lunches done right. The local favorite is Da Lau Lau Plate (with steamed pork wrapped in taro leaves) We particularly liked the spicy *kalua* pork.

Eskimo Candy
Seafood $

(☎808-891-8898; www.eskimocandy.com; 2665 Wai Wai Pl; mains $10-18; ⏰10:30am-7pm Mon-Fri; 👶) The hearty chowder here primes the palate for the top-notch fresh seafood served in this busy fish market with a takeout counter. Raw-fish fanatics should home in on the *poke*, ahi wraps and fish tacos. Parents will appreciate the under-$9 kids' menu.

Tamura's Fine
Wine & Liquors
Seafood $

(☎808-891-2420; www.tamurasfinewine.com; 91 E Lipoa St; fresh poke per lb $17.99; ⏰9:30am-8pm) What? Great *poke* from a wine and liquor store? Yep, after browsing the well-stocked alcohol aisles, head to the seafood counter for some of the island's best *poke*.

Island Gourmet Kitchen
Deli $

(☎808-874-5055; www.islandgourmethawaii.com; 3750 Wailea Alanui Dr, Shops at Wailea; breakfast mains $6-14, lunch & dinner mains $7-20; ⏰6:30am-9pm) This deli is a great quick stop for takeout. Breakfast offerings, which are available all day, include omelets, pancakes, and *huevos rancheros*, while the lunch and dinner options cover local favorites, as well as pizza, sushi, and fried chicken.

Local Boys Shave Ice
Sweets $

(☎808-344-9779; www.localboysshaveice.com; 1941 S Kihei Rd, Kihei Kalama Village; small shave ice $5.50; ⏰10am-9pm) Load up on napkins at Local Boys, where they dish up hearty servings of shave ice drenched in a rainbow of sweet syrups. Cash only.

Monkeypod Kitchen   Pub Food $$

(☎808-891-2322; www.monkeypodkitchen.com; 10 Wailea Gateway Pl, Wailea Gateway Center; lunch $16-30, dinner $16-50; ☺11am-11pm, happy hour 3-5:30pm & 9-11pm; ♠) ✿ Happy hours are crowded but convivial at this ever-popular venture from chef Peter Merriman. The gourmet pub grub comes with a delicious Hawaiian spin and incorporates organic and local ingredients, including Maui Cattle burgers and plenty of Upcountry veggies.

Café O'Lei   Hawaiian $$

(☎808-891-1368; www.cafeoleirestaurants.com; 2439 S Kihei Rd, Rainbow Mall; lunch $9-19, dinner $19-32; ☺10:30am-3:30pm & 4:30-9:30pm) This strip-mall bistro may look ho-hum at first blush, but step inside: the sophisticated atmosphere, innovative Hawaii Regional Cuisine, honest prices, and excellent service knock Café O'Lei into the fine-dining big league. For a tangy treat, order the blackened mahimahi with fresh papaya salsa. A sushi chef arrives at the sushi bar at 4:30pm (Tuesday to Saturday).

Pa'ia Fish Market Southside   Seafood $$

(☎808-874-8888; www.paiafishmarket.com; 1913 S Kihei Rd, Kihei Kalama Village; mains $10-25; ☺11am-9:30pm) This fantastic seafood joint is a spinoff from the popular Pa'ia Fish Market in the Upcountry. The open-air eatery serves *ono* and mahimahi burgers, fish and chips, and seafood pasta. Plate meals arrive with huge slabs of seasoned local fish and Cajun rice or home fries.

Lineage   Hawaiian $$

(☎808-879-8800; www.lineagemaui.com; 3750 Wailea Alanui Dr, Shops at Wailea; small plates $7-15, mains $18-22; ☺5-11pm) The hospitality at this new venture from *Top Chef* favorite and restaurateur Sheldon Simeon is warm, old-school Hawaiian. The menu spotlights Maui's diverse culinary influences, with Portuguese, Japanese and Native Hawaiian dishes on offer. Appetizers on the 'cart' menu are served dim-sum style, which contributes to an appealingly immersive dining experience.

Pita Paradise   Mediterranean $$

(☎808-879-7177; www.pitaparadisehawaii.com; 34 Wailea Gateway Pl, Wailea Gateway Center; lunch $11-22, dinner $20-34; ☺11am-9:30pm) Although this Greek taverna sits in a strip mall, the inviting patio, the townscape mural and the tiny white lights – not to mention the succulent Mediterranean chicken pita – banish any locational regrets. Owner John Arabatzis catches his own fish, which come in everything from pita sandwiches at lunch to grilled kabobs at dinner.

Restaurant at Hotel Wailea   Hawaiian Regional $$$

(☎808-879-2224; www.hotelwailea.com/rhw; 555 Kaukahi St; mains $39-62; ☺5-9:30pm) Sunsets put on an astounding performance at this romantic hilltop hideaway, the only Relais & Châteaux restaurant in Hawaii. Helmed by chef Zach Sato, a Maui native, the kitchen artfully presents an exquisite line-up of locally inspired seafood and meat dishes.The cocktails are top notch too.

Cuatro   Latin American $$$

(☎808-879-1110; www.cuatro808.com; 1881 S Kihei Rd, Kihei Town Center; mains $27-36; ☺4-10pm) Come for the amazing spicy tuna nachos, stay for the Acapulco shrimp scampi, the Asian marinated grilled rib eye and the other impeccably flavored dishes. The place is small, so reservations are recommended. The nachos and other appetizers are 25% off during happy hour (4pm to 5pm). It's BYOB with a $10 corkage fee.

🍸 DRINKING & NIGHTLIFE

Most bars in Kihei are across the street from the beach and have nightly entertainment. Kihei Kalama Village aka the Bar-muda Triangle (or just the Triangle), is a lively place at night, packed with buzzy watering holes.

5 Palms   Cocktail Bar

(☎808-879-2607; www.5palmsrestaurant.com; 2960 S Kihei Rd, Mana Kai Maui; ☺8am-11pm) For sunset cocktails beside the beach, this is the place. Arrive an hour before the sun goes down, because the patio bar, just

Kihei Caffe (p203)

steps from stunning Keawakapu Beach, fills quickly. During happy hour, selected sushi and an array of delicious appetizers are half price, with a one-drink minimum, while mai tais and margaritas are $8.

Pint & Cork
Bar

(📞808-727-2038; www.thepintandcork.com; 3750 Wailea Alanui Dr, Shops at Wailea; ⏲noon-2am) This chic gastropub and wine bar has a welcoming vibe. Big TVs overlook the 40ft soapstone bar, keeping sports fans happy. Opens early for games during football season, with a Bloody Mary bar.

Soak up the suds with gourmet pub grub specialties such as *kalua* pork sliders, garlic parmesan fries and fantastic burgers.

Maui Brewing Co
Brewery

(📞808-213-3002; www.mauibrewingco.com; 605 Lipoa Pkwy, Maui Research & Technology Park; ⏲11am-11pm, tours 11:30am-4:30pm) 🍺 Enormous windows draw your eyes toward West Maui at the glossy restaurant and bar at Maui Brewing's Kihei production facility. Over 35 craft and seasonal beers are on offer, and the food menu shines with tasty farm-to-table pizzas and pub fare (mains $14-35). The adjacent taproom is open daily

Tours (per person $15) are offered six times daily, with a tasting of the flagship beers included in the price. Reservations recommended for tours. Trivia night every other Tuesday in the tasting room (7:30pm).

❶ GETTING THERE & AWAY

A few rental car agencies can be found along North and South Kihei Rds. These are good options if you're looking for lower rates or a day-trip rental. **Kihei Rent A Car** (📞808-879-7257; www.kiheirentacar.com; 96 Kio Loop; per day/week from $35/175; ⏲7:30am-9pm) rents cars and 4WDs to those aged 21 and over, and includes free mileage. Uber and Lyft are also available.

❶ GETTING AROUND

The **Maui Bus** (📞808-871-4838; www.mauicounty.gov/bus; single ride $2, day pass $4, monthly pass $45) serves Kihei with two routes. Both operate hourly from around 6am to 8pm and cost $2.

HALEAKALĀ
NATIONAL PARK,
MAUI

Haleakalā National Park at a Glance...

To peer into the soul of Maui, make your way to the summit of Haleakalā, where the huge crater opens beneath you in all its raw volcanic glory, caressed by mist and – in the experience of a lifetime – bathed in the sublime light of sunrise. Lookouts provide breathtaking views of the moonscape below, dotted with cinder cones.

The rest of the park, which is divided into two distinct sections, is all about interacting with this mountain of solid lava and the rare lifeforms here. You can hike down into the crater, follow lush trails, or put your mountain bike through its paces.

Haleakalā National Park in One Day

Begin at the **visitor center** (p221) at the summit. Next, take an invigorating hike on the sun-warmed cinders of the unearthly **Keonehe'ehe'e (Sliding Sands) Trail** (p210).

After this, continue to Maui's highest point, **Pu'u'ula'ula (Red Hill) Overlook** (p219). Descend to the **Kalahaku Overlook** (p219), on the crater rim. Then stroll on the **Hosmer Grove Trail** (p211), in forest brimming with birdsong.

Haleakalā National Park in Two Days

Start day two in the wet and wild Kipahulu section. Stroll the **Kuloa Point Trail** (p213), savoring the ocean view. Join the **Pipiwai Trail** (p212) for a 10-minute hike to view the 200ft **Makahiku Falls** (p212), followed by a glimpse of magical bamboo forest. End at the 400ft cascade of **Waimoku Falls** (p213). Pitch a tent at **Kipahulu Campground** (p213), once an ancient Hawaiian settlement.

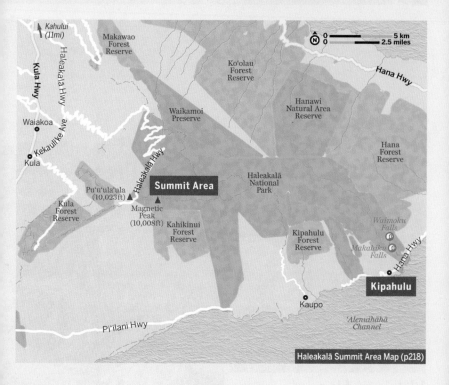

Haleakalā Summit Area Map (p218)

Arriving in Haleakalā National Park

To explore the park in depth, you will need to rent a car. The summit is 40 miles from Kahului, just over an hour's drive. Kipahulu is 55 miles from Kahului via the Road to Hana. Expect the drive to take at least two hours. Guided tours also stop at both sections of the park.

A three-day pass to Haleakalā park costs $30/25/15/15 per car/motorcycle/walk-in/bike.

Where to Stay

There are basic campsites and cabins in the Summit Area; camping permits are first come, first served, and cabins must be reserved. The campground in **Kipahulu** (p213) is first come, first served.

Kula is close to Haleakalā National Park. If you want to get a jump on the drive to the summit for sunrise, choose to stay here. The options are rustic cabins and a handful of B&Bs and rentals.

MARIDAV/SHUTTERSTOCK ©

Hiking the Summit Area

There's a trail for every type of hiker in this otherworldly place, from short nature walks ideal for families to hardy two-day treks.

Great For...

☑ Don't Miss

Snapping a picture of Haleakalā's famed ʻahinahina (silversword) plants with elegant spiked silver leaves.

Keoneheʻeheʻe (Sliding Sands) Trail

Make time for this stunning two-day, 17.8-mile round-trip hike. The high-altitude trail starts at the Haleakalā Visitor Center at 9740ft and winds down to the crater floor. There's no shade; bring a hat and water.

The path descends gently into an unearthly world of stark lava forms and ever-changing clouds. The first thing you'll notice is how quiet everything is: the only sound is the crunching of volcanic cinders beneath your feet. If you're pressed for time, just walking down 20 minutes will reward you with an into-the-crater experience and fabulous photo opportunities. Keep in mind that the return climb takes twice as long.

The full trail leads 8.9 miles to Paliku Cabin. The first 6 miles follow the southern wall. There are great views but virtually

'Ahinahina (silversword)

RAPHAEL RIVEST/SHUTTERSTOCK ©

Hosmer Grove Trail

Halemau'u Trail

Park Headquarters Visitor Center

Haleakalā Visitor Center

Holua Campground

Keonehe'ehe'e (Sliding Sands) Trail

Paliku Cabin & Campground

Kapalaoa Cabin

❶ Need to Know

Haleakalā Visitor Center (☎808-572-4400; www.nps.gov/hale; ☺8am-3pm; 3-day pass car $30, motorcycle $25, individual on foot or bicycle $15; P ♿)

✕ Take a Break

Enjoy a summit picnic overlooking a cinder cone. When you descend, fuel up at Kula Bistro (p221).

★ Top Tip

The weather can change suddenly from dry, hot conditions to cold, windswept rain. Bring layers.

no vegetation. Four miles down, after an elevation drop of 2500ft, Keonehe'ehe'e Trail intersects with a spur that leads north into the cinder desert, where it connects with the Halemau'u Trail after 1.6 miles.

Continuing on Keonehe'ehe'e, you cross the crater floor for 2 miles to Kapalaoa Cabin. Verdant ridges rise on your right, giving way to ropy *pahoehoe* (smooth-flowing lava). From here the descent is gentle and the vegetation gradually increases. At Paliku (6380ft), ohia forests climb the slopes.

Hosmer Grove Trail

Anyone who's looking for a little greenery after hiking the crater will enjoy this shaded woodland walk, as will birders. The half-mile loop trail starts at Hosmer Grove campground, 0.75 miles south of the Park Headquarters Visitor Center, in a forest of lofty trees. Fragrant incense cedar, Norway

spruce, Douglas fir, eucalyptus and various pines were introduced in 1910 in an effort to develop a lumber industry in Hawaii.

After the forest, the trail moves into native shrubland, with *'akala* (Hawaiian raspberry), mamane, pilo, kilau ferns and sandalwood.

Listen for the calls of the native *'i'iwi* and *'apapane*; both are fairly common here. The *'i'iwi* has a very loud squeaking call, orange legs and a curved salmon-colored bill. The *'apapane*, a fast-moving bird with a black bill, black legs and a white undertail, feeds on the nectar of bright red ohia flowers, and its wings make a distinctive whirring sound.

Halemau'u Trail

With views of crater walls, lava tubes and cinder cones, the Halemau'u Trail down to the Holua campground and back – 7.4 miles round-trip – is a memorable day hike. Start early, as clouds may roll in during the afternoon, obscuring visibility. Expect the ascent to take twice as long as the descent. The first mile is fairly level and offers a fine view of the crater with Ko'olau Gap to the east.

Waimoku Falls

SEKAR B/SHUTTERSTOCK ©

Hiking the Kipahulu Area

The crowning glory of the Kipahulu section of the park is 'Ohe'o Gulch, with its magnificent waterfalls and wide pools, each tumbling into the one below.

Great For...

☑ **Don't Miss**
The magical bamboo grove on the Pipiwai Trail.

Pipiwai Trail

This fun adventure trail is one of Maui's best. It ascends alongside the 'Ohe'o stream bed, has gorgeous waterfalls and includes an otherworldly trip through a bamboo grove. The trail starts near the visitor center and leads up to Makahiku Falls (0.5 miles) and Waimoku Falls (2 miles). Allow two hours return (4 miles total). The trail can be muddy.

You'll pass large mango trees and patches of guava before coming to an overlook after about 10 minutes. Makahiku Falls, a long bridal-veil waterfall that drops into a deep gorge, is just off to the right. Thick green ferns cover the sides of 200ft basalt cliffs where the water cascades – a very rewarding scene for such a short walk.

Continuing along the main trail, you'll walk beneath old banyan trees, cross Palikea Stream (bug spray advisable here)

Bamboo forest, Pipiwai Trail

Haleakalā
National
Park

*Waimoku
Falls*

*Makahiku
Falls*

**Pipiwai
Trail**

Kipahulu
Campground

Kipahulu

**Kuloa Point
Trail**

Kipahulu
Visitor Cente

*'Alenuihāhā
Channel*

❶ Need to Know

Kipahulu Campground (☎808-248-7375; www.nps.gove/hale) This campground has simple facilities, is first come, first served and stays are limited to three in any 30 days.

✕ Take a Break

Drive to Hana for delicious **Thai Food by Pranee** (5050 Uakea Rd; meals $10-15; ⊙10:30am-4pm).

★ Top Tip

Wear your grippy water shoes for the Pipiwai Trail.

---

and enter the wonderland of the Bamboo Forest, where thick groves of bamboo bang together musically in the wind. The upper section is muddy, but boardwalks cover some of the worst bits. Beyond the bamboo forest is Waimoku Falls, a thin, lacy 400ft waterfall dropping down a sheer rock face. Forget swimming under the falls: its pool is shallow and there's a danger of falling rocks.

Kuloa Point Trail

Even if you're short on time, be sure to take this 20-minute stroll. The half-mile loop runs from the visitor center down to the lower pools and back. A few minutes down, you'll reach a broad, grassy knoll with a gorgeous view of the Hana coast. On a clear day you can see Hawai'i, the Big Island, 30 miles away across 'Alenuihāhā Channel.

Best Day Hikes

Six hours If you're in decent physical shape, the phenomenal 10.2-mile hike that starts down the Keonehe'ehe'e (Sliding Sands) Trail and returns via the Halemau'u Trail is the prize. It crosses the crater floor, taking in both a cinder desert and a cloud forest, showcasing the park's amazing diversity. Hitchhiking is allowed in the park, there's a designated place to hitch on Haleakalā Hwy opposite the Halemau'u trailhead tailhead) and this is probably the best way back to your starting point.

Three hours For a half-day experience that offers a hearty serving of crater sights, follow the Keonehe'ehe'e (Sliding Sands) Trail down to where it goes between two towering rock formations before dropping steeply again. It takes an hour to get down. Careful: the way back is a 1500ft elevation rise, making the return a strenuous two-hour climb.

One hour Take to the forest on the Hosmer Grove Trail to see the green side of Haleakalā National Park.

Experiencing Sunrise

'Haleakalā' means 'House of the Sun,' so it's no surprise that since the time of the first Hawaiians, people have been making pilgrimages up to this peak to watch the sun rise.

Great For...

☑ Don't Miss
A sunrise look at Science City, whose domes turn a blazing pink.

★ **Top Tip**

The best photo opportunities occur before the sun rises. Once the sun is up, the silvery lines and subtleties often disappear.

The Sunrise Experience

Seeing the sun rise at Haleakalā is an experience that borders on the mystical. Mark Twain called it the 'sublimest spectacle' that he had ever witnessed.

First, ethereal silhouettes of the mountain ridges appear, then the gentlest colors show up in the fragile moments just before dawn. The undersides of the clouds lighten first, accenting the night sky with pale silvery slivers and streaks of pink. About 20 minutes before sunrise, the light intensifies on the horizon in bright oranges and reds. Turn around for a look at Science City, whose domes turn a blazing pink. For the grand finale – the moment when the disk of the sun appears – all of Haleakalā takes on a fiery glow.

It feels as though you're watching the earth awaken.

Come prepared: it's going to be c-o-l-d! Temperatures hovering around freezing and a biting wind are the norm at dawn, and there's often frosty ice on the top layer of cinders. If you don't have a winter jacket suitable for snow or skiing, bring a warm blanket from your hotel.

A rained-out sunrise is an anticlimactic event, but stick around: the skies may clear and you can enjoy a fantastic hike into the crater.

If you just can't get up that early, sunsets at Haleakalā are also exceptional, and they're favored by locals who want to avoid the crowds.

Haleakalā Observatory

Sunrise-Viewing Reservations

In 2017, to manage crowds and protect the park, the park service began requiring reservations for those arriving between 3am and 7am. Bookings (through www. recreation.gov) can be made up to 60 days in advance and cost $1 per car; the reservation fee is separate from the entrance fee. You can also catch the sunrise with a commercial tour group.

Visiting the Park

Pack plenty of snacks. No food or bottled water is sold anywhere in the park, and you don't want a growling stomach to send you back down the mountain before you've had a chance to see the sights.Bring extra layers of clothing. The temperature can drop dramatically at any point in the day.

A History of the Summit

Ancient Hawaiians did not inhabit the summit, but they came up the mountain and built heiau (temples) at some of the cinder cones. The primary goddess of Haleakalā, Lilinoe (also known as the mist goddess), was worshipped here. Today, Native Hawaiians still connect spiritually on the summit, and also come to study star navigation.

✕ Take a Break

After the sunrise and a bit of exploring, grab a bite at Kula Bistro (p221).

ⓘ Need to Know

The park now requires advance reservations for sunrise viewing, plus a $1 fee.

VALENTIN PROKOPETS/GETTY IMAGES ©

Haleakalā Summit Area

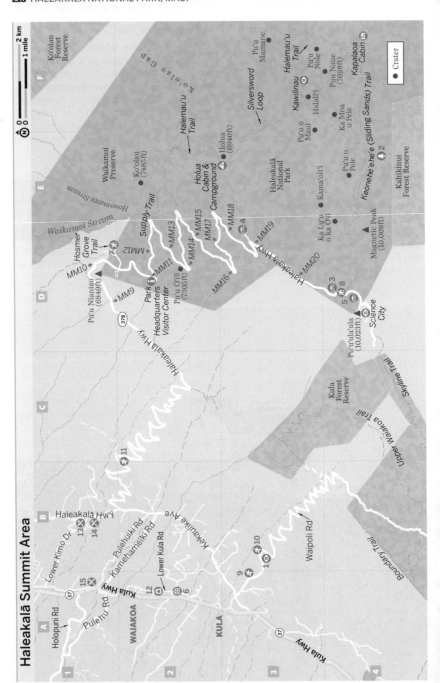

Haleakalā Summit Area

Kula

◎ SIGHTS

Puʻuʻulaʻula
(Red Hill) Overlook   Viewpoint
(www.nps.gov/hale; Summit, Haleakalā Hwy;
P) You may find yourself standing above
the clouds while exploring Puʻuʻulaʻula
(10,023ft), Maui's highest point. The summit building provides a top-of-the-world
panorama from its wraparound windows.
On a clear day you can see Hawaiʻi (Big
Island), Lanaʻi, Molokaʻi and even Oʻahu.
When the light's right, the colors of the
crater are nothing short of spectacular,
with grays, greens, reds and browns. An
ʻahinahina garden has been planted at the
overlook, making this the best place to
see these luminous silver-leafed plants in
various stages of growth.

Kalahaku Overlook   Viewpoint
(www.nps.gov/hale; Haleakalā Hwy; P) Don't
miss this one. Kalahaku Overlook (9324ft),
0.8 miles beyond Leleiwi Overlook, offers
a bird's-eye view of the crater floor and
the ant-size hikers on the trails snaking
around the cinder cones below. At the
observation deck, plaques provide information on each of the volcanic formations
that punctuate the crater floor. From the
deck you'll also get a perfect angle for
viewing both the Koʻolau Gap and the
Kaupo Gap on the rim of Haleakalā. This
overlook is only accessible on the way
down the mountain.

Aliʻi Kula Lavender   Gardens
(☏808-878-3004; www.aklmaui.com; 1100
Waipoli Rd; $3; ☺9am-4pm) On a broad
hillside with panoramic views of the West
Maui Mountains and the Central Maui
coast, this charming lavender farm is a
scenic place to relax and is ideal for families. Follow fragrant pathways, visit a gift
shop with lavender products, and enjoy a
scone and a cup of lavender tea or coffee
(surprisingly good) on a lanai (porch) with
sweeping views.

Worcester Glassworks   Gallery
(☏808-878-4000; www.worcesterglassworks.
com; 4626 Lower Kula Rd; ☺noon-5pm Mon-Sat)
This family-run studio and gallery has
produced some amazing pieces over the
years, particularly the sand-blasted glass
in natural forms (eg seashells). Visitors
can peruse the gallery, but at the time of
research artists were taking a break from
their solar-powered furnaces for a while.
The adjacent store offers gorgeous pieces
for sale. Call ahead to confirm it's open.

🏃 ACTIVITIES

Oʻo Farm   Food & Drink
(☏808-667-4341; www.oofarm.com; 651 Waipoli
Rd; tours $74; ☺farm tour 10:30am-1.30pm Mon-
Fri, coffee tour 8:30-11:30am Mon-Fri) Whether
you're a gardener or a gourmet, you're going
to love a tour of this Upcountry farm, which
supplies Pacifico restaurant and the Feast at
Lele. Where else can you help harvest your

 Nene Watch

The native nene, Hawaii's state bird, is a long-lost cousin of the Canada goose. By the 1950s hunting, habitat loss and predators had reduced its population to just 30. Thanks to captive breeding and release programs, it has been brought back from the verge of extinction and Haleakalā National Park's nene population is now 250 to 300.

Nene nest in shrubs and grassy areas from altitudes of 6000ft to 8000ft, surrounded by rugged lava flows with sparse vegetation. Their feet have gradually adapted by losing most of their webbing.

The birds are extremely friendly and love to hang out where people do, anywhere from cabins on the crater floor to the Park Headquarters Visitor Center. Their curiosity and fearlessness have contributed to their undoing. Nene don't fare well in an asphalt habitat and many have been run over by cars. Others have been tamed by too much human contact, so – no matter how much they beg for your peanut-butter sandwich – don't feed the nene. It only interferes with their successful return to the wild.

The nonprofit Friends of Haleakalā National Park runs an Adopt-a-Nene program (www.fhnp.org/nene.html). For $30 you get adoption papers, information about your nene, a certificate and a postcard. The money funds the protection of the nene habitat.

meal, give the goodies to a gourmet chef and feast on the bounty? On the seed-to-cup coffee tours, you'll learn about coffee cultivation. All tours by reservation only.

Proflyght Paragliding   Paragliding
(808-874-5433; www.paraglidemaui.com; 1598 Waipoli Rd; paraglide 1000ft $145, 3000ft $265; ⊘office 7am-7pm, flights 2hr after sunrise) Strap into a tandem paraglider with a certified instructor and take a running leap off the cliffs beneath Polipoli Spring State Recreation Area. This is thrilling stuff. Participants must be at least eight years old and under 230lb.

Skyline Eco-Adventures   Adventure Sports
(☑808-518-4189; www.zipline.com; 18303 Haleakalā Hwy; zipline tour adult/child under 18yr from $110/70; ⊘8:30am-2pm) Maui's first zipline has a prime location on the slopes of Haleakalā. The five lines are relatively short (100ft to 850ft) compared with the competition, although a unique 'pendulum zip' adds some spice. The highest jump is around 80ft and you'll zip from zero to 45mph in seconds. Good for newbies.

⊙ TOURS

A number of tour-bus companies operate half-day and full-day sightseeing tours on Maui, covering the national park and other island destinations.

Roberts Hawaii   Tours
(☑800-831-5541; www.robertshawaii.com; Hana tours adult/child 4-11yr $179/104) In operation for more than 75 years, Roberts Hawaii runs tours to Hana, the 'Iao Valley and Lahaina, and Haleakalā National Park.

Polynesian Adventure Tours   Tours
(☑888-206-4531; www.polyad.com; tours adult/child 3-11yr from $145/97) Part of Gray Line Hawaii, Polynesian is one of the major tour companies. It offers tours to Haleakalā National Park (sunrise tours from $159) and the Road to Hana (from $160.90), plus combined tours of Maui, *ahaina* and the 'Iao Valley and Haleakalā National Park (from $145).

EATING

Kula Sandalwoods
Cafe & Cottages
Breakfast $

(📞808-878-3523; www.kulasandalwoods.com; 15427 Haleakalā Hwy; meals from $9.75; ⏰8am-3pm Mon-Sat, to noon Sun; 📶) This retro diner offers a hearty breakfast – eggs Benedict, omelets, hotcakes, and French toast – and is located on the doorstep of Haleakalā National Park. There are also six rustic cottages, offering sweeping views at a good price ($190 to $200 for one to two guests).

Kula Lodge
Restaurant
Hawaiian $$$

(📞808-878-1535; www.kulalodge.com; 15200 Haleakalā Hwy; mains breakfast $13-27, lunch $16-24, dinner $27-43; ⏰7am-9pm) Assisted by its staggering view, one of the best Maui restaurants, veteran chef Marc McDowell has the kitchen humming to a farm-to-table variety menu. Outside, brick ovens provide build-your-own pizzas served under cabanas (11am to 8pm). The spectacular sunset here is the perfect ending to a day on the Haleakalā summit.

Kula Bistro
Italian $$$

(📞808-871-2960; www.kulabistro.com; 4566 Lower Kula Rd; pizza from $16, mains $35-48; ⏰7:30am-10:30am & 11am-8pm Tue-Sun, 11am-8pm Mon) This superb family-owned bistro offers a friendly retro dining room, sparkling service and delicious home cooking, including fabulous pizza and uber-fresh seafood dishes. Order a huge serving of coconut-cream pie (enough for two) to finish.

BYOB wine from **Morihara Store** (📞808-878-2502; ⏰6:30am-8pm Mon-Sat, 7:30am-8pm Sun) across the street. No corkage fee.

La Provence
Cafe $$$

(📞808-878-1313; 3158 Lower Kula Rd, Waiakoa; mains $22-35; ⏰9am-1.45pm Wed-Sun) One of Kula's best-kept secrets, this little courtyard restaurant in the middle of nowhere is a lovely spot for lunch (try the crepes). Mains include poulet cordon bleu, filet mignon with prawns, and rack of lamb with green-peppercorn sauce. Cash only.

🛈 INFORMATION

No food or beverages are sold in either section of the park. Pick up picnic supplies on the way or grab a meal before you visit. Stock up in Kula or another town in the Upcountry.

The first visitor center on the way to the crater, the **Haleakalā Park Headquarters Visitor Center** (📞808-572-4459; www.nps.gov/hale; ⏰8am-4pm) has lots of useful trail information, maps, restrooms and drinking water.

🛈 GETTING THERE & AROUND

SUMMIT AREA

Getting to Haleakalā is half the fun. Snaking up the mountain, it's sometimes hard to tell if you're in an airplane or a car – all of Maui opens up below you, with sugarcane and pineapple fields creating a patchwork of green on the valley floor. The highway ribbons back and forth, and in some places as many as four or five switchbacks are in view all at once.

Haleakalā Hwy (Hwy 378) twists and turns for 11 miles from Hwy 377 near Kula up to the park entrance, then another 10 miles to the Haleakalā summit. It's a good paved road, but it's steep and winding. You don't want to rush, especially when it's dark or foggy. Watch out for cattle wandering freely across the road. The drive to the summit takes about 1½ hours from Pa'ia or Kahului, two hours from Kihei and a bit longer from Lahaina. If you need gas, fill up the night before, as there are no services on Haleakalā Hwy.

On your way back downhill, be sure to put your car in low gear to avoid burning out your brakes. There's no public bus service to the park.

KIPAHULU AREA

The Kipahulu Area is on Hwy 31, 10 scenic miles south of Hana. There's no direct road access from here to the rest of Haleakalā National Park; the summit must be visited separately. There's no public bus service to the park. Don't feel like driving? Check for guided day tours.

You'll need a car to explore in depth.

WAIPIʻO VALLEY, BIG ISLAND

Waipi'o Valley at a Glance...

Looking like an enormous scoop that was scalloped from the emerald coastline, Waipi'o Valley is a spectacular natural amphitheatre. Waipi'o ('curving water') is one of seven valleys carved into the windward side of the Kohala Mountains; at the other end is the Polulu Valley in North Kohala. The valley goes back 6 miles, its flat floor an emerald patchwork of jungle, huts, and taro patches. Hidden (and inaccessible without crossing private property) is Hi'ilawe, a distant ribbon of white cascading 1450ft, making it the state's longest waterfall. The water flows into a river that ends at Waipi'o's black-sand beach, a rugged beauty surrounded by dramatic running cliffs.

Waipi'o Valley in One Day

Eat breakfast at **Gramma's Kitchen** (p230) then check out the view of the valley from the Waipi'o Valley Lookout. Spend the day walking the steep path to the beach or, for deeper appreciation, joining a guided tour into the valley. After your hike, eat a plate lunch followed by dessert at **Tex Drive-In** (p230).

Waipi'o Valley in Two Days

On the second day, tour a boutique farm – vanilla, tea or coffee are on offer. Dig into pasta at **Cafe il Mondo** (p231) then see what's playing at **Honoka'a People's Theatre** (p231).

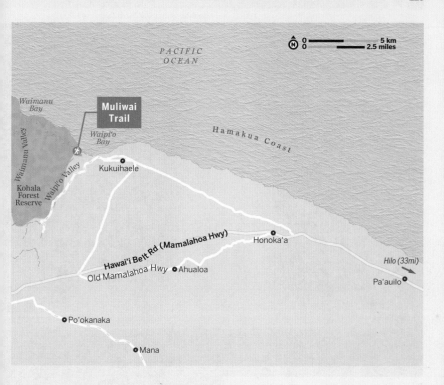

PACIFIC
OCEAN

5 km
2.5 miles

Waimanu
Bay

Waimanu Valley

**Muliwai
Trail**

Waipi'o
Bay

Hamakua Coast

Kohala
Forest
Reserve

Waipi'o Valley

Kukuihaele

Hawai'i Belt Rd (Mamalahoa Hwy)

Honoka'a

Old Mamalahoa Hwy • Ahualoa

Hilo (33mi)

Pa'auilo

• Po'okanaka

• Mana

Arriving in Waipi'o Valley

From Honoka'a, Hwy 240 runs just under 10 miles to the Waipi'o Valley Lookout. The turnoff onto Kukuihaele Rd is around the 8-mile marker, and it connects again with Hwy 240 near the lookout. There is no bus service here.

Where to Stay

You'll find memorable options in Kukuihaele, the residential community at the rim of the valley, including clifftop properties with spectacular views. In general, rates reflect the premium location.

If you plan on camping in Waimanu Valley, apply for a permit online through the **Hawaii Department of Land and Natural Resources Online Reservation System** (https://camping.ehawaii.gov/camping/welcome.html).

Rainbow across Waiʻilikahi Falls

LOKUTARA/SHUTTERSTOCK ©

Muliwai Trail

For expert trekkers only, this 8.5-mile backcountry trail goes from Waipiʻo Valley to Waimanu Valley, traversing steep, slippery and potentially treacherous ground. But it is lovely, with little waterfalls and icy pools for swimming.

Great For...

☑ Don't Miss

Waimanu Valley is a mini Waipiʻo, minus the tourists.

Hike Overview

It takes 6½ to eight hours one way and crosses 13 gulches – brutal to ascend and descend. Plan on camping in Waimanu Valley for at least two nights. For safety reasons, do not attempt this hike during or after rains. For detailed hiking information, contact **Na Ala Hele** (https://hawaiitrails. hawaii.gov/trails) in Hilo.

Trailhead & The Z Trail

The Muliwai Trail begins at the base of the cliffs on the far side of the valley. A shaded path at the end of the beach takes you to a dual trailhead: head right and up for Muliwai (straight ahead leads to the King's Trail, which local authorities discourage due to the existence of burial sites and private property). The ancient Hawaiian footpath now rises over 1200ft in a mile of

CRISTINA RAMOS HERNANDO/SHUTTERSTOCK ©

ⓘ Need to Know

Waipi'o Valley Reserve Ranger (☏808-775-7190; Waipi'o Valley; ☉7am-3pm)

✗ Take a Break

After your hike, head back to Honoka'a to refuel at Gramma's Kitchen (p230).

★ Top Tip

Park your car at the signposted 24-hour parking area.

hard laboring back and forth up the cliff face; it's nicknamed 'Z-Trail' for the killer switchbacks. Hunters still use this trail to track feral pigs. The hike is exposed and hot, so cover this stretch early.

The Hike

The trail moves into ironwood and Norfolk pine forest, and tops a little knoll before gently descending and becoming muddy and mosquito-ridden. The view of the ocean gives way to the sounds of a rushing stream. The trail crosses a gulch and ascends past a sign for Emergency Helipad No 1. For the next few hours the trail finds a steady rhythm of gulch crossings and forest ascents. A waterfall at the third gulch is a source of fresh water; treat it before drinking.

For a landmark, look for Emergency Helipad No 2 at about the halfway point

from Waipi'o Beach. Beyond that, there's an open-sided emergency shelter with pit toilets and Emergency Helipad No 3.

Rest at Helipad No 3 before making the final difficult descent. Leaving the shelter, hop across three more gulches and pass Emergency Helipad No 4, from where it's less than a mile to Waimanu Valley. This final section of switchbacks starts out innocently enough, with some artificial and natural stone steps, but over a descent of 1200ft the trail is poorly maintained and hazardous later. A glimpse of Wai'ilikahi Falls (accessible by a 45-minute stroll) on the far side of the valley might inspire hikers to press onward, but beware: the trail is narrow and washed out in parts, with sheer drop-offs into the ocean and no handholds apart from mossy rocks and spiny plants. If the descent is questionable, head back to the trail shelter for the night.

Waimanu Valley is...well, this is as good as God's green Earth gets. There was once a sizable settlement here, and the valley contains many ruins, including house and heiau (temple) terraces, stone enclosures and old *lo'i* (taro patches). In the early 19th century an estimated 200 people lived here, but the valley was abandoned by its remaining three families after the 1946 tsunami. Today you'll bask alone amid a stunning deep valley framed by cliffs, waterfalls and a boulder-strewn beach.

From the bottom of the switchbacks, Waimanu Beach is 10 minutes past the camping regulations signboard. To ford the stream to reach the campsites on its western side, avoid the rope strung across the water, which is deep there. Instead, cross closer to the ocean entry where it is shallower.

Camping requires a state permit from the **Division of Forestry and Wildlife** (http://dlnr.hawaii.gov/dofaw) for a maximum of six nights.

There are nine campsites: recommended are No 2 (full valley views, proximity to stream, grassy spots), No 6 (view of Wai'ilikahi Falls, access to the only sandy beach) and No 9 (very private at the far end of the valley, lava-rock chairs and a table). Facilities include fire pits and composting outhouses. There's a spring about 10 minutes behind campsite No 9, with a PVC pipe carrying water from a waterfall; all water must be treated.

Return Hike

On the return trip, be careful to take the correct trail. Walking inland from Waimanu Beach, don't veer left on a false trail-of-use

that attempts to climb a rocky stream bed. Instead keep heading straight inland past the camping regulations sign to the trail to the switchbacks. It takes about two hours to get to the trail shelter, and another two to reach the waterfall gulch: refill your water here (again, treat before drinking). Exiting the ironwood forest soon after, the trail descends back to the floor of Waipi'o Valley.

Trail Safety

- Streams in the valley are subject to flash floods during heavy rains. Don't cross waters above knee level.

- Don't drink unboiled or untreated water; leptospirosis is present.

- Beware of wasps and centipedes.

- Bring a signal device for emergencies, as sightseeing helicopters regularly pass the area.

❶ Waipi'o Valley Hike

To reach the valley floor and Waipi'o Beach, you must walk or drive (only with 4WD) the incredibly steep road from the lookout. Walking is recommended for those with the leg power to hike down and uphill. If not, join a guided tour that transports you into the valley. Driving is risky: the road is not only steep but narrow and winding; at the bottom, the muddy, puddle-strewn unpaved road is a quagmire during rain.

If the parking lot near the Reserve Ranger station is full, park along the road leading there. Lock your car.

GSHORIN/SHUTTERSTOCK ©

Honoka'a

SIGHTS

Honoka'a's slow-paced main street belies the town's former importance as the third-largest town in the Hawaiian Islands, after Honolulu and Hilo. Once a major hub for the dominant cattle and sugar industries, it was forced to reinvent itself when those industries crashed. By the time Honoka'a Sugar Company processed its last harvest in 1993, the town had dwindled in size and was struggling to find new economic niches. Eventually, new farmers found success with niche edibles, such as the Hamakua mushrooms now prized by gourmet chefs.

Today Honoka'a town remains a lively, if tiny, hub, as the only actual town along the Hamakua Coast. It serves the rural residents and farmers of Pa'auilo and Ahualoa, as well as tourists on their way to Waipi'o Valley, 10 miles west. The town's retro buildings have a jaunty western vibe, which bursts into full glory during Honoka'a Western Week.

ACTIVITIES & TOURS

Although nearby Waipi'o Valley is better known for activities, the back roads in Pa'auilo and Ahualoa make for terrific cycling. If hesitant to explore on your own, book a tour. **Big Island Bike Tours** (☑808-769-1308; http://bigislandbiketours.com; 65-1480 Kawaihae Rd; tours from $159), based in Waimea, offers a couple of group rides in the Honoka'a area.

If you're interested in food, local agriculture or nature and the outdoors, visit one of the small, family-run farms in pastoral Pa'auilo or Ahualoa, on the *mauka* (inland) side of the highway. They are working farms so you absolutely must book visits in advance.

Long Ears Coffee   Farm

(☑808-775-0385; www.longearscoffee.com; 46-3689 Waipahi Pl; tour $35) ✎ Try unique three- to 10-year-old 'aged' Hamakua coffee at this family farm. Wendell and Irmanetta Branco process their own and other Hamakua farms' beans, creating a sustainable agricultural economy for farmers. On tour you'll see the entire process: growing trees, harvesting cherries, pulping, drying, husking and roasting. Directions to the farm are given upon booking a tour.

Hawaiian Vanilla Company   Food

(☑808-776-1771; www.hawaiianvanilla.com; 43-2007 Paauilo Mauka Rd, Pa'auilo; tour $25, afternoon tea $48, lunch per adult/child $55/27.50; ⊙tour 1pm Mon-Fri, afternoon tea 3pm Sat (seasonal), lunch 12:30pm Mon-Fri, shop 10am-3pm Mon-Fri) ✎ The first commercial vanilla operation in the US, this family-run farm is an agritourism success story. The foodie tours (lunch or the seasonal afternoon tea – check website for schedule) are pricey crowd-pleasers, but the farm tour is too superficial to warrant the fee.

EATING

Gramma's Kitchen   American $

(www.facebook.com/grammaskitchenhonokaa; 45-3625 Mamane St; breakfast $9-13, mains $8-17; ⊙8am-3pm) The restaurant's storefront sign states 'Very homestyle cooking.' And it's true. Gramma's is your ticket for local, often Portuguese-influenced dishes, such as hearty *vinho d'alho* pork *loco* bowls, grilled *ono* (white-fleshed wahoo) with sweet onions and a slow-roasted pot roast with Hamakua mushrooms. Specials include spicy *poke* and bison burgers. Expect a casual diner setting, cheerful staff and small-town aloha.

Tex Drive-In   Bakery $

(www.texdriveinhawaii.com; 45-690 Pakalana St; malasadas $1.35-2.50, mains $6-14; ⊙6am-7pm Sun-Wed, to 8pm Thu-Sat) A malasada is a Madeiran-style Portuguese doughnut, but Tex is famous for serving them hot and fresh. They come plain or filled; either way, folks drive across the island to devour them. Tex also serves decent plate lunches and *loco moco* (a dish of rice, fried egg and hamburger patty or other main dish topped with gravy) along with other fast food.

Go elsewhere for health food; come here for local color. Adjacent to the drive-in, the Tex store (9am to 5pm) sells a variety of locally made gifts, from toiletries to T-shirts.

Cafe il Mondo   Italian $$
(☎808-775-7711; 45-3580 Mamane St; calzones $14, pizzas $13-22.25; ⊗11am-2pm & 5-8pm Mon-Sat) Honoka'a's fanciest restaurant is this longtime Italian spot, specializing in thin-crust pizzas, pastas and enormous calzones packed to bursting point. With a grand stone-tiled patio, gleaming wood furnishings, sleek bar and live music, the vibe is romantic. But the crowd is refreshingly informal, convivial and diverse.

✪ ENTERTAINMENT

Honoka'a People's
Theatre   Theater
(☎808-775-0000; www.honokaapeople.com; 45-3574 Mamane St; movie tickets adult/child/senior $6/3/4; ⊗typical showtimes 5pm & 7pm Tue-Sun) There's something wonderful about watching a movie in a huge, old-fashioned theater – like this one, with a 50ft screen and over 500 seats. Built in 1930, this theater still shows movies and hosts special events. For a bargain movie and a way to immerse yourself with locals, you can't go wrong coming here. Check the website and call to confirm show times.

🛍 SHOPPING

Hamakua Harvest
Farmers Market   Market
(www.hamakuaharvest.org; cnr Hwys 19 & 240; ⊗9am-2pm Sun) Featuring 16 or so vendors, live music and talks, this market is worth

 Waipi'o Valley Lookout

Located at the end of Hwy 240, this lookout offers a jaw-dropping view of Waipi'o's emerald amphitheater, black-sand beach and pounding surf. Feast your eyes on one of Hawaii's iconic images.

PNG STUDIO PHOTOGRAPHY/SHUTTERSTOCK ©

checking out. Everything is locally grown or made, including produce, honey, goat cheese, coconut-milk gelato, smoked fish and much more. To get here, turn *makai* (seaward) off Hwy 19 at the eastern end of Mamane St.

ℹ GETTING THERE & AROUND

From Hwy 19, there are several turnoffs toward Honoka'a town, including Plumeria St on the western end and Mamane St on the eastern end. A handy landmark is Tex Drive-In; the road just east of the drive-in leads into town. The drive from Hilo should take around an hour.

There are several **Hele-On Bus** (☎808-961-8744; www.heleonbus.org; per trip adult/senior & student $2/1, 10-ride ticket $15, monthly pass $60) per day from Honoka'a to Hilo. Check the website for details. In and around town, you'll definitely need a car.

MAUNA KEA,
BIG ISLAND

In this chapter

Mauna Kea

Mauna Kea (White Mountain) is called Mauna O Wakea by Hawaiian cultural practitioners. While all of the Big Island is considered the first-born child of Wakea (Sky Father) and Papahanaumoku (Earth Mother), Mauna Kea has always been the sacred piko (navel) connecting the land to the heavens.

For the scientific world, it all began in 1968 when the University of Hawai'i (UH) began observing the universe from the mountain. The summit is so high and pollution-free that it allows investigation of the furthest reaches of the observable universe. The summit is home to 13 observatories

Mauna Kea in Two Days

Start in Kailua-Kona, where the sunshine will switch your body clock to local time. Spend two days enjoying ocean sports, such as bodyboarding at **Magic Sands Beach** (p246), snorkeling at Kahalu'u Beach, diving or deep-sea fishing. Between dips, ground yourself in island history at **Hulihe'e Palace** (p246), where Hawaiian royalty vacationed.

Mauna Kea in Three Days

On day three begin with brunch and an ocean view at **Island Lava Java** (p250) in Kona, then spend an afternoon ascending Mauna Kea, where you'll witness an unforgettable sunset and then enjoy amazing stargazing.

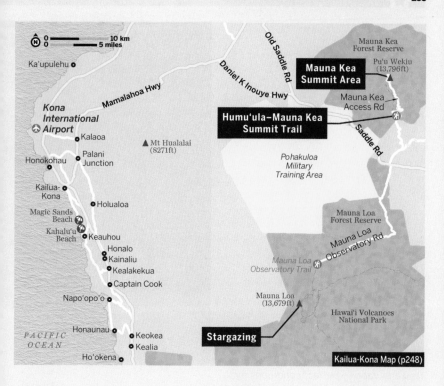

Stargazing

Kailua-Kona Map (p248)

Arriving in Mauna Kea

From Waimea or Kona take Saddle Rd (Hwy 200) or the Daniel K Inouye reroute. From Hilo, drive *mauka* (inland) on Kaumana Dr (Hwy 200) or Puainako Extension (Hwy 2000), both of which become Saddle Road. Start with a full tank of gas – there are no service stations out here.

Sleeping

The closest accommodations, besides the cabins at Gilbert Kahele Recreation Area on Saddle Road, are in Waimea and Hilo.

Mauna Kea Summit Area

At 13,796ft in the air, you are above 40% of the atmosphere and 90% of its water vapor – perfect conditions for the giant mushroom-like observatories that dot the summit.

Great For...

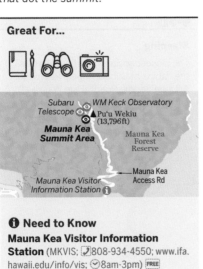

ℹ Need to Know

Mauna Kea Visitor Information Station (MKVIS; ☏808-934-4550; www.ifa. hawaii.edu/info/vis; ⊘8am-3pm) FREE

☑ **Don't Miss**

Off the visitor center parking lot is an enclosed area where rare and endangered silversword plants grow.

Mauna Kea Visitor Information Station

The modestly sized MKVIS packs a punch with astronomy and space-exploration videos, and posters galore, as well as information about the mountain's history, ecology and geology. Budding scientists of all ages revel in the gift shop, while knowledgeable staff help you pass the time acclimatizing to the 9200ft altitude.

Check the website for upcoming special events, such as lectures about science and Hawaiian culture, typically held on Saturday nights.

Normally, excellent free stargazing programs happen from 6pm until 10pm nightly, weather permitting (though this was indefinitely suspended at time of writing).

Inside the gift shop you can buy hot chocolate, coffee, packets of instant noodles and freeze-dried astronaut food to munch on; hoodies, hats and gloves to stay warm; and books about science and Hawaiian culture.

Sunset View from the Summit

Across from MKVIS, a 15-minute uphill hike crests Pu'u Kalepeamoa (9394ft), a cinder cone offering glorious sunset views.

Subaru Telescope

When it came online in 1999, Japan's 26.9ft Subaru Telescope was the most expensive observatory ever constructed. The 22-ton mirror is one of the largest optical mirrors in existence. The telescope helped create a

Astronomical telescopes, Mauna Kea

3D map of 3000 galaxies in 2016 that shows Einstein's theory of relativity still holds true.

Observatory tours (which, sadly, don't include looking through the telescope) are given in Japanese or English but not both; they fill up fast so register online early. Children under 16 years old are not allowed on tours and there are no public restrooms.

Incidentally, Subaru is the Japanese word for the Pleiades (Seven Sisters) constellation.

WM Keck Observatory

Mirrors larger than 26.2ft are so heavy that gravity distorts them as they move. In 1933 William M Keck's breakthrough design overcame that limitation by using a series of 36 hexagonal mirror segments mounted and independently adjusted that function as a single piece of glass 32.8ft in diameter. The results were so good, they built Keck II next door in 1996.

Visitors are welcome into the gallery, which has brief displays, public restrooms and views inside the Keck I dome.

Thirty Meter Telescope (Planned)

Walk behind the Keck Twins and look northwest and you'll see...nothing. But this is the ideal location for the Thirty Meter Telescope (TMT), which supersizes Keck's many-small-mirrors design to create the world's most advanced and powerful optical telescope, an estimated $1,.4 billion endeavor.

When complete, the 492 individually mounted mirrors will peer into the deepest mysteries of the universe.

We say when, not if, because the TMT will be built, just maybe not atop Mauna Kea if a vocal group of protesters have their way. In 2019, Mauna Kea Access Road and the summit were closed for six months due to protests, only to reopen under the terms of a temporary truce – check ahead for the ever-evolving situation on the ground.

★ Top Tip

Visit this sacred area with respect, and pack out your trash.

MARTIN M303/SHUTTERSTOCK ©

✕ Take a Break

After sunset drive down to Kona Brewing Company (p250) for a beer and fish tacos.

Hiking in Mauna Kea

Tackling Mauna Kea (13,803ft) and Mauna Loa (13,678ft), is Big Island bucket-list stuff. The Mauna Loa Observatory Trail and Humu'ula, The Mauna Kea Summit Trail, beckon fleet-footed summit seekers.

Great For...

☑ Don't Miss

Lake Wai'au, the sacred *piko* (navel) of the Hawaiian Islands, a 10-minute detour from Humu'ula.

Mauna Loa Observatory Trail

The easiest way to stand on the top of Mauna Loa is via this 6.4-mile (one way) trail, but easiest doesn't mean 'easy.' The 2500ft climb starts from Mauna Loa Observatory. It's a steep, exhausting adventure, but also an exceptional one.

The trail is marked by *ahu* (stone cairns; be very careful as they easily disappear in the fog), and you'll trek nearly 4 miles to the trail junction with the **Mauna Loa Trail** (end of Mauna Loa Rd). From the junction, day hikers have two choices: proceed another 2.6 miles (about three hours) along the Summit Trail to the peak at 13,677ft, or explore the caldera by following the 2.1-mile Mauna Loa Cabin Trail.

Mauna Kea
Forest
Reserve

Pu'u Wekiu
▲(13,796ft)

Mauna Kea Ice
Age Natural
Area Reserve

Mauna Kea
Access Rd

*Humu'ula–Mauna Kea
Summit Trail* 🄧

Mauna Kea Visitor
ℹ Information Station

❶ Need to Know

Overnighting at Mauna Loa Cabin requires a permit; register at the **Visitor Information Station** (MKVIS; ☏808-934-4550; www.ifa.hawaii.edu/info/vis; ⊗8am-3pm) **FREE** for Humu'ula.

✕ Take a Break

Toast post-hike with brews at Hawaii's top craft brewery, Waimea's **Big Island Brewhaus & Taqueria** (☏808-887-1717; www.bigislandbrewhaus.com; 64-1066 Mamalahoa Hwy; mains $7.50-16; ⊗11am-8:30pm Mon-Sat, noon-8pm Sun; ℗) ✿.

★ Top Tip

Start either hike very early (by 6am). Give yourself time for the unexpected.

Humu'ula–Mauna Kea Summit Trail

This strenuous, 6 mile (one way) trail begins at the Mauna Kea Visitor Information Station (start early and be prepared for serious weather – snow and 100mph winds are possible). Reflective T-posts and cairns mark the route as the trail crosses the 10,000ft vegetation zone, most of the way passing through the Mauna Kea Ice Age Natural Area Reserve as well as Millimeter Valley, nicknamed for its submillimeter and millimeter observatories. The trail officially ends at the access road's Mile 7, but the true summit is another 1.5 miles away.

If you really need to place a boot toe on **Pu'u Wekiu**, Mauna Kea's true summit, soldier on till you reach the UH 2.2m Telescope, where the short spur trail to the summit begins.

Pu'u Huluhulu Trail

This easy 0.6-mile trail (junction of Saddle & Mauna Kea Rds) up the cinder cone **Pu'u Huluhulu** (Shaggy Hill; 6758ft) makes a piquant appetizer, and an acclimatization opportunity, before going up Mauna Kea. Inside a *kipuka* (oasis), the 20-minute hike climbs through protected native forest to the hilltop, from where there are panoramic views of Mauna Kea, Mauna Loa and Hualalai on clear days. Leave gates closed.

Respectful Hiking in Hawai'i

For Native Hawaiians, Mauna Kea is a sacred mountain, which some believe has already suffered enough disrespect from development. Leave no trash behind, be wary of burial and other hallowed sites, and be respectful.

Stargazing

Studying the stars atop Mauna Loa is unique and profoundly memorable. On an average night you might move from the Ring Nebula to the Andromeda Galaxy to a galactic cluster to Jupiter's moons.

Great For...

☑ Don't Miss

At sunset, look east to see 'the shadow' – the gigantic silhouette of Mauna Kea looking over Hilo.

ℹ Need to Know

The public may drive to the summit in the daytime, but you must descend 30 minutes after sunset.

MKVIS Stargazing Program

The Mauna Kea Visitor Information Station offers a terrific nightly stargazing program, though it was indefinitely suspended in late 2018 originally due to a renovation project (but ongoing protests have delayed further).

The program normally begins at 6pm with the film *First Light,* a documentary about Mauna Kea as both a cultural and an astronomical entity. How much you'll see through the telescopes depends on cloud cover and moon phase; call ahead if you want to double check. Weekends are busiest nights, there are no reservations, and lines can get long. Special scope attachments accommodate visitors in wheelchairs.

During big meteor showers, the station staffs its telescopes for all-night star parties. On many weekends it hosts special guests and lecturers.

Stargazing Planner

Here are some tips from the experts about the best times – celestially speaking – to visit Mauna Kea.

o Lunar eclipses and meteor showers are special events in this rarefied air; the Leonides in November are particularly impressive. Check StarDate (http://stardate.org/nightsky/meteors) for meteor showers, eclipses, moon phases and more.

o The Milky Way streaks the night sky bright and white between January and March.

o Don't forget the monthly full moon. It's simply spectacular as it rises over you, seemingly close enough to touch (though it pretty much kills the stargazing).

Canada-France-Hawaii telescope

To Buy a Summit Tour or Not

Tours have many positives: transportation from other parts of the island to the visitor station, 4WD to the summit, warm clothing, a box dinner, excellent guides with deep knowledge of astronomy, and the ease of it all. The negatives to consider include the considerable cost (around $225 per individual), a fixed and limited schedule, and the herd factor.

Itinerary-wise, a typical sunset tour starts in the early afternoon, stops for dinner, arrives at the summit just before sunset, stays for about 40 minutes (this is not long enough to allow for hiking), descends to the visitor station area for private stargazing with a single telescope, and gets you home after 9pm. There is no tour of summit telescopes.

Now assess the DIY alternative. If you have the proper vehicle (or know someone who does) you can do some hiking on your own, poke into the Keck observatory, and experience a sacred mountain at your own pace. Finally, you can come back down to the visitor station for a smorgasbord of stargazing amid multiple telescopes. You'll have to pack your dinner and bring warm clothing, but the total cost is zero, apart from the car, which you may have rented anyway.

✖ Take a Break

After a chilly evening, warm up with *pho* (noodle soup) at Ba-Le Kona (p250).

★ Top Tip

There are no restaurants, gas stations or emergency services on Mauna Kea or along Saddle Rd.

The Milky Way

Kailua-Kona

⊙ SIGHTS

Magic Sands Beach   Beach

(La'aloa Beach Park; Ali'i Dr; ☉ sunrise-sunset;
P 🛁) About 4 miles south of central Kailua-
Kona, this small beach (also called White
Sands and, officially, La'aloa Beach) has
turquoise water, great sunsets, little shade
and possibly the best bodysurfing and
bodyboarding on the Big Island. A fair
warning to novice wave riders: the waves
here are usually powerful – often in a fun
way, but sometimes enough to smash
you to pieces (the north side of the bay
has more rocks). Magic Sands is almost
always packed.

During high winter surf the beach can
vanish literally overnight, earning the nickname 'Magic Sands.' When the rocks and
coral located past the disappearing sands
are exposed, the beach becomes too
treacherous for most swimmers. Gradually
the sand returns, transforming the shore
back into its former beachy self. Facilities
include restrooms, showers, picnic tables
and a volleyball court; a lifeguard is on
duty.

Hulihe'e Palace   Historic Building

(☑808-329-1877; http://hawaiistateparks.org/
parks/hawaii/hulihe'e-palace; 75-5718 Ali'i Dr;
adult/child $10/1; ☉9am-4pm Mon-Sat, 10am-
3pm Sun) ✎ This palace is a fascinating
study in the rapid shift the Hawaiian royal
family made from Polynesian god-kings to
Westernized monarchs. Here's the skinny:
Hawai'i's second governor, 'John Adams'
Kuakini, built a simple two-story, lava-rock
house as his private residence in 1838.
After Kuakini's death, the house became
the favorite vacation getaway for Hawaiian
royalty. The palace contains Western
antiques collected on royal jaunts to
Europe and ancient Hawaiian artifacts,
most notably several of Kamehameha the
Great's war spears.

Hard times befell the monarchy in the
early 20th century, and the house was
sold and the furnishings and artifacts auc-
tioned off by Prince Kuhio. Luckily his wife

Ahu'ena Heiau

STEVE BOWER/SHUTTERSTOCK ©

and other royalty numbered each piece and recorded the names of bidders.

In 1925 the Territory of Hawaii purchased the house to be a museum run by the Daughters of Hawai'i, a women's group dedicated to the preservation of Hawaiian culture and language. This group tracked down the furnishings and royal memorabilia, such as a table inlaid with 25 kinds of native woods, several of Kamehameha the Great's war spears and the (surprisingly small) bed of 6ft, 440lb Princess Ke'elikolani.

You'll learn these and other stories on 40-minute guided tours ($2 extra charged on adult tickets only) given by Daughters of Hawai'i docents. The free concert series, held at 4pm on the third Sunday of each month, is a treat, with Hawaiian music and hula performed on the grass facing sparkling Kailua Bay.

Ahu'ena Heiau   Temple

(http://ahuenaheiau.org; 75-5660 Palani Rd; 👫)
After uniting the Hawaiian Islands in 1810, Kamehameha the Great established the kingdom's royal court in Lahaina on Maui, but he continued to return to the Big Island.

After a couple of years, he restored this sacred site as his personal retreat and temple (which now sits adjacent to a hotel). Notice the towering carved *ki'i* (deity) image with a golden plover atop its helmet: these long-distance flying birds may have helped guide the first Polynesians to Hawaii.

When Kamehameha I died at Ahu'ena Heiau on May 8, 1819, his body was prepared for burial here. In keeping with ancient Hawaiian tradition, the king's bones were secreted elsewhere, hidden so securely no one has ever found them (though some theorists point to a cave near Kaloko Fishpond).

✪ ACTIVITIES

Many activity outfitters and tour companies are based either here or in Keauhou, about 5 miles south of Kailua-Kona.

Kailua Bay
Charter Company   Cruise

(📞808-324-1749; www.konaglassbottomboat.
com; 75-5660 Palani Rd, Kailua Pier; 50min tour adult/child under 12yr $50/25; ⏰11am & 12:30pm; 👫) Gain a new perspective on Kailua-Kona's coastline, underwater reef and sea life from a 36ft glass-bottomed boat with a cheery crew and onboard naturalist. Easy boarding is available for passengers with mobility issues. Times vary; check the website or call ahead.

Paradise Sailing   Boating

(📞808-883-0399; www.paradisesailinghawaii.
com; 74-380 Kealakehe Pkwy, Slip J24, Honoko-hau Marina; sunset cruise adult/child $99/69)
The beauty of the Big Island can be hard to appreciate when you're screaming past it with an outboard motor ringing in your ears, and as such, Paradise Sailing offers a nice alternative: true wind-powered sailing aboard a 36ft catamaran, with a small number of passengers as your companions. Guests are given the chance to operate the boat themselves.

SUP at Kona
Boys Beach Shack   Water Sports

(Kona Boys; 📞808-329-2345; www.konaboys.
com; Kamakahonu Beach; surfboard/SUP rental from $29, SUP lesson & tours per person group/private $99/150; ⏰8am-5pm) The Kona Boys Beach Shack organizes SUP lessons as well as more ambitious coastal paddling tours, and rents SUP sets and surfboards right on Kamakahonu Beach – which, sheltered as it is, is perfect for learning SUP basics. Call in advance to arrange group or private surfing or SUP lessons. You can also book through the shop in **Kealakekua** (📞808-328-1234; 79-7539 Mamalahoa Hwy; single/double kayak per day $54/74, tours $139-189; ⏰7:30am-5pm).

HYPR Nalu Hawaii   Surfing

(📞808-960-4667; www.hyprnalu.com; 75-5663A Palani Rd; semi-private/private surfing lessons $125/175) While this is primarily a surf and SUP gear shop, the folks at HYPR Nalu also offer solid surfing lessons. Rather than throwing you right onto the water, they're

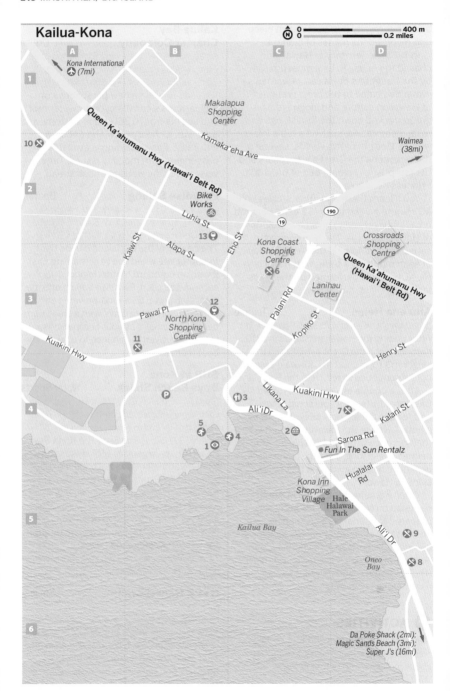

Kailua-Kona

Kailua-Kona

big on prior preparation, making a point of observing your technique in store, while giving feedback that incorporates the physics and philosophy of surfing.

Kona Coast by Air   Scenic Flights
(☏808-646-0231; www.konacoastbyair.com; 73-200 Kupipi St, Airport; 45-/75-min flight $230/330; ⊘6:30am-11am & 5-6:30pm) You can see the Big Island while hiking, and you can see it underwater, but what about seeing it from the sky? That's the promise of Kona Coast by Air, which leads powered hang glider trips through the clouds. You get to operate the flying tricycle (yup, that's what you're piloting), which is pretty damn exhilarating.

Kona Brewing Company   Brewery
(☏808-334-2739; http://konabrewingco.com; 74-5612 Pawai Pl; tours $15; ⊘30min tours 10am, noon, 3pm & 4pm) ✐ Since 1994, this eco-conscious company has anchored Hawai'i's microbrewery scene. The once-small, family-run operation is now one of the nation's fastest-growing microbreweries – from Maine to California, you can sip 'liquid aloha,' which circulates throughout 4000 kegs in Hawaii alone. Tours include tasting samples; note that kids under 15 are not allowed to tag along.

⊙ TOURS

Mauna Kea Summit Adventures   Tours
(☏808-322-2366; www.maunakea.com; tours per person $225.60) The granddaddy of Mauna Kea tours has been taking folks to the summit for over 30 years. A hot dinner outside MKVIS (p236), cold-weather parkas to borrow, and stargazing through an 11-in Celestron telescope are included. Pick-ups from Kailua-Kona, Waikoloa, and Hwys 190/200 junction. Children must be at least 13 years old.

⊗ EATING

Da Poke Shack   Seafood $
(☏808-329-7653; http://dapokeshack.com; 76-6246 Ali'i Dr, Castle Kona Bali Kai; mains & meals $5-12; ⊘10am-5pm;) Poke is a local specialty that blends ceviche and sushi: raw, marinated cubes of fish mixed with soy sauce, sesame oil, chilies, seaweed and... well, really, the sky's the limit. The point is, poke is wonderful, and Da Poke Shack is the spot to get it. You'll be eating at a picnic table or, better, bring it to the beach.

Super J's   Hawaiian $
(Ka'aloa's Super J's; ☏808-328-9566; www.facebook.com/SuperJsLaulau; 83-5409 Mamalahoa Hwy; plates $8-12; ⊘10am-6:30pm Mon-Sat;) The full name is 'Ka'aloa's Super J's Hawaiian Food,' but everyone calls it Super J's. They also call it freakin' delicious. The laulau (pork, chicken or fish wrapped inside taro and ti leaves) is steamed until it's so tender it melts under your fork, the lomi-lomi salmon is perfectly salty – you'll even want second helpings of poi (mashed taro).

Best of all is the setting: you're basically eating in a welcoming Hawaiian family's kitchen. It's on the makai (seaward) side of Hwy 11, between Miles 106 and 107.

Ba-Le Kona   Vietnamese $

(📞808-327-1212; 74-5588 Palani Rd, Kona Coast Shopping Center; mains $5-12; ⏰10am-9pm Mon-Sat, 11am-7pm Sun; 🅿) Don't let the fluorescent-lit dining room and polystyrene plates fool you: Ba-Le serves the sort of Vietnamese food that makes you want to pack it all up and move to Hanoi. Flavors are simple, refreshing and bright, from the green-papaya salad to traditional *pho* (noodle soup), and rice plates of spicy lemongrass chicken, tofu, beef or roast pork.

Ultimate Burger   Burgers $

(📞808-329-2326; www.ultimateburger.net; 74-5450 Makala Blvd; burgers $6-15; ⏰10:30am-9pm) 🍃 Kailua-Kona is likely your introduction to the Big Island; with this in mind, let Ultimate Burger be your introduction to the wonderful world of Big Island beef. There's a big focus on organic ingredients and local sourcing, and we commend such efforts, but also: these burgers are *delicious*. Wash them down with some homemade lemonade.

Big Island Grill   Hawaiian $

(📞808-326-1153; http://bigislandgrill. restaurantwebexpert.com; 75-5702 Kuakini Hwy; mains $10-20; ⏰7am-9pm Mon-Sat, 7am-noon Sun; 🅿👪) The grill serves gut-busting portions of Hawaiian soul food like plate lunches and *loco moco* (rice, fried egg and hamburger patty topped with thick gravy). Choose from fried chicken katsu (deep-fried fillets), fried mahimahi, shrimp tempura and more. All meals come with two scoops of rice, potato-mac salad and rich gravy.

Island Lava Java   Cafe $$

(📞808-327-2161; www.islandlavajava.com; 75-5801 Ali'i Drive, Coconut Grove Marketplace; breakfast & lunch mains $11-30; ⏰6:30am-9pm; 🛜🅿👪) S A convivial gathering spot for Sunday brunch or a sunny breakfast (served until 11:30am) with ocean-view dining on the sidewalk patio. This upscale diner is a little too fancy to be a greasy spoon; maybe it's a greasy complete cutlery set. Anyways, there are huge portions, Big Island–raised meats and fish, farm-fresh produce and 100% Kona coffee.

Umekes Fishmarket Bar & Grill   Hawaii Regional $$

(📞808-238-0571; www.umekesrestaurants. com; 74-5563 Kaiwi St; mains $12-20; ⏰11am-9pm Mon-Sat, to 8pm Sun; 🅿👪) Come here for several variations on delicious ahi tuna *poke*, plus a range of other island dishes, like salted Waimea beef served plate-lunch style with excellent, innovative sides such as seasoned seaweed and cucumber kimchi (along with heaping scoops of rice). The menu is huge; if in doubt, opt for the *poke*, which is prepared to a high level.

Foster's Kitchen   American $$

(📞808-326-1600; www.fosterskitchen.com; 75-5805 Ali'i Dr; mains $16-34; ⏰11am-11pm; 🅿👪) 🍃 In the midst of the booziest, cheesiest stretch of Ali'i Dr, Foster's comes out with farm-to-table New American dishes – roast chicken, fresh salads, spring lamb – served with craft cocktails and a laid-back if semi-sophisticated vibe. It's a little incongruous, and a nice break from flash-fried pub grub. There's also a kid's menu.

Sushi Shiono   Japanese $$$

(📞808-326-1696; www.sushishiono.com; 75-5799 Ali'i Dr, Ali'i Sunset Plaza; à la carte dishes $4-18, lunch plates $10-19, dinner mains $20-40; ⏰11:30am-2pm Mon-Fri, 5:30-9pm Mon-Thu, 5:30-10pm Fri & Sat, 5-9pm Sun) Inside a mini mall, wickedly fresh sushi and sashimi are complemented by a sake list that's as long as Honshu. Everything is good, but the grilled eel and special boats are standouts. The place is owned by a Japanese expat, who employs an all-star, all-Japanese cast of sushi chefs behind the bar. Dinner reservations are recommended.

🌀 DRINKING & NIGHTLIFE

Kailua-Kona's bar scene is pretty touristy, but there are a handful of places for a cocktail or a beer. Always a good fallback, **Kona Brewing Company** (📞808-334-2739; www.konabrewingco.com; 74-5612 Pawai Pl; mains $14-28; ⏰11am-10pm; 👪) 🍃 usually has live Hawaiian music from 5pm to 8pm on Sundays.

Kona Brewing Company

Ola Brew Co   Brewery
(808-339-3599; www.olabrewco.com; 74-5598
Luhia St; ⊙11am-10pm Mon-Thu, to midnight Fri
& Sat, to 9pm Sun) Ola boasts brews that are
made with local ingredients (the porter
is flavored with Kailua-Kona vanilla), or
are just good on a hot Hawai'i day (try the
citrus-y Luhia Pale Ale), a business model
that relies on community investors, and a
fresh seating area that's hugely popular
with the local after work crowd. Visit, and
enjoy. The brewery serves Hawaiian pub
food and frequently plays host to live
music, which is all a bonus.

❶ GETTING THERE & AWAY
A car is almost a necessity on Hawaii, but for
those who are not renting one upon arrival at
the airport, taxis are available curbside (book
late-night pickups in advance). Taxi fares
average $25 to Kailua-Kona or $35 to Keauhou,
plus tip. You can also use ride-sharing apps like
Lyft and Uber.

Speedi Shuttle (877-242-5777; www.speedi
shuttle.com; airport transfer to Kailua-Kona
shared $33, private $100-199; ⊙9am-last flight)

is economical if you're in a group. Book in
advance, and beware, they've been known to run
on island time.

❶ GETTING AROUND
Kailua-Kona is a bike-friendly town. You can find
kiosks for the local **bike share** (https://hawaiiis
landbikeshare.org; per half hour $3.50, per 5hrs
$20) program at six different locations, including
Kahalu'u Beach Park, Huggo's On the Rock's, and
the Courtyard King Kamehameha's Kona Beach
Hotel. The kiosks accept credit cards.

Bike Works (☑808-326-2453; www.bikeworks
kona.com; 74-5583 Luhia St, Hale Hana Center;
bicycle rental per day $25-65; ⊙9am-6pm Mon-
Sat, 10am-4pm Sun) rents high-quality mountain
and road-touring bikes.

You can also try **Kona Sports Center** (☑808-
731-6335; https://konasportscenter.com; 74-
5035 Queen Ka'ahumanu Hwy; rental per day
$30-70; ⊙9am-6pm Mon-Sat, 10am-4pm Sun).
Mopeds are a great option, too.

Get yourself set up with the folks at **Fun In
the Sun Rentalz** (☑808-990-2605; www.fun
inthesunrentalz.com; 75-5729 Ali'i Dr; per day/
three days/week $50/110/210; ⊙8am-5pm).

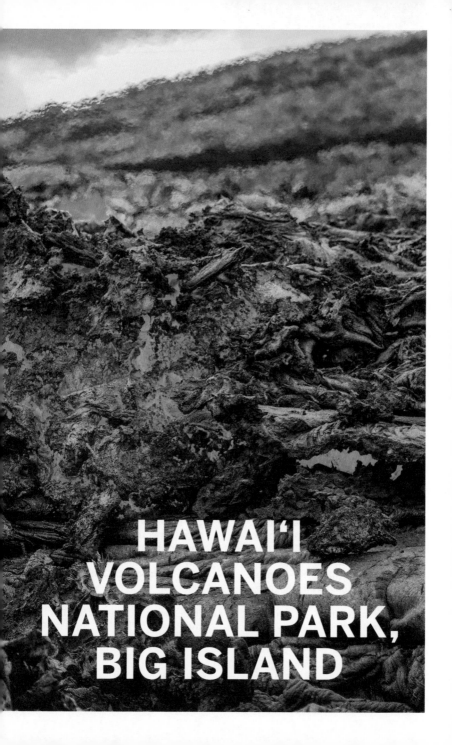

HAWAI'I
VOLCANOES
NATIONAL PARK,
BIG ISLAND

Hawai'i Volcanoes National Park at a Glance...

From the often-snowy summit of Mauna Loa, the world's most massive volcano, to the boiling coast where lava pours into the sea, Hawai'i Volcanoes National Park is a micro-continent of thriving rainforests, volcano-induced deserts, high-mountain meadows, coastal plains and plenty of geological marvels in between.

At the heart of it all is Kilauea – the earth's youngest and most active shield volcano. Between 1983 and 2018, Kilauea's East Rift Zone was erupting almost nonstop from the Halema'uma'u crater and Pu'u 'O'o vent, adding over 1000 acres of new land to the island, but Pele, the Hawaiian goddess of volcanoes, has given the island a respite. For now, anyway!

Hawai'i Volcanoes National Park in One Day

Get up to speed at **Kilauea Visitor Center & Museum** (p257), then take in the sights around the Kilauea Caldera on **Crater Rim Dr** (p264) and Chain of Craters Road (p267). Hike across a crater on the **Kilauea Iki Trail** (p257). Eat and spend the night in Volcano. Don't miss the crater view from **Rim Restaurant** (p259).

Hawai'i Volcanoes National Park in Two Days

Start day two with two easy day hikes, **Pu'u Loa Petroglyphs** (p262) and **Footprints Trail** (p262). Attend a ranger talk or two then check out the art in the **Volcano Arts Center** (p266). Eat dinner with a fantastic view of the crater as a backdrop at the **Rim Restaurant** (p259) and then attend **After Dark in the Park** (p257).

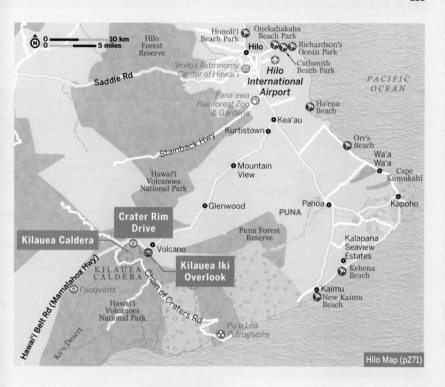

PACIFIC
OCEAN

Hilo Map (p271)

Arriving in Hawai'i Volcanoes National Park

The park is 30 miles (45 minutes) from Hilo and 95 miles (2¾ hours) from Kailua-Kona via Hwy 11. The turnoffs for Volcano Village are a couple of miles east of the main park entrance.

Sleeping

The park's two vehicle-accessible campgrounds are relatively uncrowded outside of summer months. Nights can be crisp, cool, and wet. Campsites are first-come, first-served (with a seven-night limit). Nearby Volcano Village has the most variety for those who prefer a roof over their heads.

Kilauea Iki Overlook & Trail

On Crater Rim Drive, this overlook perches beside a still-steaming 1-mile crater. The Kilaueu Iki Trail far below is as astonishing as it looks.

Great For...

☑ **Don't Miss**

A stroll through the nearby Thurston Lava Tube (p267) when it (hopefully) reopens in 2020.

Kilauea Visitor Center & Museum

Stop here first. Extraordinarily helpful (and extremely patient) rangers and volunteers can advise you about volcanic activity, air quality, road closures, hiking-trail conditions, and how best to spend however much time you have. Interactive museum exhibits are small but family friendly, and will teach even science-savvy adults about the park's delicate ecosystem and Hawaiian heritage. All of the rotating movies are excellent. Pick up fun junior-ranger-program activity books for your kids before leaving.

A well-stocked nonprofit bookstore inside the center sells souvenirs, rain ponchos, walking sticks, and flashlights. Wheelchairs are free to borrow. There are also restrooms, a pay phone, and a place to fill up your water bottles.

MARIDAV/SHUTTERSTOCK ©

ⓘ Need to Know

Kilauea Visitor Center & Museum
(☏808-985-6101; www.nps.gov/havo; Crater
Rim Dr; ◷9am-5pm; 🚻) 🅿

✕ Take a Break

Savor the rich Special Curry at **Thai Thai
Bistro and Bar** (☏808-967-7969; www.
lavalodge.com/thai-thai-bistro.html; 19-4084
Old Volcano Rd; mains $14-28; ◷11:30am-9pm
Thu-Tue; 🍴) after your hike.

★ Top Tip

Check the outdoor signboards by the
Kilauea Visitor Center entrance for
upcoming talks and ranger-led hikes.

The Crater

When 'Little Kilauea' burst open in a fiery
inferno in November 1959, it filled the
crater with a roiling lake of molten rock fed
by a 1900ft fountain that lit up the night sky
with 2 million tons of gushing lava per hour
at its peak.

Kilauea Iki erupted for five weeks at the
end of 1959, alternately filling the crater with
several meters of lava that washed against
its walls like ocean waves and then drained
back into the fissure. The lava fountain that
formed the cinder pile above reached 1900ft,
the highest ever recorded in Hawaii. This
awesome sight suddenly turned terrifying
when boulders blocked the passage like your
thumb on a garden hose, sending a jet of lava
shooting across the crater toward crowds of
visitors. The lake took more than 30 years to
completely solidify.

Kilauea Iki Trail

If you can only do one day hike, make it this
one. Do the 4.5-mile loop counterclockwise
through an astounding microcosm of the
park that descends through fairy-tale ohia
forests to a mile-wide, lava lake from the
1959 eruption.

Hit the trail before 8am to beat the
crowds. The faint footpath across the crater
floor is marked by *ahu* (stone cairns) to aid
navigation. Follow them; the crust can be
thin elsewhere.

Art After Dark in the Park

Experts in science, conservation, art, or
history unlock the mysteries of the park in
this award-winning lecture series. In our
experience, they're so fascinating we would
go even if there was more of a nightlife
scene around here.

KEITH TUCKER/ALAMY STOCK PHOTO ©

Kilauea Caldera

Once home to an astonishing fury-filled crater courtesy of former pit crater Halema'uma'u, Kilaueas fire stopped (for now!) in 2018. The now-expanded caldera remains an eye-popping marvel.

History & Geology

The main focal point of the Kilauea Caldera was its crater-within-a-crater, Halema'uma'u. The name means 'house of the 'ama'u fern,' though ancient songs also refer to it as Halemaumau without the okina (glottal stops), or 'house of eternal fire.'

In 1924, the crater floor subsided rapidly, touching off a series of explosive eruptions. Boulders and mud rained for days. When it was over, the crater had doubled in size – to about 300ft deep and 3000ft wide. Lava activity ceased and the crust cooled. But not for long.

Between 1983 and 2018, Halema'uma'u provided a near uninterrupted show of fire and flow, making it the most active area on Kilauea's summit, but Pele had backed off by the end of the unprecedented 2018 eruption. That's when its lava and lava from

Great For...

☑ **Don't Miss**

The vapor-enhanced view from Steaming Bluff on Crater Rim Dr.

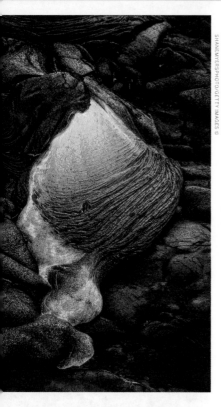

SHANEMYERSPHOTO/GETTY IMAGES ©

❶ Need to Know

808-985-6000; www.nps.gov/havo; 7-day entry per car $25

✕ Take a Break

Enjoy margherita pizza at **'Ohelo Café** (📞808-339-7865; www.ohelocafe.com; 19-4005 Haunani Rd, cnr Old Volcano Rd; lunch mains $13-20, dinner mains $13-37.50; ⏱11:30am-2:30pm & 5:30-9:30pm Wed-Mon) in Volcano after admiring the crater.

★ Top Tip

Best viewing is on a clear night at sunset from **Rim Restaurant** (www.hawaiivolcanohouse.com/dining; Crater Rim Dr, Volcano House; breakfast buffet adult/child $20/12, lunch mains $14-19, dinner mains $20-42; ⏱7-10:30am, 11am-2pm & 5-8:30pm; 🛜).

nearby Pu'u 'O'o suddenly disappeared, only to remerge through 24 fissures in lower Puna, wiping out nearly everything in Kapoho and creating 875 acres of new coastline where Kapoho Bay once stood. When all is said and done, Halema'uma'u crater had collapsed as the Kilauea summit floor sunk some 1500ft and widened by more than one square mile during the eruption.

Halema'uma'u itself increased in size from 0.5-miles wide and 200ft deep to 1.5-miles wide and 2200ft deep – it is now big enough to be considered a caldera (geologists haven't made that call yet) and too big to be considered a pit crater.

What's New: Greenish Pond

In 2019, scientists discovered Halema'uma'u's floor was cradling a greenish pond of water for the first time in recorded history. The pond was about the size of a football field and rising about 6in per day at time of research, though no visitors were to be seen. It is believed to be caused by the crater's collapse below the level of the local water table.

Lake of Fire

On March 19, 2008, Halema'uma'u Crater shattered a quarter-century of silence with a huge steam-driven explosion that scattered rocks and Pele's hair (strands of volcanic glass) over 75 acres. A series of explosions followed, widening a 300ft vent in the crater floor that continued to spew a column of gas and ash across the Ka'u desert until 2018.

Hiking on *pahoehoe* lava flow, Kilauea

Top Day Hikes

Although staring into the Kilauea Caldera, the real magic of Hawai'i Volcanoes National Park can only be found while exploring its 150 miles of trails.

Great For...

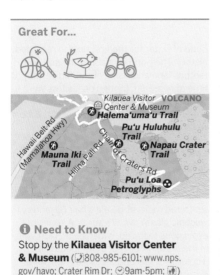

Need to Know

Stop by the **Kilauea Visitor Center & Museum** (☏808-985-6101; www.nps. gov/havo; Crater Rim Dr; ⊙9am-5pm; 👪) 🖋 before you set off to check for road closures.

★ **Top Tip**

Dress for rapidly changing weather: a hot, sunny stroll can turn cold and wet in an instant.

SAMI SARKIS/GETTY IMAGES ©

Mauna Iki Trail

For solitude in a mesmerizing lava landscape, head 2 miles across the Ka'u Desert to the barren summit of Mauna Iki (3032ft). Take in sprawling Mauna Loa and steaming Kilauea, while the vast Ka'u Desert appears to melt into the ocean. The trail's north end is sometimes referred to as **Footprints Trail**.

It's 7 miles further to Hilina Pali Rd, past craggy cinder cones, fissures, and chasms.

Take note of sulfur dioxide levels as you'll be smack in the fallout zone.

Pu'u Loa Petroglyphs

The gentle, 1.3-mile round-trip to Pu'u Loa (roughly, 'hill of long life') leads to ancient petroglyphs, some over 800 years old. Here Hawaiians chiseled more than 23,000 drawings into *pahoehoe* (smooth-flowing lava)

with adz tools quarried from Keanakako'i. Stay on the boardwalk – you might damage petroglyphs if you walk over the rocks. The trailhead parking is signed between Miles 16 and 17 on Chain of Craters Road.

There are abstract designs, animal and human figures, as well as dimpled depressions (or cupules) that were receptacles for *piko* (navel strings). Placing a baby's *piko* inside a cupule and covering it with stones bestowed health and longevity on the child. Archaeologists believe a dot with a circle around it was for a first born, while two circles were for the first born of an *ali'i* (chief).

Napau Crater Trail

This 7-mile (one way) undulating hike over rugged terrain begins with the excellent Mauna Ulu Eruption Trail before continuing across acres of *pahoehoe* to the edge of the

Pu'u Loa petroglyphs

mile-long Makaopuhi Crater. There it heads into the muddy fern forest past the Old Pulu Factory to the edge of Napau Crater with steaming Pu'u 'O'o on the horizon – an added 2-mile extension now allows for hiking all the way to Pu'u 'O'o's base.

Pu'u Huluhulu Trail

This mellower 3-mile hike starts with a closeup inspection of the multicolored 1969 fissure eruption that destroyed Chain of Craters before the road reached its 10th birthday. The trail ends atop Pu'u Huluhulu (Shaggy Hill) with a view of Mauna Ulu: the ultimate result of that eruption.

It's easy to miss the fissure, the hike's most unique feature. At the self-registration box, don't take off across the *pahoehoe* (smooth-flowing lava), but instead turn right and across the old road for the start of the 0.5-mile loop.

After that, continue toward the *kipuka* (oasis) besieged by *'a'a* (rough, jagged type of lava) and an army of lava trees as tall as you are. Lava trees form when a shell of lava cools around a tree while the rest of the molten rock drains away leaving behind a hollowed rock pillar.

Following Ancient Footprints

In 1782, Kilauea belched a massive cloud of steam, hot sand, suffocating gas, rocks, and ash that swept across the Ka'u Desert on hurricane-force winds. Warriors and civilians were caught in the sticky, wet hell-storm. As they gasped for breath, stumbling to their deaths, their feet left ghostly footprints in the muck. That muck dried, preserving the gory moment for all eternity. Or at least that's how famed geologist Dr Jaggar imagined it.

A short, 0.8-mile walk down the Mauna Iki trail from the Ka'u Desert trailhead on Hwy 11 brings you to a field of footprints preserved in fragile sediment and continually being revealed and reburied by windblown sand.

Drinking Water

Despite being bordered by rainforest, this is a dry area and dehydration comes easily. No drinking water is available, except possibly at primitive campgrounds (where it must be treated before drinking), so pack at least three quarts of water per person per day.

> ✗ **Take a Break**
>
> Pick up a grab-and-go wrap for a delicious picnic at **Eagle's Lighthouse Café** (www.eagleslighthouse.com; 19-4005 Haunani Rd; mains $10.50-14.95; ⊗7am-5pm Mon-Sat; ☞ ✐).

UMAMI LIFE/SHUTTERSTOCK ©

> ℹ **Hike With New Friends**
>
> The nonprofit **Friends of Hawai'i Volcanoes National Park** (☏808-985-7373; www.fhvnp.org; annual membership adult/student/family $30/15/45) leads weekend hikes and and organizes volunteer activities including native forest restoration.

Crater Rim Drive

This incredible 11-mile paved loop road starts at Kilauea Visitor Center and skirts the rim of Kilauea Caldera, passing steam vents and rifts, hiking trailheads and amazing views of the smoking crater.

Great For...

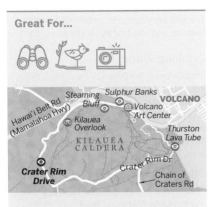

❶ Need to Know

At time of research, the road was closed between Kilauea Military Camp and Jaggar Museum with an estimated 2020 reopening date.

★ Top Tip

Get an early start. The tour buses and crowds start arriving around 10am.

Volcano Arts Center

(www.volcanoartcenter.org; 9am-5pm)
Near the visitor center, this sharp local art gallery spotlights museum-quality pottery, paintings, woodwork, sculpture, jewelry, Hawaiian quilts and more in a series of rotating exhibits. The nonprofit shop, housed in the historic 1877 Volcano House hotel, is worth a visit just to admire its construction.

Ask about upcoming art classes and cultural workshops, including the Aloha Fridays weekly immersive experiences (11am to 1pm Friday).

Sulphur Banks

A wooden boardwalk weaves between misty, rocky vents stained chartreuse, yellow, orange and other psychedelic colors by tons of sulfur-infused steam rising from deep within the earth. Once frequented by rare birds (hence the Hawaiian name, Ha'akulamanu), invasive plants and other changes to the environment have made it less hospitable to nene (native Hawaiian goose) and kolea (Pacific golden plover).

The easy 0.7-mile one-way trail, which is wheelchair accessible, connects to Crater Rim Dr near the parking lot for Steaming Bluff.

About 500 years ago, Kilauea's summit collapsed inward leaving a series of concentric cliffs stepping down towards its center. These sulphur banks are on the outermost ring and formed due to deep cracks along the fault that enable gases to escape the magma pocket below. This potent gas creates the small crystalline structures that give the rocks their hue.

Steaming Bluff

Steam Vents & Steaming Bluff

Creating impressive billowing plumes in the cool early morning, these vents make a convenient drive-up photo op. Hot rocks below the surface boil rainwater as it percolates down, producing the steam. While the vents at the parking area are perfectly fine, even more evocative is Steaming Bluff, found along a short walk out to the rim. Here, curtains of steam frame the cliffs above a post-apocalyptic view.

Kilauea Overlook

A pause-worthy panorama that was closed at time of research with an expected reopening date in 2020. It's most

remarkable for the 6-ton volcanic bomb sitting defiantly on the rim daring you to take eruptions lightly (miraculously, it survived the 80,000 earthquakes of 2018). Frustratingly, there is no view from the covered picnic tables, but there is shelter from wind and rain.

Thurston Lava Tube

On Kilauea's eastern side, Crater Rim Dr passes through a rainforest thick with tree ferns and ohia trees to the overflowing parking lot for ever-popular **Thurston Lava Tube** (Nahuku; off Crater Rim Dr;). A 0.3-mile loop walk starts in an ohia forest filled with birdsong before heading underground through a gigantic (but short) artificially lit lava tube. Unfortunately, at time of research, the tube was closed for ongoing safety assessment studies relating to the 2018 lower Puna eruption with a possible reopening date in 2020.

If open, it's normally a favorite with tour groups, so come early or late to avoid the crowds. Lava tubes form when the outer crust of a lava river hardens while the liquid beneath the surface continues to flow through. When the eruption stops, the flow drains out leaving only that hard shell behind. Nahuku, as this tube is called in Hawaiian, was 'discovered' by controversial figure Lorrin Thurston, the newspaper baron (and patron of famed vulcanogist Dr Jaggar) who was instrumental in overthrowing the Kingdom of Hawai'i.

Chain of Craters Road

This is it: possibly the most scenic road trip on an island packed with really scenic road trips. Heading south from Crater Rim Dr, paved Chain of Craters Road winds almost 19 miles and 3700ft down the southern slopes of Kilauea, ending abruptly at rivers of lava making their way to the coast.

> ✗ **Take a Break**
>
> Enjoy a world-class view with your meal at the spectacularly situated Rim Restaurant (p259).

JANICE WEI/GETTY IMAGES ©

> ★ **Top Tip**
>
> Drive slowly, especially in rainy or foggy conditions, and watch out for wildlife.

Historic Downtown Hilo

Explore Hilo's history on this stroll through the city's charming downtown heart and its numerous early 20th-century architectural standouts, cultural stops and cafes.

Start Mo'oheau Bandstand

Distance 1 mile

Duration 2-3 hours

Take a Break: Stop by **Booch Bar** (p274), a trendy boho coffee/kombucha must.

7 End browsing fascinating plantation days memorabilia at nearby Keawe St's **Local Antiques & Stuff** (p277).

Classic Photo: Federal Building

5 Head west to the dramatic **Federal Building** (1919), built by architect Henry Whitfield. The former courthouse today houses government offices, including the downtown post office branch.

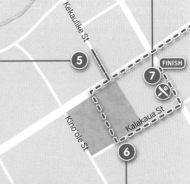

6 One block south, **East Hawai'i Cultural Center/HMOCA** (☏808-961-5711; www.ehcc.org; ⊙noon-6pm Wed-Fri, 10am-4pm Sat; donation $5) was built in 1932 and is National Register of Historic Places-listed.

0 ————— 100 m
0 ————— 0.05 miles

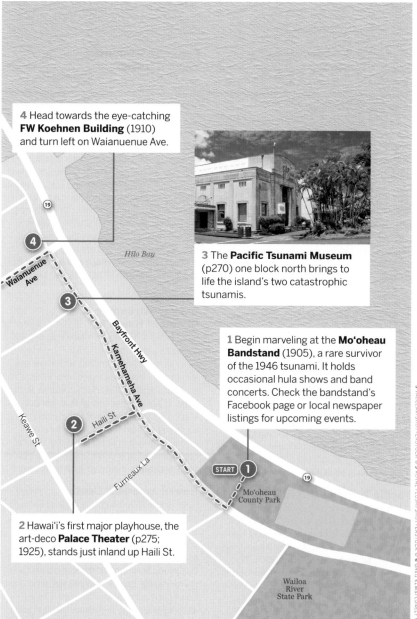

4 Head towards the eye-catching **FW Koehnen Building** (1910) and turn left on Waianuenue Ave.

3 The **Pacific Tsunami Museum** (p270) one block north brings to life the island's two catastrophic tsunamis.

1 Begin marveling at the **Moʻoheau Bandstand** (1905), a rare survivor of the 1946 tsunami. It holds occasional hula shows and band concerts. Check the bandstand's Facebook page or local newspaper listings for upcoming events.

2 Hawaiʻi's first major playhouse, the art-deco **Palace Theater** (p275; 1925), stands just inland up Haili St.

Hilo Bay

Waianuenue Ave

Bayfront Hwy

Kamehameha Ave

Keawe St

Haili St

Furneaux La

START **1**

Moʻoheau County Park

Wailoa River State Park

3 VACLAV/SHUTTERSTOCK © 5 ROYAL FLUSH/SHUTTERSTOCK © 6 GREG ELMS/LONELY PLANET ©

Hilo

Most sights are found in downtown Hilo, where historic early-20th-century buildings overlook the coast, which locals call 'bayfront.' Further east sits Hilo's landmark dock, Suisan Fish Market (p273), and the Keaukaha neighborhood, where most of Hilo's beaches are located.

Beach parking is generally not a problem but, on weekends, expect jammed lots and steady traffic along Kalaniana'ole Ave. Otherwise parking is readily available, whether on the street or not.

◎ SIGHTS

Lili'uokalani Park Park

(189 Lihiwai St; P) Arguably Hilo's most beautiful spot, these sprawling Japanese gardens are perfect for picnicking. Named for Hawaii's last queen (r 1891–93), the 30-acre county park features magnificent trees, grassy lawns, charming footbridges over ornamental ponds, and views of Hilo Bay and Mauna Kea. At sunrise and sunset, join the locals jogging or walking the perimeter.

Bordering the park is Banyan Dr, Hilo's mini 'hotel row,' best known for the giant banyan trees that line the road. Royalty and celebrities planted the trees in the 1930s and, if you look closely, you'll find plaques beneath the trees identifying Babe Ruth, Amelia Earhart and Cecil B DeMille. Also nearby is the paved footbridge to **Mokuola** (Coconut Island;), a tiny island that will captivate kids of all ages.

Pacific Tsunami Museum Museum

(808-935-0926; www.tsunami.org; 130 Kamehameha Ave; adult/child $8/4; 10am-4pm Tue-Sat) You cannot understand Hilo without knowing its history as a two-time tsunami survivor (1946 and 1960). This museum encompasses only a few rooms, but they're brimming with riveting information that reveals island life in the 1900s. Experience the multimedia exhibits, including chilling computer simulations and heart-wrenching first-person accounts. The newest section covers the Japanese tsunami of 2011, which damaged Kona.

Pana'ewa Rainforest Zoo & Gardens Zoo

(808-959-9233; www.hilozoo.org; off Hwy 11; 9am-4pm, petting zoo 1:30-2:30pm Sat; P) FREE Hilo's 12-acre zoo is a terrific, wheelchair-accessible family-friendly spot. Stroll along paved paths past tropical foliage to view a modest collection of tropical birds, monkeys, frogs, alligators, and more. The star attraction? A pair of Bengal tigers: Sriracha (orange female) and Tzatziki (white male). Two play structures and a shaded picnic area (bring your own refreshments) are perfect for kids. While by no means a major zoo, it's refreshingly low-key – and free, though donations are appreciated.

To get here, turn *mauka* (inland) off the Volcano Hwy onto W Mamaki St, just past the 4-mile marker.

'Imiloa Astronomy Center of Hawai'i Museum

(808-969-9700; www.imiloahawaii.org; 600 'Imiloa Pl; adult/child 5-12yr $19/12; 9am-5pm Tue-Sun; P) 'Imiloa', which means 'exploring new knowledge,' is a $28 million museum and planetarium complex with a twist: it juxtaposes modern astronomy on Mauna Kea with ancient Polynesian ocean voyaging. It's an educational, if rather pricey, family attraction and the natural complement to a summit tour. One planetarium show is included with admission.

Hawaii Japanese Center Museum

(808-934-9611; www.hawaiijapanesecenter. com; 751 Kanoelehua Ave; 11am-2pm Wed-Sat; P) FREE Hawaii's Japanese immigrant community is sizable and influential, especially in Hilo. Here, learn more about this group through plantation-era artifacts, memorabilia, books, and photos, all in mint condition and neatly organized. The gift shop sells vintage dishware, textiles, and other gems at reasonable prices.

Hilo

N	200 m
	0.1 miles

Honoli'i Beach Park (2mi)

Hilo Bay

Wainaku St
Wailuku River
Pu'ueo St
Shipman St
Wailuku Dr
Kekaulike St
Waianuenue Ave
Kalakaua St
Kino'ole St
Keawe St
Haili St
Kilauea Ave
Ululani St
Kapi'olani St
Bayfront Hwy
Furneaux La
Mo'oheau Bandstand
Kamehameha Ave
Mamo St
Punahoa St
Kilauea Ave
Ponahawai St

Suisan Fish Market (0.9mi);
Hilo Bay Cafe (0.9mi);
Lili'uokalani Park (1mi);
Basically Books (1.2mi);
Reeds Bay Beach Park (1.5mi);
Hilo International (3mi);
Onekahakaha Beach Park (3.5mi);
Carlsmith Beach Park (4mi);
Richardson's
Ocean Park (5mi)

Mo'oheau
County Park

Wailoa River
State Park

Restaurant Kenichi (0.4mi);
Miyo's (0.4mi);
Big Island Candies (0.4mi);
Sweet Cane Cafe (0.9mi);
Takenoko Sushi (1.5mi);
Hilo Brewing Company (1.8mi);
Hawaii Japanese Center (2.3mi);
Prince Kuhio Plaza (2.8mi)

'Imiloa Astronomy
Center of Hawai'i
(2.3mi)

Hilo

PNG STUDIO PHOTOGRAPHY/SHUTTERSTOCK ©

Japanese gardens, Lili'uokalani Park (p270)

🏊 BEACHES

Richardson's Ocean Park   Beach
(Kalaniana'ole Ave; ⏰7am-7pm; P🚻) Near the end of Kalaniana'ole Ave, this little pocket of black sand is a favorite all-round beach. When calm, the waters are popular for swimming and snorkeling, with frequent sightings of sea turtles (keep your distance; at least 50yd in the water). High surf, while welcome to local bodyboarders, can be hazardous. There are lifeguards every day, plus restrooms, showers, and picnic areas.

Onekahakaha
Beach Park   Beach
(Kalaniana'ole Ave; ⏰7am-9pm; P🚻) Ideal for kids, this spacious beach has a broad, shallow, sandy-bottomed pool, protected by a boulder breakwater. The water is only 1ft to 2ft deep in spots, creating a safe 'baby beach.' An unprotected cove north of the kiddie pool is deeper, but can be dangerous due to rough surf and needle-sharp *wana* (sea urchins). Surrounding grassy lawns shaded by trees make for pleasant picnicking. There are lifeguards on weekends and holidays, plus restrooms, showers, and covered pavilions.

Carlsmith Beach Park   Beach
(Kalaniana'ole Ave; 🚻) Although this beach may look rocky, the swimming area is protected by a reef, creating a safe lagoon. The anchialine ponds, which flow to the ocean, are tailor-made for kids. Snorkeling is good during calm water conditions. Rarely crowded, this beach has lifeguards on weekends and holidays, plus restrooms, showers, and picnic areas.

🤿 ACTIVITIES

While Hilo's beaches feature lava rock amid the sand, the lineup of beaches east of downtown are nevertheless scenic – and nice for swimming and snorkeling.

For stand-up paddle surfing (SUP), launch from **Reeds Bay Beach Park** (251 Banyan Dr; P🚻) or Mokuola (Coconut Island; p270). Diving is best on the Kona side but there are decent shore-diving spots in or near Hilo.

Hawaii Forest & Trail   Hiking

(☑808-331-3657; www.hawaii-forest.com; 224 Kamehameha Ave; all-day tours $200-275, helicopter tour $780; ☺9am-5pm Mon-Fri, to 4pm Sat) Trusted guided-tour company offers island-wide outdoor adventures: hiking, birding, ziplining, waterfall swimming, and more. Most are all-day affairs, but some shorter options are available. Hilo-based tours depart from this downtown location.

Hawaiian Crown Chocolate Farm Tour   Ecotour

(☑808-319-6158; https://hawaiiancrown chocolate.com/farmtours; 160 Kilauea Ave; adult/ child under 10yr $15/5; ☺2-3pm Mon, Wed & Fri) 🍃 Learn how cacao morphs into a smooth, rich chocolate. First meet at the 110-acre-farm with more than 1200 cacao trees growing alongside apple bananas. Then regroup at the factory store in downtown Hilo to savor the finished product. This best-value tour will heighten your appreciation of chocolate.

Nautilus Dive Center   Diving

(☑808-935-6939; www.nautilusdivehilo.com; 382 Kamehameha Ave; intro charter dive $85; ☺9am-5pm Mon-Sat) Hilo's go-to dive shop offers guided dives, PADI certification courses, and general advice on shore diving.

Orchidland Surfboards   Surfing

(☑808-935-1533; www.orchidlandsurf.com; 262 Kamehameha Ave; ☺9am-5pm Mon-Sat, 10am-3pm Sun) Board rentals, surf gear, and advice from owner Stan Lawrence, who opened the Big Island's first surf shop in 1972.

EATING

Two Ladies Kitchen   Sweets $

(☑808-961-4766; 274 Kilauea Ave; 8-piece box $6; ☺10am-5pm Wed-Sat) This hole-in-the-wall is famous statewide for outstanding Japanese *mochi* (sticky rice cake) in both traditional and island-inspired flavors, such as *liliko'i* (passion fruit) and purple sweet potato. They're sold in boxes of six to eight pieces. Study the flavor chart on the wall.

Suisan Fish Market   Seafood $

(☑808-935-9349; www.suisan.com/our-services /fish-market; 93 Lihiwai St; poke bowl $12-14, poke per lb $18-20; ☺8am-5pm Mon-Fri, to 4pm Sat) For a mouth-watering variety of freshly made *poke* (sold by the pound), Suisan is a must. Buy a takeout bowl of *poke* with rice and chow down outside or across the street at Lili'uokalani Park. Could life be any better?

KTA Super Store – Puainako   Supermarket

(☑808-959-9111, pharmacy 808-959-8700; www. ktasuperstores.com; 50 E Puainako St, Puainako Town Center; ☺grocery 5:30am-midnight, pharmacy 8am-7pm Mon-Fri, 9am-7pm Sat) 🍃 KTA's flagship store includes a bakery, pharmacy and sprawling deli. Don't miss the impressive selection of fresh *poke* (arguably the best in Hilo) and takeout bento box meals, which sell out by mid-morning.

In a pinch, stop at the **downtown branch** (☑808-935-3751; www.ktasuperstores.com; 323 Keawe St; ☺7am-9pm Mon-Sat, to 7pm Sun) 🍃, which is less extensive and spiffy, but carries the essentials.

Restaurant Kenichi   Japanese $

(☑808-969-1776; www.restaurantkenichi.com; 684 Kilauea Ave; mains $9-19; ☺10am-2pm & 5-9pm Mon-Sat; 🖐) For island-style Japanese food, this diner delivers high-volume flavor in a simple dining room filled with locals. Favorites include steaming ramen bowls made with house *dashi* (broth), succulent grilled *saba* (mackerel), boneless Korean chicken, and rib-eye steak, rushed to your table, sizzling, and aromatic.

Sweet Cane Cafe   Health Food $

(☑808-934-0002; www.sweetcanecafe.com; 48 Kamana St; mains $12-18, smoothies $7.50-9.50; ☺8am-6pm Mon-Sat, 10am-4pm Sun; 🖐) 🍃 Vegetarians rejoice, everything is fresh, locally sourced, and meat-free at this pleasant cafe. You'll find *'ulu* (breadfruit) and taro serving as the base of burgers and sandwiches – with macadamia nuts adding a dash of local flavor. Raw sugar cane juice is served, by itself and in imaginative smoothies.

Booch Bar
Health Food $

(📞808-498-4779; www.theboochbarhilo.com; 110 Keawe St; mains $13-16; ⊗8am-8pm; 🖉) This colorful downtown cafe takes health food up a notch. Breakfast hits include well-stuffed roasted veggie omelets and buckwheat pancakes, moist with apple bananas. Lunch and dinner mains range from mahimahi (white-fleshed fish) ceviche tacos to hearty quinoa bowls.

The cafe's name refers to its 'Big Island Booch' house-label products: kimchi, kraut and kombucha. Among the kombucha flavors, Super Ginger Tumeric Tonic goes down very smoothly.

Abundant Life Natural Foods
Market

(📞808-935-7411; www.abundantlifenaturalfoods. com; 292 Kamehameha Ave; ⊗8:30am-7pm Mon-Tue & Thu-Fri, 7am-7pm Wed & Sat, 10am-5pm Sun, takeout cafe to 3pm only, closed Sun; 🖉) 🌱 Located downtown, Abundant Life opened in 1977 when only hippies in Hilo ate 'health food.' Like all health-food stores predating Whole Foods, it's compact, but well stocked with essential groceries, takeout deli, natural toiletries and yoga mats.

Paul's Place
Cafe $$

(📞808-280-8646; http://paulsplcafe.wixsite.com/ paulsplacecafe; 132 Punahoa St; mains $15-19; ⊗7am-3pm Tue-Sat; 🖉) Imagine eating at a friend's home, if your friend were a gourmet chef. This six-person eatery is that small and that special. Paul serves exquisite renditions of the classics, including light and crispy Belgian waffles, robust salads and his signature eggs Benedict with smoked salmon, asparagus and a special sauce. Reservations strongly recommended.

Hilo Bay Cafe
Hawaii Regional $$

(📞808-935-4939; www.hilobaycafe.com; 123 Lihiwai St; mains $18-32; ⊗11am-9pm Mon-Thu, to 9:30pm Fri & Sat; 🖉) 🌱 As well as sweeping bay views, you'll find an eclectic omnivorous menu here, including gourmet versions of comfort food, such as Hamakua mushroom pot pie.

The ocean-facing bar serves memorable cocktails ($9.50), including a strawberry-guava mojito and GC&T ('C' = cucumber).

Moon & Turtle
Hawaii Regional $$

(📞808-961-0599; www.facebook.com/moon andturtle; 51 Kalakaua St; tapas $8-22; ⊗5:30-9pm Tue-Sat) 🌱 This tapas-style restaurant specializes in local seafood, meat and produce prepared in startlingly creative ways. The ever-changing menu is brief, but who cares? Each dish is meticulously sourced and prepared. You'll surely remember (and crave) the smoky sashimi, crispy brussels sprouts, and wild boar fried rice.

Miyo's
Japanese $$

(📞808-935-2273; http://miyosrestaurant.com; 681 Manono St; mains $15-18; ⊗11am-2pm & 5:30-8:30pm Mon-Sat; 🖉🚻) Miyo's is known for delicious home-style Japanese meals and nightly crowds. Try classics such as broiled ahi (yellowfin tuna) or *saba* (mackerel), crispy tempura or *tonkatsu* (breaded and fried pork cutlets). Located in a strip mall, the ambiance is so-so, but the food is worth it. Reservations are recommended.

Pineapples
Hawaii Regional $$

(📞808-238-5324; 332 Keawe St; mains $14-24; ⊗11am-10pm Tue-Sun; 🖉) Pineapples' open-air dining room is hopping with a convivial crowd, predominantly tourists. The food features island-inspired preparations, such as coconut-crusted fresh catch, tacos filled with *kalua* pork, and rich pumpkin curry. Go all out and order an umbrella drink!

Takenoko Sushi
Sushi $$$

(📞808-933-3939; 681 Manono St; nigiri $2.50-8, chef's choice $42; ⊗11am-1:30pm & 5-8:30pm Thu-Mon) Chances are, you won't get in. This destination sushi bar only seats eight – and it's fully booked a year in advance. Miracles can happen, however, and you might savor the upper echelon of Japanese cuisine, with premium fish (mostly flown fresh from Japan), expert sushi chef, spotless setting, and gracious service.

DRINKING & NIGHTLIFE

Temple Craft
Beer & Wine Bar   Bar
(www.thetemple.bar; 64 Keawe St; ⊙2pm–
midnight; 🛜) Nearly trendy by Hilo standards, this polished beer and wine bar is the
best bet in the city for craft-focused suds
and spirits. Expect offerings from usual sus-
pects (Hilo Brewing, Kona Brewing, Big Island Brewhaus) but also rarer options from
the mainland (barrel-aged Sierra Nevadas
etc) plus a longer bottle list than most.

Hilo Brewing Company   Brewery
(📞808-934-8211; www.hilobrewingco.com; 275 E
Kawili; ⊙noon-5pm Mon-Sat) This microbrew-
ery has a small tasting room where you
can sample excellent craft beer. Don't miss
Mauna Kea Pale Ale, a best seller, and Southern Cross, a Belgian-style double-brewed
red ale.

Bayfront Kava Bar   Bar
(📞808-345-1698; http://bayfrontkava.com; 277
Keawe St; cup of kava $5; ⊙5-10pm Mon-Sat) If
you're curious about kava ('awa in Hawaiian),

try a cup at this minimalist bar. Friendly staff
serve freshly brewed, locally grown kava root
in coconut shells. Catch live music and art
exhibitions on a regular basis.

ENTERTAINMENT

Palace Theater   Theater
(📞808-934-7010; www.hilopalace.com; 38 Haili
St; ⊙box office 10am-3pm) This historic theater is Hilo's cultural crown jewel. Its eclectic
programming includes art-house and silent
films (accompanied by the house organ),
music and dance concerts, Broadway
musicals, and cultural festivals.

SHOPPING

While locals flock to chain-store-heavy
Prince Kuhio Plaza (📞808-959-3555;
www.princekuhioplaza.com; 111 E Puainako St;
⊙10am-8pm Mon-Thu, to 9pm Fri & Sat, to 6pm
Sun) south of the airport, downtown is far
better for unique finds and fun browsing.
Be careful to distinguish between products
made in Hawaii and cheap imports.

Traditional *poke* dish

BHOFACK2/GETTY IMAGES ©

Big Island Candies
Sweets

(☏808-935-8890, 800-935-5510; www.bigisland candies.com; 585 Hinano St; ⊙8:30am-5pm) Once a mom-and-pop shop, this wildly successful confectioner is now a full-fledged destination. In an immaculate showroom-factory, enjoy generous samples, elaborate displays and beautifully packaged candies and cookies. The signature macadamia-nut shortbread is sure to please. Expect crowds of locals and Japanese tourists.

Basically Books
Books

(☏808-961-0144; www.basicallybooks.com; 1672 Kamehameha Ave; ⊙10am-6pm Mon-Fri, to 5pm Sat, to 3pm Sun) A browser's paradise, this shop carries the gamut of Hawaii-themed books – history, botany, cooking, fiction and memoir, plus the expected maps and travel guides. You'll also find a wide selection of children's books and toys.

The Knickknackery
Antiques

(☏808-747-7159; 72 Kapi'olani St; ⊙10am-6pm Mon-Sat) Keli'i Wilson, the Hilo-born shop-keeper, is a true collector. Among his hand-picked gems, you might find a 1950s koa (Hawaiian timber) dresser, a vintage Singer sewing machine, or an aloha shirt emblazoned with 'STATEHOOD.' Go to browse and learn about antiques from a pro.

Sig Zane Designs
Clothing

(☏808-935-7077; www.sigzane.com; 122 Kamehameha Ave; ⊙10am-5pm Mon-Fri, to 4pm Sat) ✐ *Kama'aina* (locally born and raised) artist Sig Zane designs unmistakable cotton fabrics, marked by rich colors and modern interpretations of Hawaiian flora. Each shirt or dress is not only beautiful, but a lesson on Hawaii's culture and geography. Aloha shirts start at $120, but they're keepers.

Hawaiian Crown Plantation & Chocolate Factory
Chocolate

(☏808-319-6158; www.hawaiiancrown.com; 160 Kilauea Ave; chocolates $6.50-8.50; ⊙8:30am-5:30pm Mon-Sat, 11:30am-4pm Sun) ✐ Hawaiian chocolate is the perfect gift – locally grown, locally made and craved by all. Cacao fans can also buy nibs, either unsweetened or agave sweetened, and learn about this crop from the owner, who's often on site and happy to chat. The shop also serves Big Island coffee and stellar acai bowls.

Pana'ewa Rainforest Zoo & Gardens (p270)

PNG STUDIO PHOTOGRAPHY/SHUTTERSTOCK ©

Still Life Books Books

(☑808-756-2919; stillife@bigisland.com; 235 Waianuenue Ave; ☺11am-3pm Mon-Sat) Bibliophiles and audiophiles shouuldn't miss this hidden trove of hand-picked secondhand books and LPs. The tiny shop doesn't look like much from outside, but contains hard-to-find gems, including the proprietor, a character worth meeting.

**Extreme Exposure
Fine Art Gallery** Photography

(☑808-989-9448; www.extremeexposure.com; 224 Kamehameha Ave; ☺10am-7pm) At this informal gallery, find striking nature photography – featuring Hawai'i's wildlife, seascapes, landscapes and lava – by photographers Bruce Omori and Tom Kuali'i. There's something for all budgets, from framed prints to greeting cards.

Local Antiques & Stuff Antiques

(104 Keawe St; ☺10:30am-4:30pm Tue-Sat) History buffs, don't miss this teeming display of local artifacts and memorabilia. Along with a few valuable furniture items, there's tons of 'stuff:' retro glass bottles, plantation-era housewares, Japanese *kokeshi* dolls, old yearbooks, and more. The mom-and-pop shopkeepers amassed their eclectic collection over many years.

Bryan Booth Antiques Furniture

(☑808-933-2500; www.bryanboothantiques. com; 94 Ponahawai St; ☺10am-5pm Mon-Sat) Transporting a rocking chair or dining table home is probably a deal breaker. But Bryan Booth's expertly restored wood furniture might convince you otherwise. In his spacious showroom, find exquisite pieces from the late 1800s and early 1900s, along with antique lamps, art, and china. Expect prices from about $500 to $5000 plus.

**Most Irresistible
Shop in Hilo** Gifts & Souvenirs

(☑808-935-9644; www.facebook.com/most irresistibleshop; 256 Kamehameha Ave; ☺9am-5pm Mon-Fri, to 4pm Sat, 10:30am-3:30pm Sun) Kids of all ages delight in the little treasures here: jewelry, Japanese dishware, children's games and toys, clothing, home textiles, and random cute stuff. The shop doesn't specialize in locally made goods, but the affordable, thoughtfully picked stock is worth a browse.

Hawaiian Force Clothing

(☑808-934-7171; www.hawaiianforce.com; 184 Kamehameha Ave; ☺10am-5pm Mon-Fri, to 4pm Sat) Craig Neff, a Native Hawaiian artist, sells aloha wear marked by bold graphics and Hawaiian motifs. While somewhat similar to Sig Zane's prints, Neff's style is more free-flowing and rough around the edges. His eye-catching T-shirts touch on local themes.

ℹ INFORMATION

Volcano Visitor Center (19-4084 Old Volcano Rd; ☺7am-7pm) Unstaffed tourist information kiosk with brochures aplenty. Next door is a coin laundromat, ATM and hardware store selling some camping gear.

ℹ GETTING THERE & AWAY

The **Hilo International Airport** (ITO; ☑808-961-9300; www.hawaii.gov/ito; 2450 Kekuanaoa St) is located at the northeastern corner of Hilo, less than three miles from downtown. Almost all flights arriving here are interisland, mostly from Honolulu. Rental car booths and taxis are located right outside the baggage-claim area.

The drive from Hilo to Kailua-Kona (via Waimea) along Hwy 19 is 95 miles and takes about 2½ hours. Driving along Saddle Road can cut travel time by about 15 minutes.

ℹ GETTING AROUND

Free parking is generally available around town. Downtown street parking is free for two hours (or more, since enforcement is slack); finding a spot is easy except when the Wednesday and Saturday farmers markets are on.

Ho'okipa Beach Park (p298)

In Focus

USS *Missouri* (p53), Pearl Harbor

History

One of humanity's greatest epics, the colonization of Hawai'i began almost two thousand years ago, when Polynesian voyagers found these tiny islands in Earth's largest ocean. Western navigators, whalers and missionaries followed much later, while migrants fro across the globe streamed in from the 19th century onwards. The kingdom founded by Kamehameha was overthrown in 1893, enabling US annexation.

30 million BCE
The first Hawaiian island, Kure, rises from the sea. Plants, insects and birds, borne by wind, wing and wave, colonize the new land.

300–600 CE
Polynesian canoe voyagers, most likely from the Marquesas, reach Hawai'i – well before Vikings start plundering Europe.

1000–1300
A second wave of Polynesians arrives from Tahiti, bringing taro, sweet potato, sugarcane, coconut, chickens, pigs and dogs.

Statue of Fr Damien, St Joseph's Church (p163)

Polynesian Voyagers

To ancient Polynesians, the Pacific was a passageway, not a barrier, and its islands were connected, not isolated. Between 300 and 600 CE, they made their way to the Hawaiian Islands, marking the northern limit of their astounding migrations. Whereas that initial discovery may have been accidental, subsequent journeys were not. In double-hulled canoes, the Polynesians crossed thousands of miles of open ocean guided by the sun, stars, wind and waves. Along with their religious beliefs and social structures, they brought more than two dozen food plants and domestic animals. The resources they lacked are equally remarkable: no metals, no wheels, no alphabet or written language, and no clay to make pottery.

Almost nothing is known about Hawai'i's earliest settlers, who probably came from the Marquesas Islands. A second wave, who arrived around 1000 CE from Tahiti, obliterated nearly all traces of their history and culture. Later legends of the *menehune* – little people who built temples and mighty stoneworks overnight – may refer to those first Marquesan inhabitants.

1778–79	1790–1810	1819
Captain Cook visits Hawai'i twice. At first welcomed and honored, he's later killed in a conflict over a stolen boat.	Kamehameha the Great unites the islands into a single Hawaiian kingdom and establishes his royal court in Honolulu, O'ahu.	Kamehameha's son Liholiho and widow Ka'ahumanu flout the *kapu* (taboo) system and end Hawai'i's traditional religion.

★ Hawaiian Temples

Pi'ilanihale Heiau (p176), Maui

Ahu'ena Heiau (p247), the Big Island

Kuan Yin Temple (pictured; p40), O'ahu

Halulu Heiau (p170), Lana'i

Ancient Hawai'i

For unknown reasons, trans-Pacific Polynesian voyages stopped around 1300 CE. Hawaiian culture continued to evolve in isolation. A highly stratified society was ruled by a royal class called *ali'i* whose power derived from their supposed descent from the gods. Clan loyalty trumped individuality, elaborate traditions of gifting and feasting conferred prestige, and shape-shifting gods animated the natural world.

Several ranks of *ali'i* ruled each island, and warfare was frequent as they jockeyed for power. The largest geopolitical division, the *mokupuni* (island), was further divided into *moku* (districts), running from mountaintops to the sea and made up in turn of smaller, similarly wedge-shaped *ahupua'a*.

Ranking just below *ali'i*, *kahuna* (experts or masters) included priests, healers and skilled craftspeople such as canoe makers and navigators. The *maka'ainana* (commoners) did most of the physical labor, while among a small class of outcasts or untouchables called *kaua*, some were forced to serve as *pua'a wawae loloa* – 'long-legged pigs,' a euphemism for human sacrificial victims.

A culture of mutuality and reciprocity infused what was essentially a feudal agricultural society. Chiefs were custodians of their people, and humans custodians of nature, all of which was sacred – the living expression of *mana* (spiritual essence). Rich traditions developed in art, music, dance and competitive sports.

Captain Cook & First Western Contact

When Captain James Cook, after a decade of traversing the Pacific, stumbled upon the Hawaiian chain in 1778, everything changed. Dropping anchor off Kaua'i, Cook bartered for fresh water and food. On the first day ashore, one of his lieutenants shot and killed 'a tall handsome man who seemed to be a chief,' but didn't even mention the incident to his captain. Cook, a representative of the British Empire, saw Hawai'i as populated by heathens. The Hawaiians knew nothing of Europeans, nor of the metal, guns and diseases they carried.

1820	1846	1848
The first Christian missionaries arrive at Kailua-Kona. Leader Hiram Bingham eventually makes his headquarters in Honolulu.	At the peak of the whaling era, 736 ships stop over in Hawai'i. Four of the 'Big Five' companies start out supplying whalers.	King Kamehameha III institutes land reforms that permit commoners and foreigners to own land in Hawai'i.

When Cook returned the following year, he anchored at Kealakekua Bay on the Big Island. A thousand canoes greeted his ships, and Hawaiian chiefs and priests honored him with rituals. Cook had landed at an auspicious moment, during the makahiki festival celebrating the god Lono. The Hawaiians were so gracious that Cook and his men felt safe to move about unarmed.

After Cook set sail some weeks later, storms forced him to turn back. The mood in Kealakekua had changed. With the makahiki over, suspicion replaced welcome. A series of minor conflicts, including the theft of a boat, prompted Cook to lead an armed party to capture local chief Kalani'opu'u. When the Englishmen disembarked, they were surrounded by angry Hawaiians. After Cook shot and killed a Hawaiian man, he was stabbed and killed in the ensuing skirmish.

A Place of Refuge

In ancient Hawai'i, the strict *kapu* (taboo) system governed daily life. For example, it was a violation of *kapu* for a commoner to eat moi – a fish reserved for ali'i (royalty). Penalties for such transgressions could be harsh, including death. Furthermore, in a society based on mutual respect, slights to honor could not be abided.

Ancient Hawai'i was a fiercely uncompromising place, but at times it could be forgiving. Anyone who broke *kapu* or was defeated in battle could avoid death by fleeing to a *pu'uhona* (place of refuge). After a kahuna (priest) had performed purification rituals, lasting from a few hours up to several days, absolved *kapu* breakers could return home in safety.

Kamehameha the Great

After the news of Cook's 'discovery' spread, and especially when Westerners learned of the deepwater anchorage in Honolulu ('sheltered bay'), explorers and traders flocked to the islands. At first, trans-Pacific commerce centered on the fur trade between China, New England and the Pacific Northwest. Hawai'i's principal commodity – salt – proved useful for curing hides, while Hawaiian chiefs wanted to obtain firearms.

Armed with European muskets and cannons, chief Kamehameha from the Big Island set out to conquer all the Hawaiian Islands. With his unyielding determination and personal charisma, he swiftly succeeded. The final skirmish in his five-year campaign, the Battle of Nu'uanu, was fought on O'ahu in 1795. The lone standout, Kaua'i, resisted invasion. but eventually joined the kingdom in 1810.

Kamehameha reigned over the most peaceful era in Hawaiian history. A savvy businessman, he created a profitable monopoly on the sandalwood trade while protecting trees from over-harvesting. He personally worked taro patches as an example to his people, and his most famous decree – Kanawai Mamalahoe, or 'Law of the Splintered Paddle' – established a *kapu* to protect travelers from harm. Most importantly, he absorbed foreign influences while honoring Hawai'i's indigenous customs.

1852	**1873**	**1893**
Indentured plantation laborers arrive from China. After completing their contracts, many stay on to start businesses and families.	Belgian priest Father Damien lands at Moloka'i's leprosy colony. 16 years later, he dies of what's now called Hansen's disease.	A group of US businessmen, backed by troops, overthrow the Hawaiian monarchy. Queen Lili'uokalani acquiesces under protest.

By the time he died in 1819, doubts were growing among Hawaiians as to the justice of the *kapu* system and the notion of a divinely ordained hierarchy. Within the year, Kamehameha's 22-year-old son Liholiho, and widow Queen Ka'ahumanu, had broken with the traditional religion in one sweeping, stunning act of repudiation.

Missionaries & Whalers

By the 1820s, whaling ships were pulling into Hawai'i's harbors for fresh water and food, supplies, and liquor. Shops, taverns and brothels sprang up around busy ports, especially Honolulu on O'ahu and Lahaina on Maui. Within 20 years, the islands were the whaling center of the Pacific.

To the ire of 'dirty-devil' whalers, Hawai'i's first Protestant missionaries sailed into Honolulu on April 14, 1820. Their timing was opportune, just a year after the traditional religion had been abolished. The missionaries expected the worst of Hawai'i's 'pagans,' and interpreted what they saw through the lens of their own prejudice. Regarding public nudity as disgraceful and hula dancing as 'lewd', they characterized kahuna as witch doctors and Hawaiians as hopelessly lazy. Although Christianity attracted Hawaiian converts, notably Queen Ka'ahumanu, few conversions were deeply felt, and many Hawaiians quickly abandoned the church's teachings. Realizing that literacy attracted avid interest, the missionaries formulated an alphabet for the Hawaiian language. Hawaiians learned to read with astonishing speed. In their oral culture, they were used to prodigious feats of memory, and *ali'i* saw literacy as the key to accessing Western culture and power.

The Great Mahele

Some 19th-century Hawaiian leaders decided the only way to survive in a world of conflicting foreign influences was to adopt Western styles of government. Traditionally, no Hawaiian ever owned land, but the *ali'i* held it in stewardship for all. – something that sat poorly with the new breed of US expatriates.

Born and raised in post-contact Hawai'i, King Kamehameha III (Kauikeaouli) promulgated Hawai'i's first constitution in 1840, establishing a constitutional monarchy with limited citizen representation. Given an inch, foreigners pressed for a mile, so Kauikeaouli set about revolutionary land reforms, starting with the Great Mahele ('Great Division') of 1848.

The Great Mahele aimed to create a nation of small freeholder farmers, but proved a disaster – for Hawaiians, at least. Confusion reigned over boundaries and surveys, and many Hawaiians simply failed to claim title to land on which they had lived for generations. Of those who did, many cashed out immediately, selling their land to eager and acquisitive foreigners.

Many missionaries ended up with sizable tracts, and left the church to devote themselves to their new estates. Within 30 to 40 years, foreigners owned three-quarters of the kingdom, and Hawaiians – who had already relinquished so much traditional culture – lost their sacred connection to the land. As historian Gavan Daws put it, 'the great division became the great dispossession.'

1898	1912	1941
President McKinley signs a resolution annexing Hawai'i as a US territory. The 1900 Hawaiian Organic Act forms a territorial government.	Duke Kahanamoku wins Olympic swimming medals, and becomes a worldwide ambassador of Hawaiian surfing.	On December 7, Japanese forces attack Pearl Harbor, sinking the USS *Arizona* and propelling the US into WWII.

King Sugar & The Plantation Era

Ko (sugarcane) came to Hawai'i with the first Polynesian settlers. But it wasn't until 1835 that Bostonian William Hooper saw a business opportunity to establish Hawai'i's first sugar plantation. Persuading Honolulu investors to put up the money, Hooper worked out a deal with Kamehameha III to lease agricultural land at Koloa on Kaua'i. The next priority was to find low-cost labor. The natural first choice was Hawaiians, but even when they were willing, there were not enough Hawaiians to meet the demand for labour. Due to diseases like typhoid, influenza, smallpox and syphilis, the Hawaiian population was in precipitous decline. Perhaps 800,000 indigenous people had lived on the islands before Western contact; by 1800 that had dropped by two-thirds, to around 250,000, and by 1860 fewer than 70,000 Hawaiians remained.

Plantation owners began to look overseas for immigrants accustomed to working long days in hot weather, and for whom even low wages might seem attractive. In the 1850s laborers were recruited from China, then Japan and Portugal – the last, incidentally, imported the miniature stringed instrument that became the ukulele. These different groups, complemented in the 20th century by influxes from Puerto Rico, Korea and the Philippines, created the unique plantation community that transformed Hawai'i into the multicultural, multiethnic society it is today.

As sugar exports to the mainland soared, during the Californian Gold Rush and the US Civil War, plantation owners grew increasingly powerful. Five sugar-related holding companies, known as the Big Five, came to dominate all aspects of the industry: Castle & Cooke, Alexander & Baldwin, C Brewer & Co, American Factors (today Amfac, Inc) and Theo H Davies & Co. All were run by haole (Caucasian) businessmen, many the sons and grandsons of missionaries, who eventually reached the same prejudiced conclusion as their forebears: Hawaiians could not be trusted to govern themselves. Behind closed doors, the Big Five developed plans to relieve Hawaiians of the job.

The Merrie Monarch

Between 1874 and 1891, King David Kalakaua fought to restore Hawaiian culture and pride. He resurrected hula and its attendant arts from near extinction. Along with his fondness for gambling and partying, this earned him the nickname 'the Merrie Monarch.' Foreign businessmen saw his pastimes as follies, and Kalakaua himself as a mercurial decision-maker given to replacing his entire cabinet on a whim.

Kalakaua spent money lavishly, piling up massive debts. Wanting Hawai'i's monarchy to match any in the world, he commissioned Honolulu's 'Iolani Palace, holding an extravagant coronation there in 1883. In 1881, he became the first king to travel around the world, meeting foreign heads of state and developing stronger ties with Japan especially.

Even so the days of the Hawaiian monarchy were numbered. The Reciprocity Treaty of 1875, which had made Hawai'i-grown sugar profitable, had expired. Kalakaua refused to

1946	1959	1961
On April 1, a destructive tsunami kills 159 people across the islands and causes $26 million in damage.	On August 21, Hawai'i becomes the 50th US state. Daniel Inouye becomes the first Japanese-American elected to the US Congress.	Elvis Presley stars in *Blue Hawaii*, the first of three on-screen romps that helped spur Hawaii's post-statehood tourism boom.

renew it, as the treaty now contained a provision giving the US a permanent naval base at Pearl Harbor – a clear threat to Hawaiian sovereignty.

In 1887, the Hawaiian League – a secret anti-monarchy group led by mostly American lawyers and 'concerned businessmen' – presented Kalakaua with a new constitution. Stripping the monarchy of most of its powers and reducing Kalakaua to a figurehead, it changed the voting laws to exclude Asians, and allowed only those who met income and property requirements to vote. Kalakaua signed under threat of violence, earning the document the moniker the 'Bayonet Constitution.' The US got its base at Pearl Harbor, and the foreign businessmen consolidated their power.

Hawai'i's Last Queen

After King Kalakaua died while visiting San Francisco, CA, in 1891, his sister Lili'uokalani ascended the throne. Fighting foreign control, the queen secretly drafted a new constitution to restore Hawaiian voting rights and the monarch's powers. It was never presented. In 1893, a hastily formed 'Committee of Safety' put in motion the Hawaiian League's long-brewing plans to overthrow the government.

First, the Committee of Safety requested support from US Minister John Stevens, who allowed American marines and sailors to come ashore in Honolulu 'to protect American citizens in case of resistance.' The Committee's own militia then surrounded 'Iolani Palace and ordered Lili'uokalani to step down. Lacking an army and seeking to avoid bloodshed, the last Hawaiian monarch acquiesced under protest.

Immediately after the coup, the Committee of Safety formed a provisional government and requested annexation by the US. Much to their surprise, US President Grover Cleveland refused: he condemned the coup as 'not merely wrong but a disgrace,' and requested that Lili'uokalani be reinstated. Miffed but unbowed, the Committee instead established their own government, the short-lived Republic of Hawai'i.

For the next five years, partly under house arrest in 'Iolani Palace, Queen Lili'uokalani pressed her case. To no avail: in 1898, spurred by new US president William McKinley, Congress annexed the republic as a Territory. In part, the US justified this act of imperialism because the ongoing Spanish-American War had demonstrated the islands' importance as a Pacific military base. Some feared that if the US didn't take Hawai'i, another Pacific Rim power – say, Japan – just might.

Pearl Harbor & the 'Japanese Problem'

In the years leading up to WWII, the US government became obsessed with the Territory of Hawai'i's 'Japanese problem.' What, they wondered, were the true loyalties of the *issei*, the 40% of Hawai'i's population who had been born in Japan? In a war, would they fight for Japan or defend the US? The identity of their children, the island-born *nisei* (second-generation Japanese immigrants), was also questioned.

1976	**1983**	**1992**
Hawaiian sovereignty activists occupy Kaho'olawe. The *Hokule'a* – a replica voyaging canoe – sails to Tahiti and back.	Kilauea volcano on the Big Island begins an eruption cycle that lasts until 2018, the longest in recorded history.	On September 11, Hurricane 'Iniki slams into Kaua'i, demolishing almost 1500 buildings and damaging another 5000.

On December 7, 1941, a Japanese force bombed Pearl Harbor and other Oʻahu military installations. This surprise onslaught propelled the US into WWII. In Hawaiʻi, the US Army took control, martial law was declared and civil rights suspended.

A coalition of forces in Hawaiʻi resisted immense federal pressure, including from President franklin D Roosevelt, to carry out a mass internment of Japanese, similar to what was happening on the US West Coast. Although around 1250 people were detained in camps on Oʻahu, most of Hawaiʻi's 160,000 Japanese citizens were spared incarceration – although they did suffer racial discrimination and deep suspicion. Hawaiʻi's multiethnic society emerged from WWII severely strained, but unbroken.

In 1943 the federal government was persuaded to reverse itself and approve the formation of an all-Japanese combat unit, the 100th Infantry Battalion. Thousands of *nisei* volunteers were sent, along with the all-Japanese 442nd Regimental Combat Team, to fight in Europe, where they became two of the most decorated units in US history. By the war's end, Roosevelt hailed these soldiers as proof that 'Americanism is a matter of mind and heart; Americanism is not, and never was, a matter of race or ancestry.' The coming decades were to test this sweeping sentiment.

Statehood

The end of WWII brought Hawaiʻi closer to the center stage of American culture and politics. Three decades had passed since Prince Jonah Kuhio Kalanianaʻole, Hawaiʻi's first delegate to the US Congress, introduced a Hawaiʻi statehood bill in 1919, to a cool reception.

Despite Hawaii's key wartime role, many US politicians saw it as too much of a racial melting pot. During the Cold War, Southern Democrats raised the specter that Hawaiian statehood would leave the US open not just to the 'Yellow Peril,' but also to Chinese and Russian communist infiltration through Hawaiʻi's labor unions. Further, they feared that elected Asian politicians from Hawaii would seek to end racial segregation, then legal on the US mainland. Conversely, proponents of Hawaiian statehood saw it as a necessary step to prove that the US did indeed practice 'equality for all.'

After Alaska beat out Hawaii to be admitted as the 49th US state in the late 1950s, Hawaiʻi finally became the 50th on August 21, 1959, with the support of over 90% of islanders. The name of the new state did not use the okina. A few years later, surveying Hawaii's relative ethnic harmony, PresidentJohn F Kennedy Kennedy pronounced, 'Hawaii is what the rest of the world is striving to become.' In the 1960s, Hawaii's two Asian American senators – WWII veteran and *nisei* Daniel Inouye and Honolulu-born Hiram Fong – helped secure the passage of America's landmark civil rights legislation.

Statehood had an immediate economic impact. Hawaiʻi's timing was remarkably fortuitous. Although the decline of sugar and pineapple plantations in the 1960s – partly the result of labor concessions won by Hawaii's unions – left the islands floundering, the advent of jet airplanes meant tourists could become Hawaii's next staple crop. Tourism

1993	**2000**	**2006**
A century after the monarchy was overthrown, President Bill Clinton signs the 'Apology Resolution,' acknowledging its illegality.	Senator Daniel Akaka introduces the so-called 'Akaka Bill,' for the recognition of Native Hawaiians as indigenous people.	Papahānaumokuākea Marine National Monument is established, to protect the reefs of the Northwestern Hawaiian Islands.

exploded, which led to a decades-long cycle of building booms. By 1970 over one million tourists each year were generating $1 billion annually, surpassing both agriculture and federal military spending.

Hawaiian Renaissance & Sovereignty

By the 1970s Hawaii's rapid growth meant new residents (mostly mainland 'transplants') and tourists were crowding beaches and roads, while runaway construction was transforming resorts like Waikiki almost beyond recognition. The relentless peddling of 'aloha' set islanders wondering: what did it mean to be Hawaiian? Some Native Hawaiians turned to *kapuna* (elders) to recover their heritage and became more politically assertive.

In 1976 a group of activists illegally occupied Kahoʻolawe, aka 'Target Island,' seized by the US government during WWII and used for bombing practice ever since. During another occupation attempt in 1977, two activist members of the Protect Kahoʻolawe ʻOhana (PKO) – George Helm and Kimo Mitchell – disappeared at sea, instantly becoming martyrs. Saving Kahoʻolawe became a rallying cry, radicalizing a nascent Native Hawaiian rights movement that continues today, long after Kahoʻolawe itself returned to Hawaiian state control in 2003.

Hawaii held a landmark Constitutional Convention in 1978, passing several amendments of special importance to Native Hawaiians. One, for example, made Hawaiian the official state language (along with English) and mandated that Hawaiian culture be taught in public schools. At the grassroots level, the islands experienced a revival of Hawaiian culture, with a surge in residents of all ethnicities joining hula *halau* (schools), learning to play Hawaiian music and rediscovering traditional crafts such as feather lei-making.

In 1993, President Clinton signed an official Apology to Native Hawaiians, acknowledging that the US had illegally overthrown the Hawaiian monarchy. The federal government has yet, however, to recognize Native Hawaiians as an indigenous people, and thereby give them equivalent legal status to Native American tribes. For some activists, such a move would help the islands' indigenous people heal from the violence and injustices of the last two centuries. For others, the goal is for Hawaii to become a sovereign independent nation once again, while opponents argue that electing a Native Hawaiian self-governing body would be racially exclusionary.

Forever at the mercy of economic forces far beyond its shores, and overly dependent on tourism, Hawaii has experienced major boom and bust cycles in recent years. The climate crisis too has emphasized the vulnerability of the world's remotest islands, and their interdependence with the rest of the planet. Small wonder that the sense of Hawaiian identity seems to grow ever stronger, or that perceived threats to the islands' spiritual essence, like the proposed construction of the Thirty Meter Telescope on Hawaii's highest peak, arouse such deep local feelings.

2008	2016	2018
Born and raised on Oʻahu, Barack Obama is elected US President, winning more than 70% of the vote in Hawaii.	President Obama accompanies Japanese Prime Minister Shinzo Abe on a historic visit to Pearl Harbor.	Bearing witness to Hawaiian cultural pride, protestors block construction of the proposed Thirty Meter Telescope atop Mauna Kea.

King Kamehameha Day Parade (p23)

G WARD FAHEY/SHUTTERSTOCK ©

People & Culture

Whatever form your romanticized image of Hawaii might take – an idyll of sandy beaches, emerald cliffs and azure seas, peopled by falsetto-voiced ukulele strummers, swaying hula dancers and sun-bronzed surfers – it exists somewhere on the islands. Just out of frame, however, lies a very real place, where a multicultural mix of folk actually make their homes.

Island Style

Polynesian paradise it may be, but Hawaii is one with shopping malls, landfills and industrial parks, cookie-cutter housing developments and sprawling military bases. In many ways, it's much like the rest of the USA. On O'ahu especially, a first-time visitor may be surprised to find a thoroughly modern environment where interstate highways and McDonald's look pretty much the same as back home.

Beneath the tourist glitz and veneer of consumer culture lies a different world, defined by – and proud of – its separation, its geographic isolation and its unique blend of Polynesian, Asian and Western traditions. While those cultures don't always merge seamlessly, there are few places in the world where so many ethnicities, with no single group forming a majority, get along.

Memorial Day, Honolulu

Perhaps it's because they live on tiny specks in a vast ocean that Hawaii residents strive to treat one another with aloha (kindness), act politely and respectfully, and 'make no waves' (ie be cool). As the Hawaiian saying goes, 'We're all in the same canoe.'

In his anthem to life in Hawaii, guitarist John Cruz sang 'On the islands, we do it island style.' He may not explicitly define 'island style,' but he doesn't have to; every local understands. Island style is easygoing, low-key, casual; even guitar strings are more relaxed here. Islanders take pride in being laid-back – everything happens on 'island time,' aloha shirts are preferred over suits and no one minds when a *tutu* (grandmother) holds up a line to chat with the checkout person at Longs Drugs. 'Slow down! This ain't da mainland!' reads one popular bumper sticker.

Even urban Honolulu has something of a small-town vibe. Shave ice, surfing, 'talking story,' ukulele, hula, baby luau, pidgin, 'rubbah slippah' (flip-flops) and particularly '*ohana* (extended family and friends) – these are the touchstones of everyday life. Working overtime is uncommon, and weekends are reserved for playing and potlucks at the beach.

Local vs Mainland Attitudes

That Hawaii often seems overlooked by the 49 other US states has both advantages and disadvantages. While there's a genuine celebration of Hawaii's uniqueness, it reinforces an insider-outsider mentality that can manifest itself as exclusivity or, worse, blatant discrimination.

Mainland transplants tend to stick out, even after they've lived in the islands for some time. For example, in public meetings and such situations in Hawaii – where as a rule, brash assertiveness is discouraged – the loudest speakers tend to be recent arrivals from the mainland. Locals take justifiable umbrage at outsiders who presume to know what's best for Hawaii. To get anywhere here, it's better to show aloha – and a bit of deference – toward people who were island-born and raised, popularly called *kama'aina*.

Island Identity

Honolulu is 'the city,' not only for those who live on O'ahu but for all of Hawaii. Slower paced than New York or LA, Hawaii's capital is still cosmopolitan, technologically savvy and fashion-conscious. With sports stadiums, the state's premier university and actual (if relatively tame) nightlife, Honoluluans see themselves at the center of everything. Kaua'i, Maui, the Big Island, Lana'i and especially Moloka'i are considered 'country.'

Neighbor Island residents tend to dress more casually and speak more pidgin. Status isn't measured by a Lexus but by a lifted pick-up truck. *'Ohana* is important everywhere, but on the islands it's at the very heart of life. Just as ancient Hawaiians compared genealogies, locals often define themselves not by their accomplishments but by the communities to which they belong: island, town and high school.

Island Values, Multiculturalism & Diversity

That a man from Hawaii was twice elected president was a source of huge pride for island residents. Barack Obama, who spent most of his boyhood in Honolulu, was embraced by local voters because his calm demeanor and respect for diversity represent Hawaii values. It also didn't hurt that he can bodysurf, and, more importantly, that he displayed true devotion to his *'ohana*. To many locals, these are the things that count.

What didn't matter to Hawaii is what the rest of the country seemed fixated on: his race. That Obama is of mixed-race parentage was barely worth mentioning. Of course he's mixed race – who in Hawaii isn't? One legacy of the plantation era is Hawaii's unselfconscious mixing of ethnicities. Cultural differences are freely acknowledged, even carefully maintained, but don't normally divide people. For residents, the relaxed lifestyle and inclusive cultural values are probably the most defining, best-loved aspects of island life.

Among older locals, plantation-era stereotypes still inform social hierarchies and interactions. Long after whites ceased to be the wealthy plantation owners, minorities would joke about the privileges that came with being a haole *luna* (Caucasian boss). But in a growing generational divide, Hawaii's youth often dismiss these distinctions even as they continue to speak pidgin. Many locals these days can rattle off four or five different ethnicities in their ancestry – Hawaiian, Chinese, Portuguese, Filipino and Caucasian, for example.

While Hawaii is as ethnically diverse as California, Texas or Florida – and more racially intermixed – it noticeably lacks the significant African American and Latinx populations that help define those other states. Politically, most residents are middle-of-the-road Democrats who vote along party, racial/ethnic, seniority and local/nonlocal lines.

An Unequal Paradise

By most social indicators, life is good. Hawaii consistently ranks as the healthiest state in the nation, with the longest life expectancy (81.3 years) and the second-highest rate of health-care coverage. Unemployment – at 2.7% in late 2019 – and violent-crime rates are also below average, while the obesity rate is third lowest in the US. In 2017 Hawaii's median annual household income ($77,765) ranked fourth among US states, and its poverty rate (9.5%) was third lowest.

Such statistics, however, gloss over glaring inequalities. Wealthy locals and mainland transplants who own magnificent estates and vacation homes skew the averages, while a much larger number of locals, particularly Native Hawaiians and those of other Pacific-island descent, struggle with poverty and its attendant challenges. Hawaii, for example, faces one of the highest rates of ice (crystal meth) abuse in the US.

Who's Who

Hawaiian A person of Native Hawaiian ancestry. To call just any Hawaii resident 'Hawaiian' is to ignore the islands' indigenous people.

Local A person who grew up in Hawaii. Locals who move away retain their local 'cred,' at least in part. But transplant residents never become local, even if they've lived in the islands for many years.

Malihini 'Newcomer,' someone who has just moved to Hawaii and intends to stay.

Resident A person who lives but might not have been born and raised in Hawaii.

Haole White person (except local Portuguese people); further subdivided as 'mainland' or 'local' haole. Can be insulting or playful, depending on context.

Hapa A person of mixed ancestry; *hapa* is Hawaiian for 'half.' One common racial designation is *hapa* haole (part white and part other, such as Hawaiian and/or Asian).

Kama'aina Literally a 'child of the land.' A person who is native to a particular place, eg a Hilo native is a *kama'aina* of Hilo, not Kona. In a commercial context, though, *kama'aina* discounts apply to any resident of Hawaii.

Around 6500 people remain homeless in Hawaii. Rents in Honolulu are more than 70% above the national average, and it's a telling reflection on the cost of living that up to 42% of Hawaii's homeless people are employed, but still can't make ends meet. Sprawling tent communities pop up at beach parks and other public areas, to be dispersed by police, but the problem is never solved, only moved.

Native Hawaiians continue to confront the colonial legacy that has marginalized them in their own homeland. They constitute more than a third of Hawaii's homeless, while their children are more likely to drop out of school. Hawaiian charter schools have achieved remarkable successes using culturally relevant approaches, but many Hawaiians feel that only some form of political sovereignty can correct the deeply entrenched inequities.

Being faced with a constant flow of tourists purchasing paradise at resorts so few locals visit is enough to sap the aloha spirit of many residents. For Hawaiians in particular, tourism can seem a Faustian bargain; it may bring jobs and economic stability, but many question whether it's worth the cost.

Hawaiian Arts & Crafts

Stop, look and listen. The sensory experience of the Hawaiian Islands is manifold, reflecting the creativity of its diverse inhabitants. Native Hawaiian song and dance convey a powerful aloha 'aina, respect for the land, while waves of immigration have augmented the cultural milieu in ways ranging from the embrace of the ukulele to the emergence of the islands' own form of pidgin.

Hula

In the oral culture of ancient Hawai'i, long complex chants known as *mele* were composed to record and celebrate anything from the creation of the world to the genealogies of the *ali'i* (chiefs) or the latest island stories. Sometimes the chants were solemn and unaccompanied; others were blended with music and dance in a performance known as *mele hula*.

When chief and *kama'aina* (commoners) danced together, such as during the annual makahiki harvest festival, hula could be lighthearted entertainment. Many chants contained *kaona* (hidden meanings), which might be spiritual, but also slyly amorous or sexual.

Traditional wood carving, Big Island

GEORGE BURBA/SHUTTERSTOCK ©

★ **Hawaiian Folktales, Proverbs & Poetry**

The Legends and Myths of Hawai'i, by King David Kalakaua

Folktales of Hawai'i, compiled by Mary Kawena Pukui and illustrated by Sig Zane

Hawaiian Mythology, by Martha Beckwith

Any musical accompaniment was simple, using gourds, rattles and small drums made from coconuts. In legend, warriors from Tahiti introduced a larger kind of drum, the shark-skin *pahu*, a thousand years ago, heralding their arrival with its forbidding beat as they approached the shore.

Dancers would learn hula during rigorous training in a *halau* (school), guided by their *kumu* (teacher). All their movements were precise, with their hand gestures interpreting and complementing the words of the chant while their feet and legs kept the rhythm.

Island Music

During the 19th century, foreign missionaries and sugar plantation workers brought new melodies and instruments to Hawaii, which were incorporated and adapted to create a unique local musical style. Thus *paniolo* cowboys introduced guitars from Mexico, while Portuguese migrants arrived from the sugar-growing islands of the Azores carrying the small guitar-like *braguinha*, which swiftly became the ukulele.

Remarkably, the Hawaiian royal family were in the forefront of developing what came to be seen, despite its already world-spanning influences, as traditional Hawaiian music. As well as reinstating public performances of hula, which had been banned by the missionaries, King David Kalakaua co-wrote the national anthem *Hawaii Pono*, while Hawaii's last monarch, Queen Liliu'okalani, wrote the even better-known *Aloha Oe*, as recorded by Elvis Presley among others.

Distinctive singing styles emerged too. *Leo ki'eki'e* (falsetto, or 'high voice') vocals, sometimes just referred to as soprano for women, became popular. They remain characterized by a signature *ha'i* (vocal break, or split-note), in which the singer moves abruptly from one register to another. The Hawaiian version of a yodel, it was picked up from the original Prussian bandmaster of the Royal Hawaiian Band.

Tune your rental car radio to today's island radio stations, and you'll hear everything from US mainland hip-hop beats, country-and-western tunes and Asian pop hits to reggae-inspired 'Jawaiian' grooves. A few Hawaii-born singer-songwriters, like Jack Johnson, have achieved international stardom. To discover new hit-makers, check out the latest winners of the Na Hoku Hanohano Awards (www.nahokuhanohano.org), Hawaii's version of the Grammys.

Slack Key & Steel

The style of guitar playing known as slack key (*ki ho'alu*) first emerged in the late 19th century. It's based on a system of tuning in which, unlike conventional guitars, players tune their instruments so a simple strum across the open strings will produce a pleasing chord. The thumb plays the bass and rhythm chords, while the fingers play the melody and improvisations, in a picked style. With infinite variations possible, specific tunings were kept as closely guarded family secrets.

A further variation came with the development of the *kika kila* (steel guitar). O'ahu schoolboy Joseph Kekuku was the first to experiment with sliding assorted objects along his guitar strings in 1885. As the method caught on, new kinds of guitar were constructed to optimize the effect.

Briefly, a century ago, Hawaiian music became the most popular genre in the US. Touring Hawaiian musicians are even credited with having introduced their guitar sound to the Mississippi Delta, where it became the defining feature of the Delta blues.

The legendary guitarist Gabby Pahinui launched the modern slack key era with his first recording of 'Hi'ilawe' in 1946. In the 1960s, Gabby and his band the Sons of Hawaii embraced the traditional Hawaiian sound. Along with guitarists such as Sonny Chillingworth, they spurred a renaissance in Hawaiian music that continues to this day. The list of contemporary slack key masters is long and ever growing, including Keola Beamer, Ledward Ka'apana, Martin and Cyril Pahinui, Ozzie Kotani and George Kuo.

Mention must also be made of the extraordinary Israel Kamakawiwo'ole (1959–97). Raised in Waimanalo, O'ahu, 'Iz' was the living embodiment of the power, grace and beauty of Hawaiian music. His signature recording of *Somewhere Over The Rainbow/ What A Wonderful World* spread the music he loved around the globe, and alongside Gabby, his work remains the bedrock on which modern Hawaiian music stands.

Traditional Crafts

During the 1970s, the Hawaiian renaissance revived interest in artisan crafts. The most beloved traditional craft is lei-making, in which flowers, leaves, berries, nuts or shells are strung into garlands. Less ephemeral souvenirs include wood carvings, woven baskets and hats, and Hawaiian quilts. All have become so popular with tourists that cheap imitation imports have flooded into Hawaii from across the Pacific; shop carefully and always buy local.

Woodworking

Ancient Hawaiians were expert woodworkers, carving seaworthy canoes out of logs and hand-turning lustrous bowls from beautifully grained hardwoods. Native koa remains prized over all other woods. A traditional bowl (often called a calabash) is not decorated or ornate, but smoothly finished to highlight the wood's natural beauty. *Ipu* gourds were similarly dried and used as containers and hula implements.

Contemporary woodworkers use native and introduced woods to handcraft wide-ranging pieces, from bowls and boxes to exquisite furniture, such as handsome rocking chairs and sweeping dining tables. Expect to pay top dollar for collectible items, whether antique or modern. Don't be fooled by cheap monkeypod bowls imported from the Philippines.

Lei

Greetings. Devotion. Respect. Peace. Celebration. Love. A Hawaiian lei – a handcrafted garland of tropical flora – can signify myriad meanings. Giving or receiving a lei is a symbol of heartfelt aloha, not a throwaway gesture. Fragrant and fleeting, lei exemplify the beauty of nature and the embrace of *'ohana* (extended family and friends). When offered to visitors, a lei means "welcome!"

In choosing their materials, lei makers express emotions and tell stories, since flowers and other natural artifacts often embody Hawaiian places and myths. In addition to subtly

Lei Dos & Don'ts

○ Do not wear a lei hanging down from your neck. Instead, drape a closed (circular) lei over your shoulders, ensuring that equal lengths hang over your front and back.

○ When presenting a lei, bow your head slightly and raise the lei above your heart. Do not drape it over the head of the recipient yourself; let them do it.

○ Never refuse a lei, and do not take one off in the presence of the giver.

○ It's bad luck to wear a lei intended for someone else.

○ Closed lei are considered unlucky for pregnant woman, so give an open (untied) lei or *haku* (head) lei instead.

○ When you stop wearing your lei, don't trash it. Return its natural elements to the earth.

scented flowers, traditional lei makers use feathers, nuts, shells, seeds, seaweed, vines, leaves and fruit. The most common ways to make lei are by knotting, braiding, winding, stringing or sewing raw materials together.

Worn daily, lei were integral to ancient Hawaiian society. They were important elements of sacred hula dances and given as special gifts to loved ones, as healing medicine to the sick and as offerings to the gods, all practices that continue today. So powerful a symbol were they that on ancient Hawaii's battlefields, a lei could bring peace to warring armies.

Today, locals wear lei for special events, such as weddings, birthdays, anniversaries and graduations. Performers in ceremonial hula are often required to create their own lei, gathering raw materials by hand, never taking more than necessary and always thanking the tree and the gods. Otherwise, though, it's no longer common to make them yourself.

EPICSTOCKMEDIA/SHUTTERSTOCK ©

Outdoor Activities

Nature has given Hawaii such awesome scenery you could do nothing here but lie on your beach towel admiring the view. But you didn't come all this way just to rest on your elbows. To experience the outdoor adventures of a lifetime, the only real question is – how much time have you got?

In the Water

Beaches & Swimming

When it comes to swimming beaches, your options seem endless in Hawaii. Coastal strands come in a rainbow of hues and infinite textures – with sand that's sparkling white, tan, black, charcoal or green and orange, or scattered with sea glass, pebbles and boulders, and cratered with lava-rock tide pools.

By law, all Hawaiian beaches are open to the public below the high-tide line. Private landowners can prevent access to the shoreline from land, but not by water. Resort hotels provide limited beach-access public parking, occasionally for a small fee.

★ Top Island Adventures

Surfing Waikiki (p80), O'ahu

Kayaking Na Pali Coast (p110), Kaua'i

Stargazing Mauna Kea (p242), the Big Island

Hiking & Backpacking Haleakalā National Park (pictured; p210), Maui

Diving Cathedrals (p170), Lana'i

Most of Hawaii's many state and county beach parks have basic restrooms and outdoor cold-water showers; about half are patrolled by lifeguards. A few parks have gates that close during specified hours or are signposted as off-limits from sunset until sunrise.

Nudity is legally prohibited on all public beaches. However, at a few beaches going nude or topless sunbathing by women is grudgingly tolerated.

Diving

In Hawaiian waters, you can dive shipwrecks and 100ft-long lava tubes, listen to whales singing and see sharks and manta rays. Ocean temperatures average 71°F to 83°F year-round, and the visibility is usually ideal. November through March, when winter rainstorms and winds bring rougher seas, are the worst months. Dive costs depend on gear, dive length and location. Two-tank boat dives including all gear typically cost $125 to $180.

Hawaii is a great place to learn to dive. Some operators offer a 'discover scuba' option, following brief instruction with a shallow beach or boat dive, for $110 to $200. **PADI** (Professional Association of Diving Instructors; www.padi.com) open-water certification courses can be completed in as few as three days, and cost $300 to $600.

Kayaking

Heavenly bits of coastline and offshore islets beckon sea kayakers throughout the archipelago. Many beaches, bays and valleys can only be reached from the open ocean. The greatest challenge is kayaking the 17-mile Na Pali Coast on Kaua'i, which is also the only island to offer river kayaking.

Guided kayaking tours, usually including basic instruction, cost from $60. Kayak rentals are available near popular put-ins, typically for $40 to $75 per day.

Kitesurfing

Kitesurfing, or kiteboarding, is like strapping on a snowboard, grabbing a parachute and sailing over the water. If you know how to surf or windsurf, you may well master it quickly. The best winds usually blow in summer.

Maui dominates the kitesurfing scene. Shops offer rentals and instruction at **Kanaha Beach Park** (Alahao St; ☉6:30am-8pm), while experts brave **Ho'okipa Beach Park** (☑808-572-8122; www.mauicounty.gov/facilities; Hana Hwy, Mile 9; ☉7am-7pm; ℗) in Pa'ia. O'ahu's **Kailua Beach Park** (526 Kawailoa Rd) is a great place to learn. On Kaua'i, **'Anini Beach Park** ('Anini Rd; 👫) and **Kawailoa Bay** are popular.

Snorkeling

Coming to Hawaii and not snorkeling is like climbing the Eiffel Tower and closing your eyes – the world's most beautiful underwater city lies at your feet, and all you need is some molded plastic and antifog gel to see it. If you can swim, Hawaii's magnificent coral reefs are yours. Along with over 500 species of neon-colored tropical fish, you may see endangered sea turtles, plus manta rays, spinner dolphins, jacks, sharks and other predators.

Every island has fantastic shoreline snorkeling spots, while snorkel cruises can deliver you to places you could never swim to.

Reef-Safe Sunscreen

It's a legal requirement, enforced by tour-boat operators, to wear reef-safe sunscreen lotion in Hawaiian seas. Many modern lotions are reef killers; avoid those with oxybenzone and other chemical UV-radiation filters. Titanium dioxide and zinc oxide are safe ingredients.

Stand-Up Paddleboarding

As the name implies, stand-up paddleboarding (SUP) means standing on a surfboard and using a paddle to propel yourself along flat water or waves. It takes coordination to learn, but is a lot easier than regular surfing. Always paddle with a buddy and use a leash. Carry water and a whistle or a cellphone in a waterproof case for emergencies, and don't forget sun protection.

You'll see SUP fans paddling on all the main islands, anywhere from ocean beaches and calm bays to flat-water rivers. Outfitters offer two-hour group lessons for $75 to $130, rentals (from $25 to $75 per day) and occasionally guided tours (from $120).

Surfing

Ancient Hawaiians invented surfing, which they called *he'e nalu*, 'wave sliding.' In Hawaii today, surfing is both its own intense subculture and part of everyday life. The biggest waves roll in to the north shores of the islands from November through March. Summer swells, breaking along the south shores, are smaller and more infrequent.

All the major pro surfing competitions happen on O'ahu, where the **Triple Crown of Surfing** (www.vanstriplecrownofsurfing.com) draws thousands of roadside spectators to the North Shore every November and December. All the main islands, though, have good, even great surfing breaks. Surf lessons and board rentals are available at just about every tourist beach that has rideable waves.

Windsurfing

With warm waters and steady winds, Hawaii is a major windsurfing destination. Generally, the best winds blow from June through September, but trade winds will keep windsurfers – somewhere, at least – happy all year.

As O'ahu's North Shore is to surfing, so Maui's Ho'okipa Beach (p298) is to windsurfing: a dangerous, fast arena where the top international competitions sort out who's best. The other islands have windsurfing, but don't reach Maui's pinnacle. Only Moloka'i, bracketed by wind-whipped ocean channels, provides an equivalent challenge for experts.

Mere mortals might prefer windsurfing Maui's Kanaha Beach (p298) or **Ma'alaea Bay** (N Kihei Rd). If you're looking to learn, O'ahu's Kailua Beach (p298) is windy year-round and home to top-notch schools. Other spots on O'ahu include Diamond Head, **Fort DeRussy**

Beach (off Kalia Rd; 🚻) in Waikiki and the North Shore's **Backyards** (59-104 Kamehameha Hwy) and **Malaekahana State Recreation Area** (📞808-587-0300; www.hawaiistateparks.org; 56-075 Kamehameha Hwy; ⏱7am-7:45pm Apr-early Sep, to 6:45pm early Sep-Mar; 🚻) **FREE**. Kaua'i has only one prime spot for windsurfers: 'Anini Beach (p298). On the Big Island, check out **'Anaeho'omalu Beach** (A Bay; Waikoloa Beach Dr; ⏱6am-8pm; 🚻).

On Land

Caving

Funny thing, lava. As the top of a flow cools and hardens, the molten rock beneath keeps moving. When the eruption stops and the lava drains, it leaves an underground maze of tunnels like some colossal ant farm. Many such lava tubes were used by ancient Hawaiians as burial chambers, water caches, housing and more.

Still volcanically active, Hawai'i (Big Island) is a caving hot spot, with six of the world's 10 longest lava tubes. Ka'u's Kanohina cave system holds 20 miles of complex tunnels – take a peek at **Kula Kai Caverns** (📞808-929-9725; www.kulakaicaverns.com; 92-8864 Lauhala Dr; tours adult/child 6-12yr from $28/16; ⏱by reservation; 🚻). Kea'au's **Kazumura Cave** (📞808-967-7208; www.kazumuracave.com; off Volcano Hwy, past Mile 22; from $45; ⏱Mon-Sat by reservation) is even longer.

Other islands have fewer opportunities. but even kids can explore Maui's **Hana Lava Tube** (Ka'eleku Caverns; 📞808-248-7308; www.mauicave.com; 305 'Ula'ino Rd; self-guided tour adult/child under 5yr $12.50/free; ⏱10:30am-4pm; 🅿🚻), also called Ka'eleku Caverns.

Cycling & Mountain Biking

Quality trumps quantity when it comes to cycling and mountain biking in Hawaii. Cyclists will find the most bike-friendly roads and organizational support on O'ahu, but all of the main islands offer bicycle rentals, as well as trails and 4WD roads that double as two-wheel, pedal-powered adventures.

Hiking & Backpacking

Hikers will find that, mile for mile, these tiny islands cannot be topped for heart-stopping vistas and soulful beauty. As even the most rugged spots are usually accessible as day hikes, backpacking is seldom necessary. When it is, the rewards far outstrip the effort. Explore Hawaii's public trails online via **Na Ala Hele Trail & Access** (http://hawaiitrails.hawaii.gov).

Best Islands for Hiking

For sheer variety, **Hawai'i (Big Island)** wins by a nose. As well as an active volcano, Hawai'i Volcanoes National Park holds steaming craters, lava deserts and rain forests. Then there are two nearly 14,000ft mountains to scale – Mauna Loa and Mauna Kea.

Kaua'i ranks a close second, with the Kalalau Trail edging the spectacular cliffs of the Na Pali Coast, and abundant paths crisscrossing mountaintop Koke'e State Park and Waimea Canyon.

On **Maui**, awe-inspiring descents traverse the eroded moonscape of Haleakalā, while the Road to Hana tempts with short hikes to waterfalls.

On **O'ahu,** you can escape Honolulu in the forests of the Manoa and Makiki Valleys around Mt Tantalus, or lose the crowds at Ka'ena Point.

SARAH MICHALS/SHUTTERSTOCK ©

Hana Lava Tube (p179)

Trespassing on private land or government land not intended for public use is illegal, no matter how many people you see doing it. Respect all 'Kapu' or 'No Trespassing' signs – not just for legal reasons, but also for your own safety.

Stargazing

For astronomers, Hawaii's night sky is beyond compare. The view from Mauna Kea volcano on Hawai'i, the Big Island, is unmatched in clarity, and the urge to construct ever larger observatories has increasingly clashed with traditional reverence for the mountain. On the summit road, the **visitor information station** (MKVIS; ☑808-934-4550; www.ifa.hawaii.edu/info/vis; ⊘8am-3pm) hosts free public stargazing programs nightly (weather permitting). During the day, catch a family-friendly planetarium show at Hilo's '**Imiloa Astronomy Center** (p270), also on the Big Island, or at Honolulu's **Bishop Museum** (p46) on O'ahu.

While the observatories on Maui's Haleakalā volcano aren't open to the public, the summit visitor center stocks star maps, and you can rent high-powered binoculars from island dive shops before you head up. Some resort hotels, especially on Maui and the Big Island, offer stargazing programs for guests.

Lomilomi salmon

Food & Drink

Forget pineapple-topped pizza: Hawaii's cuisine is no cliché. It's a multicultural taste sensation, rooted in the natural bounty of the islands and influenced by the entire Pacific. Over the years, the wildly different flavors introduced by migrants from across the ocean and around the world have fused to become 'local,' as savored today in a heaping, island-style plate lunch.

The Island Diet

Until humans reached Hawaii, the only indigenous edibles in the islands were ferns and *'ohelo* berries. In their wooden sailing canoes, the earliest Polynesian voyagers carried seedlings to propagate that included *kalo* (taro), *niu* (coconut), *'ulu* (breadfruit), *'uala* (sweet potato), *mai'a* (banana) and *ko* (sugarcane), along with chickens, pigs and dogs for meat, and they were of course skilled in harvesting seafood from the ocean.

From 1793 onwards, when Captain George Vancouver presented Kamehameha with six cows and a bull, Europeans introduced their animals to the islands. Later on, American missionaries imported macadamia nuts, coffee and tropical fruits such as pineapple that have come to symbolize Hawaii. When growth of the sugar industry in the 19th century

Spam *musubi* (p304)

resulted in the arrival of immigrants from China, Japan, Portugal, Puerto Rico, Korea and the Philippines, Hawaii's cuisine developed an identity all of its own. While mixing in imported ingredients, especially from around Asia, it never abandoned Hawaiian staples such as *kalua* pork and *poi* (steamed, mashed taro).

What does all this mean for visitors? Always sample the unknown during your trip, take another bite and travel the world on a single plate. Hawaii isn't a place to diet – it's a *broke da mout* (delicious) reward.

Native Hawaiian Food

With its earthy flavors and Polynesian ingredients, Hawaiian cooking is like no other. Smoky, salty and succulent, *kalua* pig was traditionally roasted whole in an underground *imu*, a pit of red-hot stones layered with banana and *ti* leaves. You'll see pigs cooked like that at most commercial luau, but it's usually just for show – it couldn't feed 300-plus guests anyway. Instead, *kalua* pork these days is typically seasoned with salt and liquid smoke, and oven-roasted.

Ancient Hawaiians held *poi* sacred. A purplish paste made of pounded taro root, often steamed and fermented, it's highly nutritious, low in calories and easily digestible. Tasting bland to mildly tart or even sour, it's usually eaten as a starchy counterpoint to strongly flavored dishes such as *lomilomi* salmon (minced, salted salmon with diced tomato and green onion).

★ Best Restaurants

Da Poke Shack (p249) Kailua-Kona, Big Island

Monkeypod Kitchen (p204) Wailea, Maui

Senia (pictured; p70) Honolulu, Oʻahu

Kauaʻi Ono (p132) Princeville, Kauaʻi

Another traditional favorite, *laulau*, is a bundle of pork or chicken and salted butterfish wrapped in taro or *ti* leaves and steamed until it has a soft sautéed spinach-like texture. Other Hawaiian staples include baked *'ulu* (breadfruit), with a feel similar to a potato; *'opihi*, tiny limpets picked off reefs at low tide; *pipikaula* (beef jerky); and *haupia*, a coconut-cream custard thickened with arrowroot or cornstarch.

Local specialties

Cheap, tasty and filling, local 'grinds' (food) is the stuff of cravings and comfort. Start with the classic plate lunch, typically eaten on a disposable plate with disposable chopsticks: a fixed-plate meal of 'two scoop' rice, macaroni-potato salad and a hot protein dish, such as fried mahimahi, tender *kalua* pork, teriyaki chicken or *kalbi* short ribs. *Loco moco*, the compact cousin of a plate lunch, consists of a scoop of rice, fried egg and choice of main dish, topped with gravy.

Poke (rhymes with *okay*), long an island craze, has recently swept the world. In its original Hawaiian form, *poke* is made of bite-sized raw fish (typically ahi) seasoned with sea salt, *ogo* (stringy, crunchy seaweed) and *'inamona* (a condiment made of roasted, ground *kukui* nuts). For a satisfying meal to go, a *poke* bowl – *poke* on rice – takes some beating.

Look out too for saimin, a soup of chewy Chinese egg noodles swimming in Japanese broth, garnished with green onion, dried seaweed, steamed fish cake and barbecued pork. And be sure to sample Spam *musubi* (rice balls), neat little parcels of sticky white rice, surrounding a slice of Spam sautéed in soy sauce and wrapped in seaweed.

Sticky white rice, incidentally, is much more than a side dish. It's an essential culinary building block. Just so you know, sticky white rice means exactly that. Not fluffy rice. Not wild rice. And definitely not instant.

Manapua, the much-loved local version of the Chinese *bao* (steamed or baked filled bun), probably owes its name to either of two Hawaiian phrases: *mea 'ono pua'a* ('good pork thing') or *mauna pua'a* ('mountain of pork').

Hawaii Regional Cuisine

Hawaii was considered a culinary backwater until the early 1990s, when a handful of island chefs – including Alan Wong, Roy Yamaguchi, Sam Choy and Peter Merriman, all of whom still have restaurants on the islands – created a new cuisine, borrowing liberally from Hawaii's multi-ethnic heritage. Partnering with island farmers, ranchers and fishers, these chefs highlighted fresh, local ingredients, and transformed childhood favorites into gourmet Pacific Rim masterpieces. Suddenly macadamia-nut-crusted mahimahi, miso-glazed butterfish and *liliko'i* (passion fruit) anything-at-all were all the rage.

At first, 'Hawaii Regional Cuisine' was seen as exclusive, and found only at high-end dining rooms. Its original hallmarks included Eurasian fusion flavors, gastronomic techniques and elaborate plating, but in the 21st century the focus shifted toward island-grown, organic, seasonal and handpicked ingredients. Upscale restaurants are still the mainstay for star chefs, but now neighborhood bistros and even plate-lunch food trucks serve dishes inspired by Hawaii Regional Cuisine, with island farms lauded like designer brands on menus.

> **Organic Farming**
>
> Learn all about local agriculture, farm tours, farmers markets and more on the Hawaii Organic Farming Association (HOFA) website, www.hawaiiorganic.org.

Hawaii also has a strong tradition of organic farming. You can learn all about local agriculture, farm tours, farmers markets and more on the Hawaii Organic Farming Association (HOFA) website, www.hawaiiorganic.org.

Coffee, Tea & Traditional Drinks

Coffee first reached Hawaii early in the 19th century. Grown on the upland slopes of Mauna Loa and Hualalai volcanoes in the Kona district of the Big Island, Kona coffee is now world-famous for its mellow flavor and lack of bitter aftertaste. While 100% Kona coffee has the most cachet, commanding $20 to $40 per pound, crops from elsewhere on the island, as well as Maui, Kaua'i and Moloka'i, have won accolades and impressed aficionados. When buying coffee, always look for the '100%' designation. Anything less, and that 'Kona' coffee bargain, by definition, consists of cheap imported beans laced with a smattering of the real stuff.

Ancient Hawaiians never got buzzed on caffeine. Instead, Hawaii's original intoxicants were plant-based Polynesian elixirs: 'awa (a mild, mouth-numbing sedative made from the roots of the kava plant) and noni (Indian mulberry), which some consider a panacea. Both are pungent in smell and taste, so they're often mixed with other juices, but it's not hard to find drinkable kava. If it tastes like dirt, as some allege, just imagine you're tasting the earth.

Tea, incidentally, was introduced to Hawaii in the late 19th century, but never took hold as a commercial crop due to high labor and production costs.

Tropical fruits may seem to grow wild everywhere you look, but don't expect to find fresh fruit juice in chain supermarkets. Look out instead for roadside fruit stands, farmers markets and the deli counters in health food stores. Fresh-fruit smoothies, juices and acai bowls can easily cost as much as a light meal, especially if they're organic and local, but they're an absolute treat for visitors.

Once a novelty, microbreweries have now become firmly established on Hawaii's major islands. According to brewmasters, the mineral content and purity of Hawaii's water makes for excellent-tasting beer. Another hallmark of local craft beers is added hints of tropical flavor, such as Kona coffee, macadamia nuts, coconut, honey or liliko'i.

Hawaiian Green Sea Turtle

SHANE MYERS PHOTOGRAPHY/SHUTTERSTOCK ©

Survival Guide

Directory A–Z

Accessible Travel

○ Hawaii's larger, newer hotels have elevators, wheelchair-accessible rooms (reserve well in advance) and TDD-capable phones.

○ Telephone companies provide relay operators (TTY/TDD dial 711) for the hearing-impaired.

○ Many banks provide ATM instructions in Braille.

○ Traffic intersections in cities and some towns have dropped curbs and audible crossing signals.

○ Guide and service dogs are not subject to the same quarantine requirements as other pets, but must arrive via Honolulu International Airport. Contact the Dept of Agriculture's **Animal Quarantine Station** (☏808-483-7151; http://hdoa. hawaii.gov/ai/aqs/aqs-info; ⊙8am-5pm) in advance.

○ Visit the 'Community Resources' section of the **Disability & Communication Access Board** (☏808-586-8121; www.hawaii.gov/health/dcab)

website to download free 'Traveler Tips' guides to all islands except Lana'i.

○ On O'ahu, Honolulu's Dept of Parks & Recreation (www.honolulu.gov/parks. html) can provide free all-terrain beach mats and wheelchairs at beaches including Ala Moana, Hanauma Bay, Sans Souci and Kailua.

Transportation

○ Where available on the islands, public transportation is wheelchair-accessible. Buses will usually 'kneel' if you're unable to use the steps – let the driver know you need the lift or ramp.

○ Some major car-rental agencies offer hand-controlled vehicles and vans with wheelchair lifts; reserve these well in advance. **Wheelchair Getaways** (☏800-638-1912; www.accessiblevans. com) rents wheelchair-accessible vans on Hawai'i (Big Island), Maui and Kaua'i, while **Wheelers Van Rentals** (☏800-456-1371; http://wheelersvanrentals. com) operates on those three islands plus O'ahu.

○ If you have a disability parking placard from home, bring it with you. Hang it from your vehicle's rearview mirror when using designated disabled-parking spaces.

Accommodations

It's almost always necessary to book accommodations in advance. For peak times, the sooner you book the better – reserve up to a year ahead for Christmas and New Year's.

Hotels & Resorts Close to popular tourist beaches; expect daily resort and/or parking fees.

Condos Plentiful on the larger islands, offering apartment-style amenities and often weekly discounts.

B&Bs & vacation rentals Generally reliable, with more space and amenities than comparably priced hotels.

Hostels For cheap private rooms and dormitory beds - but they're scarce.

Camping & cabins In some national, state and county parks; bring your own camping gear.

Book Your Stay Online

For more accommodation reviews by Lonely Planet authors, check out http://hotels.lonely planet.com/Hawaii. You'll find independent reviews, as well as recommendations on the best places to stay. Best of all, you can book online.

Electricity

120V/60Hz

120V/60Hz

Entry & Exit Requirements

o Double-check current visa and passport requirements *before* traveling to the USA.

o For current information about entry requirements and eligibility, check the visas section of the **US Department of State** (http://travel.state.gov) website and the travel section of the **US Customs and Border Protection** (CBP; www.cbp.gov) website.

o Upon arrival in the USA, most foreign citizens (excluding for now, many Canadians, some Mexicans, all children under age 14 and seniors over age 79) must register with the **Department of Homeland Security** (DHS; www.dhs.gov), which happens automatically at airports, and entails taking electronic fingerprints and a digital photo.

Customs Regulations

Currently, each international visitor is allowed to bring into the USA duty-free:

o 1L of liquor (if you're over 21 years old)

o 200 cigarettes (1 carton) or 100 cigars (if you're over 18 years old)

Amounts higher than $10,000 in cash, travelers' checks, money orders and other cash equivalents must be declared. For detailed, up-to-date information,

check with **US Customs and Border Protection** (CBP; www.cbp.gov).

Most fresh fruits and plants are restricted from entry into Hawaii (to prevent the spread of invasive species), and customs officials strictly enforce these regulations. Because Hawai'i is a rabies-free state, the pet quarantine laws are draconian. Questions? Contact the **Department of Agriculture** (http://hdoa.hawaii.gov).

All checked and carry-on bags leaving Hawai'i for the US mainland, Alaska or Guam must be checked by an agricultural inspector at the airport using an X-ray machine. Make sure that any fresh food, produce or flowers in your baggage has been commercially packaged and approved for travel, or you'll be forced to surrender those pineapples and orchids at the airport. For more information, contact the **US Department of Agriculture** (☑808-834-3240; www.aphis.usda.gov).

Passports

o All foreign citizens wishing to enter the USA must have a machine-readable passport (MRP).

o Your passport must be valid for six months beyond your expected dates of stay in the USA.

o Any passport issued/renewed after October 26, 2006, must be an 'e-passport' with digital photo and an integrated chip containing biometric data.

Island Dos & Don'ts

Island residents are mostly casual and informal in everyday life, but there are some (unspoken) rules of etiquette you should follow:

○ Take off your shoes when entering someone's home. Most residents wear 'rubbah slippah' (flip-flops) – easy to slip on and off, no socks required.

○ Try to pronounce Hawaiian place names and words correctly. Even if you fail, the attempt is appreciated.

○ Ask permission before you pick fruit or flowers or otherwise trespass on private property. Drive slowly. Unless you're about to hit someone, don't honk your car horn.

○ Don't be pushy. You'll get what you want (this time), but you'll get no aloha with it.

○ Don't grumble about high prices. You're (probably) not being gouged by the local business owner: over 80% of consumer goods are shipped in, adding significantly to costs. If you're miffed about paying $8 for a gallon of milk, consider how residents feel.

○ Don't collect (or move) stones at sacred sites. If you're not sure whether something's sacred, consider that in Hawaiian thinking, everything is sacred, especially in nature.

○ Don't stack rocks or wrap them in *ti* leaves at waterfalls, heiau (temples) etc. This bastardization of the ancient Hawaiian practice of leaving *hoʻokupu* (offerings) at sacred sites is littering.

Visas

○ Under the US Visa Waiver Program (VWP), citizens of 39 countries do not require visas for stays up to 90 days (no extensions).

○ For the VWP program, you must have a return ticket (or onward ticket to any foreign destination) that's nonrefundable in the USA.

○ All VWP travelers must register online at least 72 hours before arrival with the **Electronic System for Travel Authorization** (ESTA; https://esta.cbp.dhs. gov), which currently costs $14. Once approved, regis-tration is valid for two years (or until your passport expires, whichever comes first).

○ Canadian citizens are generally admitted visa-free for stays up to 182 days total during a 12-month period; they do not need to register with the ESTA.

○ All other visitors who don't qualify for the VWP and aren't Canadian citizens must apply for a tourist visa. The process costs a nonrefundable fee (minimum $160), involves a personal interview and can take several weeks; apply early.

○ www.usembassy.gov has links for all US embassies and consulates. Apply for a visa in your home country rather than on the road.

Food

The price ranges in this book refer to an average main course at dinner in a res-taurant – lunch is cheaper, usually half-price – or a meal at a casual take-out joint. Unless otherwise stated, tax-es and tip are not included.

$ less than $15
$$ $15–$25
$$$ more than $25

LGBT+ Travellers

The state of Hawaii prides itself on having strong minority protections and a constitutional guarantee of privacy that extends to sexual behavior between consenting adults.

Locals tend to be private about their personal lives, so you won't see much public hand-holding or open displays of affection, either same-sex or opposite-sex. Everyday LGBTIQ life is low-key, and more about picnics and potlucks than nightclubs. Even in Waikiki, the laid-back gay scene comprises just a half dozen or so bars, clubs and restaurants.

That said, Hawai'i is a popular destination for LGBTIQ travelers, who are served by a small network of gay-owned and gay-friendly B&Bs, guesthouses and hotels. For recommendations on places to stay, beaches, events and more, check out these resources:

Out Traveler (www.outtraveler.com/hawaii) LGBTIQ-oriented Hawaii travel articles, available free online.

Pride Guide Hawaii (www.gogayhawaii.com) Free island visitor guides for gay-friendly activities, accommodations, dining, nightlife, shopping, festivals, weddings and more.

Hawai'i LGBT Legacy Foundation (http://hawaiilgbtlegacyfoundation.com) News, resources and a community calendar of LGBTIQ events, mostly on O'ahu.

Purple Roofs (www.purpleroofs.com) Online directory of gay-owned and gay-friendly B&Bs, vacation rentals, guesthouses and hotels.

Health

● For emergency medical assistance anywhere in Hawaii, call 911 or go directly to the emergency room (ER) of the nearest hospital. For nonemergencies, consider an urgent-care center or walk-in medical clinic.

● Some insurance policies require you to obtain preauthorization for medical treatment from a call center before seeking help. Keep all medical receipts and documentation for claims reimbursement later.

Insurance

Purchasing travel insurance to cover theft, loss and medical problems is highly recommended. Some insurance policies do not cover 'risky' activities such as scuba diving, trekking and motorcycling, so read the fine print. Make sure your policy at least covers hospital stays and an emergency flight home.

Certain insurers require policyholders to get preauthorization before receiving medical treatment – contact the call center. Retain your medical receipts and documentation so you can seek reimbursement at a later date.

Paying for your airline ticket or rental car with a credit card may provide limited travel accident insurance. If you already have private US health insurance or a homeowners or renters policy, find out what those policies cover and only get supplemental insurance. If you have

---

Vog

Vog, a visible haze or smog caused by volcanic emissions from the Big Island, is often (but not always) dispersed by trade winds before it reaches other islands. On the Big Island, vog can make sunny skies hazy in West Hawai'i, especially in the afternoons around Kailua-Kona.

Although short-term exposure to vog is not generally hazardous, high sulfur-dioxide levels can create breathing problems for sensitive groups (eg those with respiratory or heart conditions, pregnant women, young children and infants). Avoid vigorous physical exertion outdoors on voggy days.

prepaid a large portion of your vacation, trip cancellation insurance may be a worthwhile expense.

Worldwide travel insurance is available at www.lonelyplanet.com/travel-insurance. You can buy, extend and claim online any time – even on the road.

Internet Access

○ While it's unusual for any accommodations option not to provide free wi-fi for guests, no service may be available in remote locations such as cabins or campsites in state parks.

○ Most coffee shops, along with some bars, restaurants, shopping malls and other businesses offer public wi-fi access, sometimes free for paying customers only.

○ Cities and larger towns may have cybercafes or business centers like **FedEx Office** (📞800-463-3339; http://local.fedex.com/hi) offering pay-as-you-go internet terminals (typically $12 to $20 per hour) and sometimes wi-fi.

○ Hawaii's **public libraries** (📞808-586-3500; www.librarieshawaii.org) provide free internet access via computer terminals if you get a temporary nonresident library card ($10). A few library branches also offer free wi-fi.

Tipping

Tipping is *not* optional; only withhold tips in cases of outrageously bad service.

Airport and hotel porters $2 per bag, minimum $5 per cart

Bartenders 15–20% per round, minimum $1 per drink

Concierges Nothing for simple information, up to $20 for securing last-minute restaurant reservations, etc.

Housekeeping staff $2–4 per night, left under the card provided; more if you're messy

Parking valets At least $2 when your keys are returned

Restaurant servers and room service 18% to 20%, unless a gratuity is already charged (common for groups of six or more)

Taxi drivers 10 to 15% of metered fare, rounded up to the next dollar

Legal Matters

If you are arrested, you have the right to an attorney; if you can't afford one, a public defender will be provided for free. The **Hawaii State Bar Association** (📞808-537-9140; http://hawaiilawyerreferral.com; Suite 1000, 1100 Alakea St, Honolulu; ⏲8:30am-4:30pm Mon-Fri) makes attorney referrals. International visitors may want to call their nearest consulate or embassy for advice; police will provide the telephone number upon request.

Money

ATMs are widespread in cities and larger towns. Credit cards are almost universally accepted and are usually required for reservations.

ATMS

○ ATMs are available 24/7 at banks, shopping malls, airports and grocery and convenience stores.

○ Most ATMs are connected to international networks like Plus and Cirrus.

○ Expect a surcharge of around $3 per withdrawal, in addition to fees charged by your home bank.

Credit Cards

○ Credit cards are widely accepted and generally obligatory for car rentals, hotel reservations etc. Some B&Bs and vacation rentals refuse them (pay in US dollar travelers' checks or cash instead), or add a 3% surcharge.

○ Visa, MasterCard and American Express are widely accepted, followed by Discover and JTB.

Exchange Rates

Australia	A$1	$0.67
Canada	C$1	$0.75
China	Y10	$1.43
Euro zone	€1	$1.08
Japan	¥100	$0.91
New Zealand	NZ$1	$0.64
UK	UK£1	$1.30

For current exchange rates see www.xe.com

Money Changers

○ Exchange foreign currency at Honolulu International Airport or main branches of bigger banks, such as **Bank of Hawaii** (808-643-3888; www.boh.com) or **First Hawaiian Bank** (808-844-4444; www.fhb.com).

○ Outside cities and larger towns, exchanging money may be impossible; be sure to carry enough cash and/or plastic.

Public Holidays

On state and national holidays, banks, schools and government offices (including post offices) close, and museums, transportation and other services operate on a Sunday schedule. Holidays falling on a weekend are usually observed the following Monday.

New Year's Day January 1

Martin Luther King Jr Day Third Monday in January

Presidents' Day Third Monday in February

Prince Kuhio Day March 26

Good Friday Friday before Easter Sunday in March/April

Memorial Day Last Monday in May

King Kamehameha Day June 11

Independence Day July 4

Statehood Day Third Friday in August

Labor Day First Monday in September

Veterans Day November 11

Thanksgiving Fourth Thursday in November

Christmas Day December 25

Telephone

Cell Phones

International travelers need a multiband GSM phone to make calls in the USA. With an unlocked multiband phone, popping in a US prepaid rechargeable SIM card is usually cheaper than using your own network. SIM cards are available at any telecommunications or electronics store. Such stores also sell inexpensive prepaid phones, including some airtime – useful if your phone doesn't work.

Check with your service provider whether you can use your cell phone in Hawaii. Among providers, Verizon has the most extensive network. Coverage is best on O'ahu, but sometimes spotty outside major towns (especially on Neighbor Islands) and nonexistent in many rural areas, including on hiking trails and at remote beaches.

Payphones & Phonecards

○ Payphones are very much a dying breed, but can sometimes be found at shopping centers, hotels, beaches, and parks.

○ Some payphones are coin-operated (local calls usually cost 50¢); others only accept credit cards or phone cards.

○ Prepaid phone cards are available from convenience stores, newsstands, supermarkets and pharmacies.

Dialing Codes

○ Hawaii phone numbers consist of a three-digit area code (808) followed by a seven-digit local number.

○ To call long-distance from one Hawaiian Island to another, dial 1 + 808 + local number.

○ Always dial 1 before toll-free numbers (800, 888 etc). Some toll-free numbers only work within Hawaii or from the US mainland (and possibly Canada).

○ To call Canada from Hawaii, dial 1 + area code + local number (international rates still apply).

○ For all other international calls from Hawaii, dial 011 + country code + area code + local number.

• To call Hawaii from abroad, use the international country code for the USA 1.

Useful Numbers

Emergency (police, fire, ambulance)	911
Local directory assistance	411
Long-distance directory assistance	1-808-555-1212
Toll-free directory assistance	1-800-555-1212
Operator	0

Time

• Hawaii-Aleutian Standard Time (HAST) is GMT minus 10 hours.

• Hawaii doesn't observe Daylight Saving Time (DST).

Tourist Information

Airport arrivals areas hold tourist information desks. While you wait for your bags to appear, you can peruse racks of brochures and magazines, containing discount coupons for tours and activities.

For pre-trip planning in several languages, browse the information-packed website of the **Hawaii Visitors & Convention Bureau** (800-464-2924; www.gohawaii.com).

Transportation

Getting There & Away

Air

Hawaii is a competitive market for US domestic and international airfares, which vary tremendously by season, day of the week and demand. Competition is greatest between the airlines that fly to Honolulu from major US cities.

The 'lowest fare' fluctuates constantly. In general return fares from the US mainland to Hawaii range from $400 (in low season from the West Coast) to $800 or more (in high season from the East Coast). **Pleasant Holidays** (www.pleasantholidays.com) offers vacation packages from the US mainland. For flights and packages from Canada, check low-cost carrier **WestJet** (888-937-8538; www.westjet.com).

Airports

The majority of incoming international flights arrive at **Honolulu International Airport** (HNL; 808-836-6411; www.airports.hawaii.gov/hnl; 300 Rodgers Blvd;) on O'ahu. Direct flights do connect Maui, Kaua'i and the Big Island with the mainland, while most flights to Lana'i and Moloka'i originate from Honolulu or Maui.

The main Neighbor Island airports include:

Hilo International Airport (ITO; 808-961-9300; www.hawaii.gov/ito; 2450 Kekuanaoa St) East Hawai'i (Big Island).

Kahului International Airport (OGG; 808-872-3830; www.airports.hawaii.gov/ogg; 1 Kahului Airport Rd) Maui.

Kona International Airport at Keahole (KOA; 808-327-9520; http://airports.hawaii.

Climate Change & Travel

Every form of transport that relies on carbon-based fuel generates CO_2, the main cause of human-induced climate change. Modern travel is dependent on airplanes, which might use less fuel per kilometer per person than most cars but travel much greater distances. The altitude at which aircraft emit gases (including CO_2) and particles also contributes to their climate change impact. Many websites offer 'carbon calculators' that allow people to estimate the carbon emissions generated by their journey and, for those who wish to do so, to offset the impact of the greenhouse gases emitted with contributions to portfolios of climate-friendly initiatives throughout the world. Lonely Planet offsets the carbon footprint of all staff and author travel.

gov/koa; 73-200 Kupipi St) **West Hawai'i (Big Island)**.

Lana'i Airport (LNY; ☑808-565-7942; http://hawaii.gov/lny) **Lana'i**.

Lihu'e Airport (LIH; ☑808-274-3800; http://airports.hawaii.gov/lih; 3901 Mokulele Loop) **Kaua'i**.

Moloka'i Airport (MKK, Ho'olehua; ☑808-567-9660; http://hawaii.gov/mkk; 3980 Airport Loop, Ho'olehua) **Moloka'i**. Among the domestic and international airlines serving the islands, the only Hawaii-based carrier is **Hawaiian Airlines** (☑800-367-5320; www.hawaiianairlines.com).

Sea

Most cruises to Hawaii include stopovers in Honolulu and on Maui, Kaua'i and the Big Island. Cruises typically last two weeks, with ship-only fares starting around $120 per person per night, in double occupancy.

Popular cruise lines include:

Holland America (☑877-932-4259; www.hollandamerica.com) Departures from San Diego, Seattle and Vancouver, British Columbia.

Norwegian Cruise Line (NCL; ☑855-577-9489; www.ncl.com) Departures from Vancouver, British Columbia.

Princess Cruises (☑800-774-6237; www.princess.com) Departures from Los Angeles, San Francisco, Seattle and Vancouver, British Columbia.

Royal Caribbean (☑866-562-7625; www.royalcaribbean.com) Departures from Vancouver, British Columbia.

Getting Around

Almost all interisland travel is by plane, while traveling around the individual islands usually requires renting a car.

Air

Interisland flights are short, frequent and surprisingly expensive. The airports that handle the most interisland air traffic are Honolulu (O'ahu), Kahului (Maui), Kona and Hilo on Hawai'i (Big Island) and Lihu'e (Kaua'i).

Smaller airports, served by commuter airlines and charter, include Lana'i City (Lana'i); Kaunakakai and Kalaupapa (Moloka'i); Kapalua and Hana (Maui); and Kamuela (Waimea) on the Big Island.

Boat

Only Moloka'i and Lana'i are served by regular, passenger-only public ferries, both to/from Lahaina, Maui.

Norwegian Cruise Line operates a seven-day cruise between the four biggest islands, starting and ending in Honolulu. Fares start at $1299 per person, based on double occupancy.

Bus

○ Thanks to **TheBus** (☑808-848-5555; www.thebus.org), O'ahu is the easiest island to get around without a car. Schedules are frequent, service reliable, and fares low. That said, TheBus doesn't go everywhere – to most hiking trailheads, for example.

○ Public bus systems on the larger Neighbor Islands are geared toward resident commuters; service tends to be infrequent and limited to main towns. After O'ahu, the next best system is **Maui Bus** (☑808-871-4838; www.mauicounty.gov/bus), but it doesn't run to Hana or Haleakalā National Park.

○ The Big Island's **Hele-On Bus** (☑808-961-8744; www.hele-onbus.org) will get you to many island towns (albeit slowly and not always on Sundays), but schedules are too limited for sightseeing. It stops at Hawai'i Volcanoes National Park's main visitor center.

○ **Kaua'i Bus** (www.kauai.gov/busschedules) runs between the main towns, but not to the Na Pali Coast, Waimea Canyon or Koke'e State Park. The **North Shore Shuttle** (☑888-409-2702; https://kauainsshuttle.com; single ride/day pass/week/month $5/10/20/40) connects Hanalei and Princeville on North Shore with the Kalalau Trail.

○ On Moloka'i, the free **MEO Bus** (☑808-553-3216; www.meoinc.org; bus trips free; ◷Mon-Fri) trundles east and west of Kaunakakai every couple of hours on weekdays. Call ahead to confirm schedules.

Car

Most visitors to Hawaii rent their own vehicles, particularly on the Neighbor Islands. If you're only visiting Honolulu and Waikiki, is not necessary. Free parking is usually plentiful outside of cities and major towns. Bigger hotels and resorts, especially in Waikiki, typically charge $10 to $40 or more for overnight parking, either self-parking or valet.

Glossary

'a'a – type of lava that is rough and jagged

ahu – stone cairns used to mark a trail; an altar or shrine

ahupua'a – traditional land division, usually in a wedge shape that extends from the mountains to the sea (smaller than a *moku*)

'aina – land

'akala – Hawaiian raspberry or thimbleberry

ali'i – chief, royalty

ali'i nui – high chiefs, kingly class

aloha – the traditional greeting meaning love, welcome, good-bye

aloha 'aina – love of the land

'amakihi – small, yellow-green honeycreeper; one of the more common native birds

anchialine pool – contains a mixture of seawater and freshwater

'apapane – bright red native Hawaiian honeycreeper

'aumakua – protective deity or guardian spirit, deified ancestor

'awa – see *kava*

e komo mai – welcome

ha'i – voiced register-break technique used by women singers

haku – head

hala – pandanus tree; the leaves (*lau*) are used in weaving mats and baskets

haole – Caucasian; literally, 'without breath'

hapa – portion or fragment; person of mixed blood

hapa haole – Hawaiian music with predominantly English lyrics

he'e nalu – wave sliding, or surfing

heiau – ancient stone temple; a place of worship in Hawaii

ho'okupu – offering

hula – Hawaiian dance form, either traditional or modern

hula halau – hula school or troupe

hula kahiko – traditional and sacred hula

'i'iwi – scarlet Hawaiian honeycreeper with a curved, salmon-colored beak

'iliahi – Hawaiian sandalwood

'ilima – native plant, a ground cover with delicate yellow-orange flowers; O'ahu's official flower

ipu – spherical, narrow-necked gourd used as a hula implement

kahuna – knowledgeable person in any field; commonly a priest, healer or sorcerer

kama'aina – person born and raised, or a longtime resident, in Hawaii; literally, 'child of the land'

kapa – see *tapa*

kapu – taboo, part of strict ancient Hawaiian social and religious system

kapuna – elders

kava – a mildly narcotic drink ('awa in Hawaiian) made from the roots of *Piper methysticum*, a pepper shrub

ki ho'alu – slack key

kiawe – a relative of the mesquite tree introduced to Hawaii in the 1820s

ki'i – see *tiki*

kilau – a stiff, weedy fern

ko – sugarcane

koa – native hardwood tree often used in making Native Hawaiian crafts and canoes

kukui – candlenut, the official state tree; its oily nuts were once burned in lamps

kumu – teacher

Kumulipo – Native Hawaiian creation story or chant

kupuna – grandparent, elder

la'au lapa'au – plant medicine

lanai – veranda; balcony

lauhala – leaves of the *hala* plant, used in weaving

lei – garland, usually of flowers, but also of leaves, vines, shells or nuts

leptospirosis – a disease acquired by exposure to water contaminated by the urine of infected animals, especially livestock

limu – seaweed

lomilomi – traditional Hawaiian massage; known as 'loving touch'

Lono – Polynesian god of harvest, agriculture, fertility and peace

loulu – native fan palms

luau – traditional Hawaiian feast

luna – supervisor or plantation boss

mahalo – thank you

mai ho'oka'awale – leprosy (Hansen's disease); literally, 'the separating sickness'

maile – native plant with twining habit and fragrant leaves; often used for lei

makahiki – traditional annual wet-season winter festival dedicated to the agricultural god Lono

makai – toward the sea; seaward

malihini – newcomer, visitor

mana – spiritual power

mauka – toward the mountains; inland

mele – song, chant

menehune – 'little people' who, according to legend, built many of Hawaii's fishponds, heiau and other stonework

milo – a native shade tree with beautiful hardwood

moku – wedge-shaped areas of land running from the ridge of the mountains to the sea

mokupuni – low, flat island or atoll

Neighbor Islands – the term used to refer to the main Hawaiian Islands except for O'ahu

nene – a native goose; Hawaii's state bird

niu – coconut palm

'ohana – family, extended family; close-knit group

'olelo Hawai'i – the Hawaiian language

'opihi – an edible limpet

pahoehoe – type of lava that is quick and smoothflowing

pali – cliff

paniolo – cowboy

pau – finished, no more

pau hana – 'stop work'; happy hour

Pele – goddess of fire and volcanoes; her home is in Kilauea Caldera

pidgin – distinct local language and dialect, originating from Hawaii's multiethnic plantation immigrants

piko – navel, umbilical cord

pohaku – rock

pono – righteous, respectful and proper

pukiawe – native plant with red and white berries and evergreen leaves

pulu – the silken clusters encasing the stems of tree ferns

pupu – snack or appetizer; also a type of shell

pu'u – hill, cinder cone

pu'uhonua – place of refuge

raku – a style of Japanese pottery characterized by a rough, handmade appearance

rubbah slippah – flip-flops

sansei – third-generation Japanese immigrants

shaka – hand gesture used in Hawaii as a greeting or sign of local pride

talk story – to strike up a conversation, make small talk

tapa – cloth made by pounding the bark of paper mulberry, used for Native Hawaiian clothing (*kapa* in Hawaiian)

ti – common native plant; its long shiny leaves are used for wrapping food and making hula skirts (*ki* in Hawaiian)

tiki – wood- or stone-carved statue, usually depicting a deity (*ki'i* in Hawaiian)

tutu – grandmother or grandfather; also term of respect for any member of that generation

ukulele – a stringed musical instrument derived from the *braguinha,* which was introduced to Hawaii in the 1800s by Portuguese immigrants

'ulu – breadfruit

Wakea – sky father

Behind the Scenes

Acknowledgements

Climate map data adapted from Peel MC, Finlayson BL & McMahon TA (2007) 'Updated World Map of the Köppen-Geiger Climate Classification', *Hydrology and Earth System Sciences*, 11, 1633–44.

Cover photograph: North Shore, Waimea Bay, Hawaii, tropicalpixsingapore/ Getty Images ©

This Book

This 2nd edition of Lonely Planet's *Best of Hawaii* guidebook was researched and written by Amy Balfour, Jade Bremner, Kevin Raub, Ryan Ver Berkmoes and Greg Ward. The previous edition was written by Amy Balfour and Sara Benson.

This guidebook was produced by the following:

Senior Product Editor Vicky Smith

Regional Senior Cartographer Corey Hutchinson

Product Editors Claire Rourke, Fergus O'Shea

Book Designer Ania Bartoszek

Cover Designer Fergal Condon

Assisting Editor Ronan Abayawickrema, Sarah Bailey, Bailey Freeman, Kate Morgan

Cartographer Diana Von Holdt

Cover Researcher Brendan Dempsey-Spencer

Assisting cartographer Valentina Kremenchutskaya

Thanks to Sasha Drew, Sandie Kestell, Amy Lynch, Angela Tinson

Send Us Your Feedback

We love to hear from travelers – your comments keep us on our toes and help make our books better. Our well-traveled team reads every word on what you loved or loathed about this book. Although we cannot reply individually to postal submissions, we always guarantee that your feedback goes straight to the appropriate authors, in time for the next edition. Each person who sends us information is thanked in the next edition, the most useful submissions are rewarded with a selection of digital PDF chapters.

Visit lonelyplanet.com/contact to submit your updates and suggestions or to ask for help. Our award-winning website also features inspirational travel stories, news and discussions.

Note: We may edit, reproduce and incorporate your comments in Lonely Planet products such as guidebooks, websites and digital products, so let us know if you don't want your comments reproduced or your name acknowledged. For a copy of our privacy policy visit lonelyplanet.com/privacy.

Index

Symbols & Map Key

Look for these symbols to quickly identify listings:

- ◎ Sights
- ✚ Activities
- ◉ Courses
- ◉ Tours
- ✱ Festivals & Events
- ✖ Eating
- ◉ Drinking
- ✪ Entertainment
- ◉ Shopping
- ❶ Information & Transport

These symbols and abbreviations give vital information for each listing:

🍃 Sustainable or green recommendation

FREE No payment required

- ☎ Telephone number
- ✆ Opening hours
- P Parking
- ⊖ Nonsmoking
- ✳ Air-conditioning
- @ Internet access
- 📶 Wi-fi access
- ▣ Swimming pool

- ▣ Bus
- ⬇ Ferry
- ▣ Tram
- ▣ Train
- ▣ English-language menu
- ✎ Vegetarian selection
- ✚ Family-friendly

Find your best experiences with these Great For... icons.

 Art & Culture

 Beaches

 Budget

 Cafe/Coffee

🚲 Cycling

 Detour

 Drinking

 Entertainment

 Events

 Family Travel

 Food & Drink

 History

 Local Life

 Nature & Wildlife

 Photo Op

 Scenery

 Shopping

🎒 Short Trip

🏀 Sport

🥾 Walking

❄ Winter Travel

Sights

- Beach
- Bird Sanctuary
- Buddhist
- Castle/Palace
- Christian
- Confucian
- Hindu
- Islamic
- Jain
- Jewish
- Monument
- Museum/Gallery/ Historic Building
- Ruin
- Shinto
- Sikh
- Taoist
- Winery/Vineyard
- Zoo/Wildlife Sanctuary
- Other Sight

Points of Interest

- Bodysurfing
- Camping
- Cafe
- Canoeing/Kayaking
- Course/Tour
- Diving
- Drinking & Nightlife
- Eating
- Entertainment
- Sento Hot Baths/ Onsen
- Shopping
- Skiing
- Sleeping
- Snorkelling
- Surfing
- Swimming/Pool
- Walking
- Windsurfing
- Other Activity

Information

- Bank
- Embassy/Consulate
- Hospital/Medical
- Internet
- Police
- Post Office
- Telephone
- Toilet
- Tourist Information
- Other Information

Geographic

- Beach
- Gate
- Hut/Shelter
- Lighthouse
- Lookout
- Mountain/Volcano
- Oasis
- Park
- Pass
- Picnic Area
- Waterfall

Transport

- Airport
- BART station
- Border crossing
- Boston T station
- Bus
- Cable car/Funicular
- Cycling
- Ferry
- Metro/MRT station
- Monorail
- Parking
- Petrol station
- Subway/S-Bahn/ Skytrain station
- Taxi
- Train station/Railway
- Tram
- Underground/ U-Bahn station
- Other Transport

Ryan Ver Berkmoes

Ryan Ver Berkmoes has written more than 110 guidebooks for Lonely Planet. He grew up in Santa Cruz, California, which he left at age 17 for college in the Midwest, where he first discovered snow. All joy of this novelty soon wore off. Since then he has been travelling the world, both for pleasure and for work — which are often indistinguishable. He has covered everything from wars to bars. He definitely prefers the latter. Ryan calls New York City home. Read more at ryanverberkmoes.com and at @ryanvb.

Greg Ward

Since youthful adventures on the hippy trail to India, and living in Spain, Greg Ward has written guides to destinations all over the world. As well as covering the USA from the Southwest to Hawaii, he has ranged on recent assignments from Corsica to the Cotswolds, and Dallas to Delphi. Visit his website, www.gregward.info, to see his favourite photos and memories.

Our Story

A beat-up old car, a few dollars in the pocket and a sense of adventure. In 1972 that's all Tony and Maureen Wheeler needed for the trip of a lifetime – across Europe and Asia overland to Australia. It took several months, and at the end – broke but inspired – they sat at their kitchen table writing and stapling together their first travel guide, *Across Asia on the Cheap*. Within a week they'd sold 1500 copies. Lonely Planet was born.

Today, Lonely Planet has offices in Franklin, Dublin, Beijing and Delhi, with a network of over 2000 contributors in every corner of the globe. We share Tony's belief that 'a great guidebook should do three things: inform, educate and amuse'.

Our Writers

Amy Balfour

Amy practiced law in Virginia before moving to Los Angeles to try to break in as a screenwriter. If you listen carefully, you can still hear the horrified screams of her parents echoing through the space-time continuum. After a stint as a writer's assistant on Law & Order, she jumped into freelance writing, focusing on travel, food, and the outdoors.

Jade Bremner

Jade has been a journalist for more than 15 years. She has lived in and reported on four different regions. It's no coincidence many of her favourite places have some of the best waves in the world. Jade has edited travel magazines and sections for Time Out and Radio Times and has contributed to The Times, CNN and The Independent. She feels privileged to share tales from this wonderful planet we call home and is always looking for the next adventure. @jadebremne

Kevin Raub

Atlanta native Kevin Raub started his career as a music journalist in New York, working for Men's Journal and Rolling Stone magazines. He ditched the rock 'n' roll lifestyle for travel writing and has written over 95 Lonely Planet guides, focused mainly on Brazil, Chile, Colombia, USA, India, Italy and Portugal. Raub also contributes to a variety of travel magazines in both the USA and UK. Along the way, the self-confessed hophead is in constant search of wildly high IBUs in local beers. Find him at www.kevinraub.net or follow on Twitter and Instagram (@RaubOnTheRoad).

--- More Writers ---

STAY IN TOUCH LONELYPLANET.COM/CONTACT

IRELAND
Digital Depot, Digital Hub
Roe Lane (off Thomas St)
Dublin 8, D08 TCV4

USA
230 Franklin Rd, Building 2B
Franklin, TN 37064
☏ 615 988 9713

 twitter.com/
lonelyplanet

 facebook.com/
lonelyplanet

 instagram.com/
lonelyplanet

 youtube.com/
lonelyplanet

 lonelyplanet.com
newsletter